D0240158

life,
inter-
rupted

life,
inter-
rupted

James McConnel

headline
review

First published in 2006
by HEADLINE BOOK PUBLISHING

2

Cataloguing in Publication Data is available from the British Library

Hardback ISBN 0 7553 1503 0
Trade paperback IBSN 0 7553 1556 1

Typeset in Frutiger and Din by Avon DataSet Ltd,
Bidford-on-Avon, Warwickshire

Designed by Viv Mullett

Printed and bound in Great Britain by
Mackays of Chatham plc, Chatham, Kent

Headline's policy is to use papers that are natural, renewable and recyclable
products and made from wood grown in sustainable forests. The logging and
manufacturing processes are expected to conform to the environmental
regulations of the country of origin.

Headline Book Publishing
A division of Hodder Headline
338 Euston Road
London NW1 3BH

www.headline.co.uk
www.hodderheadline.com

For my mother and Amanda

The End

There's no music.
Guilt.
Shame.
Anger.
Yes.
But not music.
Half awake.
Apart from the *fucking* bass beat from next door.
Thump, thump, thump, thump, thump . . .
Never changing.
Relentless.
Mindless.
Shit . . . feel terrible.
My stomach.
Nausea.
Thump, thump, thump . . .
'Oh, turn that **fucking** noise off!' Only half-hearted.

More awake.

I'm cold.

Neck's stiff.

Headache.

And my heart's racing.

Thump, thump, thump . . .

Fucking noise! **Fuck**ing neighbours! **Fuck**ing bass beat!

Suddenly, uncontrollably: 'SHUT **THE FUCK UP!**'

Rage, acidic, addictive; undercut with the fear of being heard.

Hit the chair arm five times.

One two three four five!

Shit! Not right. **Again.** Five times.

One – two – three – four – five!

SHIT! Ten, need one more . . .

Kill it, for fuck's sake, **KILL IT!** Eleven!

No! Not RIGHT!

Again! NO! One more!

'Nna! Nna! Nna! Nnn nnn nnn.' One more.

'**Nnn.**'

Yes, seven . . .

'Look, JUST . . . **F-U-C-K** . . . **OFF**, will you!'

'Ba! Ba! Ba!'

STOP IT!

Fucking **stop** it!

'WHY . . . CAN'T . . . YOU . . . *STOP*?'

Chapter 1
The Beginning

'Morning, old boy.' Daddy, whispering. He pokes his head around my bedroom door. It's still dark outside.

'Morning,' I whisper back, only half awake.

I'm four.

'Got to go and milk the cows,' he whispers, as if it's unusual and important. 'See you later.'

'See you later,' and I doze off again.

We have lots of cows.

And pigs.

And three donkeys; and eight chickens, four cats, 'that *bloody* dog' called Honey – a golden Labrador who chews everything and does 'unspeakable' things on the floor – and Peggy, who's small, yaps a lot and chases the postman. I don't like her much because she has sticky stuff coming out of her eyes. There are five of us living here: me, Mummy and Daddy, my baby sister Polly and Jane, our nanny.

Daddy smells of pigs. And petrol.

Always.

Except in the mornings when he's had a bath. Then for a while he smells of soap and aftershave.

'Morning, darling.'

Mummy comes in later and gives me a kiss before going next door to check Polly in her cot. Then she goes downstairs and I hear her clattering away in the kitchen, making laying-the-table-for-breakfast noises followed by the rattling sound of Honey's dog biscuits being poured from paper sack into metal bowl. Then the smell of frying bacon and eggs drifts up the stairs and my tummy starts rumbling.

I leap out of bed. I *can* dress myself but I like to wait for Jane to come and help me because she makes everything fun; even dressing.

I love Jane. She calls me 'sweetheart' and brings me chocolate buttons in the evening after her day off. But she's got spots and I don't like kissing her cheek too often in case they come off on me.

Jane looks after Polly as well and when she's not changing nappies and making 'goo goo' noises, she plays games with me and takes me for long walks, pushing Polly in the pram.

When I'm dressed, Jane gets Polly up while I dash downstairs to the kitchen.

'What do you want for breakfast, darling?'

Mummy asks me this every morning, even though I always have the same things: Rice Krispies, bacon and egg, then toast. I have to wait until Daddy comes in – soap and aftershave already giving way to pig and petrol – carrying the small silver-coloured 'breakfast' churn full of freshly squeezed milk before I can start my cereal.

Daddy hands the churn to Mummy, and while she pours

some milk into a jug, he sits next to me at the table, a small shower of hay dropping from his thick blue jersey on to the kitchen floor. Then he slurps loudly at the cup of coffee waiting for him, before tipping up the packet of cornflakes – some of which go into his bowl.

All these things annoy Mummy, but she settles on one of them. 'Oh, Adrian! Even James can pour his cereal without spilling it, for heaven's sake! Why can't *you*? Honestly!' And she sighs.

'Sorry, sorry,' he replies, beaming good-naturedly at me, completely unconcerned.

I pour out my Rice Krispies slowly, carefully spilling none.

'Morning, old boy. Sleep well?'

'Yes, thanks.'

I think he forgets he's already seen me.

He calls me different things at different times. When he's in a good mood it's 'old boy' or 'Jamie', which he pronounces 'Jemmy'. When I've done something naughty it's 'Come here, boy!' or 'Stop that, boy!'

Mummy calls me 'Jamie' or 'darling' usually, but she uses 'sweetie' as well sometimes.

'Jolly good; how about coming out and giving me a hand later on?'

'Can I give the pigs their water?' This is my bargain. I want to use the hose.

'Yes, all right.'

Mummy pipes up, 'Yes, but *do* be careful. I don't want him going in by himself, he's too young. Promise?'

'Promise,' he says.

'I *mean* it, Adrian.'

'I *promise*!'

He pauses to eat a mouthful of cornflakes. Then:

5

'Damned nuisance, I'm going to have to go into Romsey again.'

'Why? What's happened?'

'Oh, nothing. The weaners have *still* got scour, that's all.'

'Oh, Adrian, not *again*!' She drops the bread knife heavily on the chopping board and turns to him. 'I thought the vet had sorted that out last week.'

'So did I, but it's back, for some reason.'

'Well, you must simply ring him and tell him to come out again! This is the third time! I think you should give him a piece of your mind, really I do.'

'All right, all right. I'll ring him.'

'And make sure he comes out today!'

'Okay, okay.'

She goes over to the sink, looking a bit cross. He winks at me and, putting on a childish voice, leans over and half whispers, 'Isn't Mummy silly!'

I smile and nod, slightly embarrassed because I know he wants me to be on his side.

There's a lull while we eat. Mummy joins us and, with a sigh, sits down with half a grapefruit and some disgusting lemon juice stuff called PLJ, which is good for her diet.

Then Jane appears carrying Polly, who's complaining loudly because she wants to be fed. Mummy abandons her own breakfast, takes Polly in her arms and, as if in complete surprise, says in a high-pitched voice, 'Hello! Who have we got here! Ooh, are you a hungry little girl? Are you, darling? (kiss) Well, Mummy's got some lovely (kiss) scrumptious (kiss) apple (kiss) just . . . for (kiss) you! So there! (kiss)'

And while Jane has breakfast, Mummy straps Polly into the high chair and starts feeding her.

Mummy's always in the kitchen. Twice a day, it becomes a

quiet room and no one is allowed in while she listens to *Mrs Dale's Diary* and *The Archers*. She gets very annoyed if she's interrupted. 'Can't I have some peace, just for once!' she always says if we disturb her.

Daddy finishes his breakfast, stands up, dusting toast crumbs off his jersey on to the floor, and after kissing my head with a 'See you later, Jamie,' he walks round the table and kisses Polly, then Mummy on her forehead.

'See you later,' he repeats.

'Now, darling, you *are* going to ring him, aren't you? Promise?'

'Yes, all right, I'll do it later, I've got to give Bert a hand first.'

As he leaves, Mummy lets out an enormous sigh, 'Ahhhh', before loading the next spoonful of apple sauce for Polly.

Bert helps Daddy on the farm. He's very old (I reckon about a hundred) and he has a black bicycle. He wears a dark blue jacket with leather pads at the shoulders and elbows, and *he* smells of pigs and petrol too, except it's a different smell because he drives the tractor, which takes different petrol. He always has a cigarette dangling from his mouth, which he re-lights from time to time because they keep going out. Bert rolls his own cigarettes. Daddy just buys *his* in packets called Tipped Woodbines. They never go out until he wants them to.

Bert doesn't say much; but when he does, he speaks in a funny accent which I can only just understand. He calls me 'young'n', and says things like 'Get doon off 'ee tractorrr, young'n!' (I'm not allowed on the tractor.)

Our house is made of red bricks and it's bendy in places

because it's so old. It has three floors and it stands back from a winding country lane. In front, you can see a marshy paddock that leads through trees to the river where Daddy sometimes takes me fishing. To the left of the house there are farm buildings which we use as cow sheds and pigpens, and further on, there's a huge barn where we keep hay and straw. This is my favourite place to climb and play.

Behind the house there's a cottage. Mr and Mrs Flint live there with their son Derek, who's interested in cranes and drives one for his job. Mrs Flint helps Mummy in the house three times a week, and Mr Flint does the gardening.

Mrs Flint wears skin-coloured tights, which are see-through, so you can see the bandage that she wears to protect her bad knee. Once a week she cleans the silver teapot with horrible-smelling cotton wool which turns black and she does hoovering too. Mr Flint calls her 'babe', which is funny because she's very old. She smells of cleaning stuff and dust.

It's warm in the kitchen and I like listening to the music on the wireless. Jane likes it too and she taught me to sing 'I lost my poor meatball', which came on the other day.

When we have elevenses, me and Mummy and Mrs Flint sit at the kitchen table and I have a biscuit. Mummy and Mrs Flint have coffee. Mrs Flint talks and talks and talks about her daughter, who is 'in the family way', and Derek, who's courting Shirley, and Mummy says 'Yes' and 'Yes' and 'Oh yes' and 'Oh really' and 'Gosh' and 'Heavens' and 'Of course not' and 'Oh no'. And Mummy looks at me in a funny way and I think she wishes Mrs Flint wouldn't talk so much.

Mr Flint is always singing. His voice wobbles when he sings, but it's a nice voice. He sings songs that have the word 'baby' in them. I don't know any songs about babies except

'Rock-a-bye baby on the tree top', but he doesn't sing that one. He smokes a pipe, which is like Bert's cigarettes because it always goes out and he has to light it again.

When it's cold, drips hang off the end of his nose. I keep wanting them to fall off but they never do, which is really annoying; they just hang there and I wonder what the drips would taste like if I licked them. Yuck! He calls me 'nipper', and I'm cross with him because he dug up my bean, which I planted all by myself. He thought it was a weed and I'm cross with Mummy, too, because she won't give him a telling-off.

We have about two hundred pigs. The biggest one is a huge boar called Alf. I'm not allowed to go into the pen with him because boars can be vicious. Alf has huge balls the size of saucers which jiggle about when he walks. When he wants to have some piglets he jumps on to the sow's back and tries to put his spend-a-penny thing in her bottom. Daddy usually has to help him because his spend-a-penny thing is very long and thin and curly like a corkscrew and it wobbles every-where. I wonder how Alf would manage if Daddy wasn't there to help him.

'You've always got to think a couple of seconds ahead of a pig, Jemmy; they're very intelligent, you know.' Daddy always says this when they're being moved across the yard to a different pen. I love pigs. I like watching them as they grunt and sniff and jostle each other at feeding time. I even like the sweet, overpowering smell of their wee and poo.

Sometimes a lorry comes to take the fatteners away to be slaughtered.

'Come on, you buggers, get in there!' yells Mr Flint.

'Go on with yer!' the lorry driver shouts. I hate the way they are slapped and punched, kicked and electrocuted with prods to force them up the ramp to stand inside like raisins in a box, trying to get comfortable.

And yet when Daddy gives me a pig bat, a long thin piece of wood to 'guide' them in the right direction, a small part of me, a cruel part of me, likes the power I have and I grip the pig bat and I hit hard, to show off to Daddy and Bert and Mr Flint and the lorry driver . . . and I know it's wrong.

One day, Mummy takes me to the dentist. Trips with Mummy, just the two of us, are fun. I like having her to myself. We climb into the car, a dark blue Morris Traveller, which Daddy calls a 'shooting brake'. It's a car that smiles at you; the lines of the bonnet and windscreen curve so that it looks like a face and the back half and rear doors are covered with bright yellowish shiny wooden strips. The number plate is POU 892G and before I get in I always check that we have the right car. The reason is that Mummy's best friend has a car exactly the same in every way except that the number plate on hers is POU 895G. Sometimes when she's been for a visit I worry that she might have taken our car home by mistake. She never has yet, though.

Mummy's a jerky driver. It's okay getting out of the drive, but once we're on the road she presses the foot pedal until the engine screams and when she changes gear the car shudders as though it's sneezing. Sometimes when she's driving she touches her cheek with her forefinger, makes a funny face and jiggles her head sharply once. She does it when she's concentrating or trying to think what to make for lunch.

I like the dentist, Mr Wakeford. I like the 'eeeeeeeeee' sound the chair makes as he raises me up on it. I like the taste of the purply-pink mouthwash his white-coated lady assistant puts beside me. Mr Wakeford has an odd-shaped bushy moustache and while he's poking around in my mouth with long bits of metal he tells me jokes and gives me a peppermint afterwards because I've been good.

When he's finished and it's Mummy's turn, she says, 'I won't be long, sweetie. Can you go and sit in the waiting room?'

Why aren't I allowed to watch? I want to watch. She watched *me*.

The waiting room's boring. There are no picture books, no one to play with and no toys. The leather chairs are shiny, hard and uncomfortable and the only sound is the slow ticking coming from a round clock on the wall which has large black Vs, Xs and Is on it instead of numbers.

After sitting for what feels like ages, swinging my legs to try and pass the time, humming to myself, I hear quiet voices in the hallway, and a few moments later the door opens and in shuffles a very old lady, head bent forward, wearing a brown coat, round brown hat, brown handbag and carrying a brown wooden walking stick. She moves slowly, painfully almost, panting a little, each step an effort, the rubber bottom on the end of her stick making soft thumping noises on the wooden floor as she walks. She reaches a chair across the room and as she sinks down cautiously on to the leather with a deep 'Ahh,' she looks over at me.

And I stop breathing.

She has a beard.

Covering her whole chin.

It's grey, curly and wiry, with gaps of smooth skin between the tufts. I've seen beards before; of course I have. Big Ears has one. So does Jesus. *And* Tom – who helps Daddy with the cows sometimes. But they're men! Men are hairy. Men are *supposed* to be hairy. Daddy's hairy. He doesn't have a beard, but I know he could grow one if he wanted to.

This is a lady!

I find myself comparing her with Mummy, Jane, Mrs Flint, Polly even. They all have smooth, soft skin. This lady does too, in some places. The lined skin around her eyes is soft and smooth, and so are her cheeks. But suddenly it goes wrong around her chin and for some reason it's . . . hairy.

The seconds pass, long and silent, apart from the clock. Something tells me I shouldn't be staring quite so hard. I move about in the chair restlessly. I look away, trying to find something, *anything* in the room that could be interesting; the curtains, the carpet, the door. But all the time I can't stop thinking about it and I *need* to look back at the 'thing' again.

Look at it! Just once!

No, don't!

Yes! Just once, only once!

I can't help myself, I *have* to look again, just for an instant. A quick look, disguised as a sweep of the room, a look that would make anyone think that my eyes were just passing through on their way to the ceiling.

And there it is! Like the roots of a leek.

What would happen if I said, 'Urghh! You've got a beard! Yuck!'

What would she do?

Get cross? Shout at me? Smack me?

Or if I went over and pulled it – right off her face – pop pop pop pop pop as each hair came out . . . like a cartoon.

Just *one* more look – quick!

Suddenly our eyes lock.

Oh no!

I snatch mine away instantly, feeling myself blush at having been caught.

But then I hear the sound of the surgery door opening and Mummy comes out, Mr Wakeford following her.

'Penny, if you'd just like to have a seat here for a moment, I'll go and see when we can fit you in.'

How do people know whether to call my parents by their first names or not? Jane calls Mummy 'Mrs McConnel' but Mummy calls her 'Jane'. Mrs Flint and Mummy call each other 'Mrs Flint' and 'Mrs McConnel'. But if Jane is 'Jane' to Mummy, why is Mrs Flint not 'Rosie'? And Mr Wakeford. He calls Mummy 'Penny', but she calls *him* 'Mr Wakeford'. It's confusing.

While Mr Wakeford disappears through the other door to talk to the receptionist, Mummy sits down beside me.

'Hello, darling. You okay?'

'Mm hmm,' I reply.

I glance up at her, watching, waiting for her to discover 'the thing' for herself, expecting the same reaction that I had.

Finally, she looks across at the old lady and . . . she nods . . . and smiles!

As though nothing was wrong!

She *must* have noticed! *Surely!*

How could she *not*?

But maybe she hasn't.

I lean over and, keeping my voice low in case the old lady hears, but pointing my finger to make sure Mummy knows who I'm talking about, I whisper as quietly as I can, 'Mummy? Why's that lady got a beard?'

I *was* whispering. I *know* I was, but Mummy reacts in the way she would if I shouted 'biggies' in church. Her face turns red like Noddy's shirt, her eyes widen in horror, she puts her mouth next to my ear, and in a desperate whisper splutters, 'Shh, darling! Not now.'

This puzzles me. She can't have heard; so I try again, a little louder this time. 'Mummy, that lady's got a beard!'

It may have been a bit too loud because, glancing across the room, I can see by her face that the old lady has also heard.

Mummy says, 'Be quiet, darling, that's enough!' Then, looking at the old lady, she says, 'I'm *so* sorry. I *do* apologise – he's only four.'

Actually, I'm nearly five, and I say so.

The old lady, however, says nothing. She just stares at us, looking cross, which somehow makes her beard seem to fit the rest of her face, while for the next few minutes Mummy fidgets. First she examines her fingernails very closely, scraping away any old bits of the red nail varnish she always wears. Then she brushes her skirt with the back of her fingers to get rid of any stray dog hairs. Finally, looking at me and frowning slightly, she picks up her handbag from the floor beside her and rummages about in it for some time, at last bringing out a crumpled tissue with a perfect image of her mouth already stamped upon it in lipstick. She licks the tissue, cups my chin with her hand and starts wiping a mystery smudge off my cheek. I hate it when she does this, and impatiently I try to wriggle away from her, protesting loudly, but she holds on tight, scrubbing hard in a way that makes me think she's cross, until she's satisfied herself that I'm clean.

When Mr Wakeford comes back and she's fixed a date for her next appointment, for some reason Mummy seems impatient to leave.

In the car on the way back, she tells me it's very rude to make 'personal remarks' and that if I ever see anybody who looks a 'bit strange' I should ignore them. A few minutes later she starts laughing quietly to herself, looks across at me, strokes my hair and says, 'Honestly! You are a funny one sometimes, but I do love you.'

When we get home, I leap out of the car and dash inside to find Jane to tell her about the lady with the beard. But running into the drawing room, I come to a halt, speechless for the second time that day, all thoughts of old ladies and beards vanishing instantly from my mind; because there, where the bookcase should be – where *is* the bookcase? – is a monster, a brown monster, standing on three monstrous legs and tiny, shiny wheels. It's huge, bigger than anything in the house! The biggest thing I've ever seen. It's new, with curvy bits and straight bits, and sticking-up bits, and I can see my bent reflection in the highly polished wood. Daddy's sitting next to it.

How can anything be this big?

I move closer to Mummy, absent-mindedly clutching her skirt and rubbing the soft material against my upper lip.

Daddy looks very proud of himself. 'What do you think?'

'Heavens!' says Mummy. 'Makes the room look terribly small, doesn't it? Can't we push it nearer the wall?'

'No, it'll warp the wood if it's too close to the radiator.'

'What is it, Mummy?'

'It's a piano, darling.'

'Come over here, old boy, I'll show you.' When I hesitate, he adds, 'It's all right, it won't bite.'

Trusting him, I let go of Mummy, keeping my thumb in

my mouth but transferring my skirt-stroking forefinger to the tip of my nose. I approach cautiously, still overwhelmed by its size, still not convinced it won't attack me, and see that the piano monster has teeth – lots of teeth, long white ones and short black ones, evenly spaced; two then three, then two, then three . . . then two . . . then three, then two, then three, then two . . . then . . . one, at the very end.

'Come on, come and sit next to me.'

He helps me up on to the stool beside him, spreads out his hands – enormous hands marked with cuts from barbed-wire fences; rough, brown, thick-skinned hands, toughened from years of hefting bales and sacks of pig food, hands I could never imagine doing anything other than hammering or painting or digging or mowing or lifting – and presses down on the teeth. Immediately, incredibly, music comes from deep within the monster and I realise at once that I recognise the sound. I've heard it before on the gramophone and the wireless lots of times, but I never knew how the sound was made; never thought to *think* how it was made. Daddy's fingers are moving so fast they're almost a blur. He makes it look so easy, but how does he know which teeth to press? There are so many of them. He's playing something Mummy knows, and she's humming along to the tune, her head swaying slowly from side to side. I look up at Daddy's face, and there's a look there I haven't seen before. He's completely happy.

I'm hooked. I've *got* to have a go on it. There's something exciting about the clean white smoothness of the teeth, the way they pop up again by themselves when they've just been played. Like magic. When he comes to the end of the music and gets up, I shuffle along the stool and try to copy what I've just seen and heard. I spread my hands out and push down on the teeth with all my fingers at once, lifting and pressing, lifting and pressing as fast and as hard as I can, expecting it to be as easy as Daddy has just made it look. But it doesn't work. It's just lots of loud noises.

'Jamie! No, no, no! Not so hard, you'll break the strings. Press the notes gently. Like this.' He takes the forefinger of my right hand and uses it to play something. I want to help, and without thinking I push down, wanting to control it but going against what he's trying to do.

'Hang on, old boy. Just let go and relax your arm. Relax. Let *me* do it.'

I do, and suddenly he's making my finger play a tune I know. It's 'Baa baa black sheep'.

I'm amazed. Utterly . . . amazed.

'Again, again!' I beg, when he comes to the end.

And we do it again, and Mummy claps and says, 'Gosh, well *done*, darling, you *are* clever!'

And then I make him do it once more.

And then we have tea.

But I can remember, and all the way through tea, while Mummy is telling Daddy about the lady with the beard – 'Honestly, Adrian, I could have *died* of embarrassment' – I can think of nothing else and after we've had tea and Daddy's gone to feed the animals, I sit down at the piano again and I can still remember the first four notes of 'Baa baa black sheep' all by myself.

After I've played them again and again and again and again, I can hear in my head what's meant to come next and I know it's higher than the note before. So I experiment until I find the right note and then I start from the beginning and play the first five notes all together. Again and again and again and again.

There is such a lovely feeling in the repetition of these notes, so much joy. Each play-through gives me a jolt of happiness. Then, when I can tear myself away, I look for the sixth and seventh notes and when I find them I play the whole thing from the beginning again. And again and again and again. And by the time Jane comes down to say it's time for my bath, I can play up to 'have you any wool?' And it's wonderful. Everything is wonderful and I dance round the bathroom singing and Jane's getting annoyed with me.

'Jamie! Sweetheart! Will you *please* get in the bath or I'm going to get cross!'

But I don't care because I can play 'Baa baa black sheep' and I'm incredibly happy and filled up and powerful and almost shaking with excitement because I've discovered this fantastic thing which makes me feel like nothing else matters.

And it's the next morning and the first thing I think of is the piano. So I jump out of bed and go downstairs and start playing. Something has happened while I was asleep. Now I can play 'Baa baa black sheep, have you any wool?' much better than I could last night. It's easy, and then I can do 'Yes sir, yes sir, three bags full' straight off, first time. I don't need to look for the notes; they just happen. So I start again from the beginning and . . .

'Darling, what are you *doing* here?'

It's Mummy, standing in the doorway in her blue dressing gown, shoulders raised, arms crossed as though she's cold.

'Mummy, I can play "Baa baa black sheep"!'

There's a pause while she takes this in.

'Lovely, sweetie . . . but it's five o'clock in the morning, darling. It's still the middle of the night!'

She walks slowly over to me.

'Come on now. Let's get you upstairs again. It's not time to get up yet.' She takes my hand and as she gently leads me up the stairs, my thumb in my mouth, I can hear both amusement and disapproval in her voice as she says, 'Honestly, darling, you are a funny old thing sometimes, aren't you?'

Now I have a ritual, an unbreakable routine. First thing after breakfast, after cleaning my teeth – I'm not allowed to do anything in the mornings until I've cleaned my teeth – I clamber on to the piano stool. This act alone is exciting, before I even touch the keys. I can feel the expectant, gentle (as it's now become) giant, waiting like a patient pet, a live thing, wanting me to touch it. It's what I'm for.

Having discovered that the harder you press the notes, the louder they sound, I realise that the opposite is also true. I become obsessed with trying to play as quietly as possible, placing one ear against the notes, playing so softly that only I can hear. It makes a completely different sound then, a soft, stringy hum that reverberates around inside, mingling with the subtle sliding and tapping noises of wood against wood, felt against steel, even when you've released the note. I love the delicate balance of each key as it springs up again immediately. And there's the lid, like a seesaw which swings down to cover the keys, and if you bang it shut, the strings vibrate and you can hear all the notes at once. The lid is finely balanced too, and sometimes I try to find the centre, the midpoint in its swing, where it's neither up nor down, but I never can.

I don't like the black notes very much. They feel strange and awkward. I don't like the gaps between them, and pressing in the gaps makes the white notes harder to play and the balance is lost, which is annoying. The black notes are thinner as well, and the sounds they make aren't as pure.

I move on to 'Frère Jacques', and in the same way as 'Baa baa black sheep', I learn that too. And after several months I can play lots of one-fingered nursery rhymes and the first half of the 'Marseillaise' – which Daddy taught me.

My next discovery is that you can play more than one note at a time. By adding harmony in my left hand, 'Baa baa black sheep' and 'Frère Jacques' suddenly move to a whole new level.

But I long to be able to play like Daddy. At night, I lie awake listening to the music drifting up from below. Some nights I even sneak out of bed and watch him secretly from halfway up the stairs. From this distance, he makes it look so easy. His huge hands seem to glide over the keys, barely touching them, yet making all these rich sounds that I can't wait to be able to play myself. And as he sits there he looks so peaceful, and yet distracted almost, as if nothing else really matters. And I know just how he feels.

The End

Relax.

Calm down.

Calm . . . down.

Glance around me.

Scan the room.

'Look at this place.'

Chaos.

Unwashed plates iced with congealed fat.

Empty beer cans doubling as ashtrays.

There, an old, cold cup of coffee, skinned with green velvet.

Uneaten pizza crusts and takeaway boxes.

Crushed cigarette packets and dust.

Decayed entertainment.

Empty vodka bottle, topless, standing by itself . . .

Like an exhibit.

Hate this brown carpet.

Wicker waste-paper basket lying on its side, spewing its contents . . .

Cellophane wrappers, brown apple core, butt ends, empty matchbox.

Urghh! Stinks in here . . . stale smoke, beer, pizza.

'Stinks! Stinks stinks **stinks stinks!'**

And still the mindless bass beat.

Thump, thump, thump.

Not just *through* the wall.

Under the wall.

I can feel it.

Along the ground.

Through the chair.

Into my feet, up my legs.

Infecting me, *becoming* me.

Till I'm 'thump' myself.

I *am* thump.

Sickening. Fucking vibration.

A disease.

Threatening.

And the fucking neighbours don't realise it.

They don't *know* it's driving me mad.

And that's what grates . . .

The not knowing-ness of it . . .

I feel dismissed . . .

'Dismissed! Dsmissed! Smissed! Smisst! Mss ss ss ss ss ss st!'

Chapter 2
The Controller

'*Mild He lays His glory by . . .*'

School carol service. I'm nearly seven.

I'm singing at the top of my voice.

So's everyone else – mostly.

The church is packed with children, parents and teachers; two hundred mouths opening and closing like dying fish.

It's so loud I can hardly hear myself, the congregation competing with the organ for supremacy. I can almost *see* the sound as it reverberates around the thick, carved wooden beams, high above.

The atmosphere is heavy with Christmas. Togetherness; a collective excitement.

I belong.

I'm playing in the recorder ensemble and we're crammed in with the choir up by the altar.

Nearby, the giant Christmas tree bristles with presents,

tinsel, silver balls, lights, an angel with gold wings at the very top.

'Born that man no more may die . . .'

Strange seeing Miss Paget not *being* head teacher, just one of a crowd singing. I can't think of her as a 'normal' person. I can't imagine her needing to sleep or clean her teeth or go to the loo.

What would she look like on the loo?

Does she fart?

Does she fold the paper *exactly* in half twice – like me – before she wipes her bottom?

Bottoms . . .

Yuck!

'Born to raise the sons of earth . . .'

Mummy and Daddy are near the back with Jane, who's holding Polly. Mummy's looking at me and smiling slightly. Daddy's standing up very straight, like the vicar, Mr Newman.

Newman . . .

New Man . . .

New man . . . new . . . man.

How do people get their names?

My friend David's doing his best to sing along even though he's got a terrible voice. Next to him is Mrs Fuller, the geography teacher with a lined face, who never stops talking about her years living in Australia, who tries to improve my concentration by making me read boring passages about the Stone Age, then firing questions at me to see whether I've taken it in or not.

'Born to give them second birth . . .'

This is the good bit. The organ gets louder, ready for the big ending. Everyone takes a deep breath; four notes up from 'birth', to . . .

'Hark the herald angels . . .'
Sniff!
'Glory to the newborn King.
Hark the herald angels sing
Glory to the newborn . . .'
Sniff, sniff!
An interruption.
A command.
Getting in the way of 'sing' and 'King'.
A tiny urge . . . an itch . . . not a real itch . . . not like on your leg. Just a need . . .
To sniff . . .
Nothing disturbing or worrying or frightening.
And again: Sniff, sniff!
'Let us pray.'
A wave of purposeful rustling. I kneel. So do the other children. We have to. Grown ups are allowed to sit and lean forward to pray. We aren't.
Wish I was a grown-up.
Apart from the vicar's voice echoing round the church, it's suddenly quiet. Everyone's still. There's a hush.
And again: Sniff, *sniff*! The accent on the second sniff this time.
It seems important.
I could . . . *not* do it . . . if I really wanted to; I know I could.
I don't absolutely *have* to.
I could just . . . *not* sniff. I *could* control it.
But if I don't . . . somehow it'll *feel* wrong; uncomfortable.
Again: Sniff, *sniff*! To get it right, the last sniff must be loudest.

To my left, Charlie Philips, a year older, throws me a quick, curious glance, then, sensing nothing important, looks away.

Sniff, **sniff!**

Louder this time. Much louder.

Loud enough, in fact, for pure 'sniff' to be snatched by the surrounding air; thrown up and outwards, echoing, reverberating, competing with the vicar.

Audible. Noticeable.

Two or three of my recorder colleagues simultaneously rotate their heads in my direction. Mrs Ferguson, my arithmetic teacher, kneeling in the front row of the congregation, glares at me with her angry, piggy little eyes. She frowns and mouths, 'Stop it!'

I can't do arithmetic. I hate it. She makes me cry when I get it wrong.

I *hate* her! Hate hate hate hate **hate** her!

I'm embarrassed because she's seen me, but it makes the urge stronger. I bend my head forward and bury my face in my hands.

Sniff, sniff! – very quietly.

And again: Sniff!

And again: Sniff!

As well as the itch, this time there's the need to have the last word, the last sniff, which she can neither see nor hear.

'In the name of the Father, the Son and the Holy Spirit . . .'

'Amen,' everyone growls quietly.

The service ends. The organ plays; the congregation gets to its feet and slowly leaves the church.

Outside in the crisp coldness I see Mrs Ferguson

approaching and because I'm with my parents she's all smiles and sweetness, regarding me with feigned fondness, every inch the concerned teacher politely suggesting, in her stupid Scottish accent, that perhaps if I have a cold I should carry a handkerchief: '. . . because you had a wee bout of the sniffles during the service, didn't ye, Jamie?'

She never calls me Jamie at school, just James.

God, I hate her! I want to scrape her thick make-up off with a fork. I wish she would die!

Mummy turns to me. 'You haven't got a cold, have you, darling?'

'No,' I say.

But something's shifted.

Awakened within me.

Something that wasn't there before.

Something that is exterior; but at the same time interior.

A part of me, and yet not a part of me.

Not a voice.

A feeling.

A gentle reminder.

A presence.

A Controller.

Which stays with me. Putting down roots, growing slowly; developing and increasing over the following weeks and months.

And each time it interrupts I stop to give it room; I have to . . . I *need* to . . .

Even though it lasts a millisecond, the tiniest fraction of time, smaller than the smallest atom of time.

It feels like a competition, a task; the Controller

challenging me to create the 'perfect' sniff, the sniff that scores ten out of ten, the super-sniff that'll be good enough for me to stop; to satisfy; to make me comfortable.

To make *us* comfortable, maybe.

But it forgets.

The Controller forgets I've just *done* a super-sniff, and it challenges me again a few minutes later.

It's not intrusive. It's too quick to be intrusive. Nor is it strange.

It's just me. It's natural.

Jane notices first.

'You getting a cold, sweetheart?'

'No.'

'Are you sure? I think you might be; you're sniffing quite a lot, aren't you?'

I shrug.

'Oh well, I expect it'll go away soon.'

Then Mummy.

'Darling, what's the matter? Why do you keep sniffing all the time?'

'I don't know; I can't help it.'

'You're not feeling ill, are you?'

'No.'

'Oh dear, I do hope you're not going to have trouble with your sinuses.'

She presses the skin just above my eyebrows.

'Does that hurt?'

'No.'

She turns to Daddy. 'Marigold had to have her sinuses drained.'

'Hah! Marigold would! Knowing her, she probably enjoyed it.'

Mummy laughs. 'Yes, she probably did.'

She puts her hand on my forehead.

'I don't *think* you've got a temperature.'

'Come on, darling,' Daddy says, 'leave the boy alone; it's probably just a phase. He'll be all right.'

Mummy sighs. 'Oh well, I hope so.'

Then others.

'Got a bitta cold therrrre, young'n, eh?' says Bert, in rare talkative mood.

'I don't know,' I say, although I do.

'Sniff sniff sniff. Sounds like a cold t'me. Tell Mum a cup o' warrrm lemon'll sorrrt you oat; soon paaaass.'

'James, I know you've got a cold, but could you please try not to sniff; it's rather annoying for other people.'

'Sorry, Miss Paget.'

And later:

'Darling, do you *really* need to make that awful noise? You haven't got a cold. *Please* try and stop it.'

'I can't help it.'

'Come on, old boy, that's enough now.'

The urges become stronger at certain times; especially before doing anything delicate or poised. Lifting a loaded fork, I hold it about six inches from my face, needing to sniff gently a couple of times before I'm allowed to open my mouth to eat.

Not to smell the food.

Just to sniff.

Correctly.

The same goes for cleaning my teeth: there's a pause, to sniff, before the toothbrush is granted permission to brush.

Likewise putting on my pyjama bottoms, stroking Honey, writing, opening the car door . . .

There's always a delay . . . to get the sniff right.

And later still, the Controller issues a new instruction: to make a short staccato 'mm' sound, mouth closed. It must be closed.

A grunt, like an expression of mild surprise tinged with humour.

Quiet but definite.

Sometimes it needs to accompany the sniffs; at others it can be independent of them. 'Mm mm mm mm . . .' the shorter the better, striving to find that 'perfect' grunt of grunts; an endless search, a quest, to find the one *perfect* grunt that will mean I never have to grunt again as long as I live. To make it . . . finally . . . right.

Mummy's worried now.

She takes me to the doctor.

He looks me over, checks my breathing, my sinuses, my throat, my reflexes, my spend-a-penny thing.

'Well, I can't find anything wrong with him,' he says. 'His sinuses are clear and his chest's fine. Seems like a perfectly healthy young man. It's probably just a phase; I wouldn't worry about it if I were you.'

But my parents aren't convinced and gradually they start experimenting with various forms of alternative home therapy to try and ease the symptoms – to make them go away.

'For God's sake, boy, stop that awful noise!' . . . is one method.

'Look, darling, if you don't stop that dreadful racket, I'm going to get really cross!' . . . is another.

'Right, that's it! I warned you! Now go upstairs to your room and don't come down until you can behave!'

Thus my sniffing and grunting moves from mild – possibly medical – concern, to 'bad habit'.

An offence.

Punishable.

I start seeing it as naughtiness because they do. I don't know what else to say other than 'I can't help it.' I don't understand it myself. I *can* stop it, and yet I *can't*. They tell me I'm being naughty; they are my parents; they must be right. 'Shut up!' and 'Stop it!' therefore seem perfectly appropriate reactions to my repeated 'misbehaviour'.

One evening after supper, Daddy calls me into the drawing room.

'Jamie, come and have a listen to this.'

As I walk in from the kitchen he's standing by the gramophone holding a record carefully between the fingertips of both hands, light glancing off the black, faintly grooved shiny surface.

'Thought you might like to hear this. It's a piece of music by a man called J.S. Bach.'

He pronounces 'Bach' with a rasping sound at the back of his throat.

He places the record on the spindle and presses the start lever. I move closer and, as always, I watch intrigued as the machine 'does it by itself'. But this time it's different. This time, once the record has dropped on to the turntable, I feel an impatience as the robot-like arm moves agonisingly, painfully, annoyingly slowly from its cradle across to the outside edge of the record, before lowering itself with a 'chonk' as it makes contact, followed by a rhythmic pulsing hiss before the music starts.

But I can't concentrate on the music. I hear it, but it doesn't make any impact. This time it's the robot arm that has my complete attention. It sits there, resting gently on the surface like a small boat, rising and falling with the slightly warped contours of the record. It's so delicately balanced, so undecided, frustrating and maddening. I *need* to move it, to press it, to make it do something more than just sit there unconcerned, undecided. The impulse is overwhelming. I reach out, unable to stop myself, wrap my hand round it and pull. There is a sharp screeching sound as the needle slides across the vinyl. I let go immediately, horror-struck.

There's a shocked silence. Then: 'What the *bloody hell* are you doing, boy?' He is furious, and frightening. 'What the *hell* do you think you're *doing*? Come *here*!'

And in a burst of fury he grabs my collar, turns me round and smacks me hard, three times on my bottom.

'How *dare* you, you silly little boy! Look what you've done!'

I start crying, as much from the suddenness of his anger as from the pain of the smacking, while he goes to the gramophone to inspect the damage.

Hearing the noise, Mummy comes running in from the kitchen.

'What on earth's going on?'

'He's just broken the gramophone!'

'What d'you mean! How?'

'Oh God, and he's *ruined* my Brandenburg Concerto!' He lifts the record off the spindle and examines it. 'Look, he's *ruined* it! Scratched to buggery!'

'Oh, Adrian, do stop swearing!'

'Well, *look* at it!'

She examines the record cursorily and then turns to me.

'Jamie, what on earth were you doing?'

'I don't know, I didn't mean to,' I murmur, between sobs.

'Well, I think you'd better go straight up to bed, don't you? Go on, up with you!'

As I go upstairs, I can hear Mummy trying to restore calm.

'Come on, Adrian, it's not the end of the world. He's only seven; I'm sure he didn't mean to do it.'

'Little bugger, it's completely wrecked.'

Later on, when she comes up to tuck me in and say goodnight, she sits on my bed and says quietly, 'Darling, I think you've upset Daddy quite a lot. It wasn't a very *nice* thing to do, now was it?'

'I didn't mean to,' I mumble.

'Well, you must tell Daddy you're sorry and then we'll say no more about it. All right?'

It was true. I hadn't meant to do it. But why? Why did I *need* to do it? Why did it feel uncomfortable *not* to do it?

I don't know why. Do other people feel like this? What is the Controller? Do other people have one as well? Maybe everyone does but you're not supposed to talk about it. Or maybe *their* Controllers make them do different, less noticeable things. I don't know.

*   *   *   *   *

Jane's the one person who seems to understand; or at least she doesn't shout at me or tell me to stop it the whole time. When we're playing games or she's taking me for walks I can sniff and grunt freely without worrying.

Sometimes she'll say gently, 'Shh, sweetheart. Come on now, take a deep breath.Try and relax.'

When I do, she says, 'That better?' And I nod, even though it isn't; and because I'm grateful I try and hold it in for a while.

'Funny old sniffles and grunts you've got, haven't you?'

And I love her for *talking* about it; accepting it; not getting cross.

'Jamie, clear the table, will you?'

We've finished Sunday lunch. I turn to Mummy in outrage. 'But I *laid* the table; why can't Polly clear it?'

'Because, my darling, you're seven and she's only four. Anyway, she's not well; you know that.'

'But that's not fair! She never does *anything*.'

'Come on! Hop to it, boy!'

Daddy says this a lot. 'Hop to it, boy!', as if he himself is a trained hopper who has earned the right to teach *me*, though his tone suggests he doesn't hold out much hope of my ever becoming a proper hopper.

'Listen, darling,' Mummy says, 'we have to look after Polly. You know her asthma makes her very wheezy. Please, be a good boy and clear the table, just this once.'

Polly *is* ill all the time. We share a bedroom now and she always wakes up in the middle of the night.

'Mu-mmy!' she wheezes.

Then again . . .

'Mu-*mmy*!'

In comes Mummy to sit with her once more, trying to comfort her, always for an hour minimum, often two.

I can sleep, but only fitfully. I wake up every fifteen minutes or so when Polly has another coughing fit. I can see Mummy on the edge of the bed, the light from the corridor silhouetting her figure. I know Mummy loves me, but sometimes I think she loves Polly more. I think they both love Polly more.

On Sunday mornings, Polly and I have to play 'quietly' in our bedroom because Mummy and Daddy like having a lie-in. Today I'm trying to persuade her to hang herself from the tallboy. She seems quite keen at first, though I don't know how you're supposed to do it. The nearest thing I can think of is Jesus on the cross, but I can't understand how they managed to keep him up there.

'Stand on the chair,' I say, finally, 'then I can tie the string round your chest.'

'I don't want to.'

'Yes you do; it won't hurt. You'll really *like* it, I promise.'

'I don't want to.'

'Come on. Please! And then it'll be long enough and it can reach the handle on the top drawer.' I help her up on to the chair, then climb on next to her. 'Stand still a minute.' And I thread the string around her chest, under her arms and tie it off.

'I don't want to.'

'It's all right. It's nearly done. Stay there.'

I climb down off the chair.

'I don't yike it,' she says. Polly can't pronounce her ls yet.

'It's okay, don't move, I'm just going to take the chair away.'

'No! I don't *yike* it!' And she leans forward, trying to get down, and the string breaks.

'You've broken the string now!' I'm furious. She's *ruined* my experiment.

She climbs off the chair.

'Get up there again,' I order.

'No!'

I soften my tone. 'Please, Poll . . .'

'No! I don't want to.'

Which is typical; she never wants to do what I want to do. When I want her to play football with me, she won't. Mummy makes excuses for her, saying it's not good for her asthma. It's always her bloody asthma.

We start having a fight on my bed and I get a strange pleasure from hitting Polly and pulling her hair. I really want to hurt her; to punish her. Then I push her, even though I know what'll happen next. I can see it coming, but I can't help it, I'm so angry.

She falls off the bed and crashes headfirst into the red-brick fireplace.

Suddenly there's blood everywhere and screaming, lots of it.

Oh God! Instantly my anger disappears, to be replaced by panic. How can I get out of this without being punished? I rush into my parents' room.

'Mummy! Polly's had an accident!' Using the word 'accident' plants the idea in their heads.

Mummy reacts with the words she always uses in a crisis. 'Oh my hat!' she cries.

She and Daddy jump out of bed. I follow them, all the time wondering if Polly will give the game away. It's awful; my heart's pumping, adrenaline surging – will I get caught? I need a safety valve. The radiator! The old, white, over-painted radiator with its smooth gaps and angular ridges that I trace with the tips of my fingers, tapping and pushing on the sharp edges to lessen the load – hit it, push it, meld with it, 'become' radiator myself.

'Polly, *darling*!'

This is something entirely different from the anxiety I hear when she comforts Polly during her asthma attacks. This is an out-of-control, primeval scream. It's shocking and it's frightening. I realise this is something Mummy can't fix. She's powerless. I'm not used to my parents being powerless. They know everything – don't they?

'It's all right, darling; you're going to be all right, my poor darling. Adrian, get the car; we've got to take her straight to hospital.'

'Shouldn't we call the doctor?'

'Oh, Adrian! Don't be so bloody ridiculous! Can't you see she's bleeding! For heaven's sake, get the car!'

I don't like seeing Mummy like this. She's so upset, but she's also being brave for Polly. I suddenly feel very sorry for what I've done, the fear and guilt coming into direct conflict with the need to avoid blame. I wish I could undo it all and put the clock back. I want to cry.

'Is she going to be all right, Mummy?'

I'm trying to soften up the ground for a confession. I keep thinking that at any moment Mummy will turn to me and say accusingly, 'This is all *your* fault!'

'Sorry, Polly,' I mutter.

Polly's screaming has subsided to a muffled sobbing, but there's blood everywhere.

'It's not your fault, darling, it was an accident,' Mummy says.

This is much, much worse. I feel terrible. If only she knew the truth . . . but I can't come out and say it. So I watch while Polly gets all the sympathy and the love. Whenever I hurt myself or get ill, I get it too, and sometimes I pretend it's much worse than it is, just to squeeze every last ounce of 'there theres' out of Mummy.

Daddy reappears. 'The car's outside. I'll drive her into Southampton.'

'No, Adrian. You stay here and look after James. I'll take Polly and I'll ring you from the hospital. Come on, help me get her into the car.'

Later on, Polly comes home with stitches in her head. She wasn't very badly hurt after all, but it looked as if she was because there was so much blood. I feel terrible for days afterwards, but for the first time the Controller helps me to feel better by making me twiddle small strands of my hair with my fingers until they get into a tangle and I have to pull them out.

But the Controller also decides it's time to introduce a new kind of urge, a mental urge; an urge that controls only my thoughts, not my physical movements at all.

Gazing out of the car window, one morning, I find myself idly counting the cars swishing by on the way to school. Only moving cars; parked ones don't count.

Over the following days and weeks, almost unnoticeably, the need to find patterns within the numbers emerges, and mentally I split the school run into three separate zones. Zone one lies between the house and the main road about a mile away. Zone two begins as we turn left on to the main road itself and travel for a further two miles. Then, when we turn left into a smaller road leading directly to the school – again, about a mile – this is zone three. I have to count the number of cars we pass in each zone.

Initially, the Controller is happy. I reach school with three separate numbers in my head, the total number of cars from each zone, and as long as I can remember them all, it feels right; finished; done. As a rough average it's usually about two – fifteen – five. This only happens on the way to school, never on the way back.

But before long this doesn't seem quite enough and I start noticing whether each total is an odd or an even number. Even numbers feel more 'right' than odd, and it soon becomes important that at least two of the zones are even, knocking any remaining odd number off balance, cancelling it out, leaving the pureness, the whiteness of the even numbers. I experience a sense of unease if odd outweighs even.

Later, zones one and two lose their power, their significance fades. I still count them but it's zone three which matters now, and on the days when odd triumphs in this zone, I worry I won't have a good day at school. Zone three is my fortune teller and the nagging feeling of an odd day stays with me, pulling my internal worry strings in the background, often taking until break-time to wear off.

But still it isn't enough, and soon the colours of cars become important. Red cars feel right and only red cars will do. So passing a red car anywhere on the journey is good, but a red car in zone three is magical and can undo some of the damage caused by an odd number. A red car *and* an even number in zone three is rare, but when it happens I feel comfortable inside.

And as though the Controller had merely been experimenting, it decides that the trial period with cars was so successful that numbers and counting and patterns should play a larger part in my life, steadily infecting everything I do. The gates open wide. Nothing is left to chance any more. Every tiniest little detail of my day-to-day activities must be made safe, checked and double-checked for 'rightness'.

I am assigned a magic number.

That number is four.

It's a perfect number, an even number, symmetrical, square, the root number, the key, the password, the cure, the gateway to all 'numberness', the magic code to unlock my safeness.

Four needs to be everywhere.

I have to make it everywhere.

Walking in Romsey, I have to walk in the middle of four paving slabs, treading on each slab only once before I'm allowed to step on a crack. Because my reach is limited, the size of the paving slabs means I have to take gigantic steps to accomplish this before being allowed to walk normally again.

'Darling, will you please walk *properly*!'

The process repeats itself a few seconds later and in my head I carry a ridiculous image of what I must look like to passers-by.

I'm instructed by the Controller to count other things.

Cat's-eyes on the road are easy if we're driving slowly – one two three four one two three four – but difficult at speed, because I worry that I may have missed one. And even if I know I haven't really, it won't feel right until I've done it again and again and again and again.

One two three four one two three.

Rewind: one two.

Rewind: one.

Rewind: one two three.

Rewind: one two three four.

When I finish my cup of milk at breakfast I can't just put it down. I have to put it down four times – tap tap tap tap – and continue until each tap feels comfortable.

And when I clean my teeth I have to brush each row of teeth four times, stop, then another four times and so on. Always groups of four.

This becomes complicated because soon I need to count the groups of four themselves, and they too must add up to four. And if I brush too many times, the groups become the groups of the groups, and they too must be counted.

The Controller, recognising the problem, adjusts by adding further, larger numbers, so that grouping doesn't need to happen so often. These are eight, sixteen and, finally, thirty-six, which replaces four as the super number of numbers. It too is perfect, divisible by all the others – four, eight and sixteen. Okay, sixteen doesn't go into thirty-six, but it *feels* like it ought to, which is the important thing.

Counting and magic numbers take over. They become the main focus for my urges. On the upside, I find the sniffings and gruntings gradually subside to make way for them. This is a relief in some ways, especially at home, for while the urges come just as frequently as ever, to my parents – still irritated by my intrusive noises – counting and an obsession with patterns and numbers is far less noticeable.

But I dread situations where I have to applaud. At a school play or speech day or at the pantomime, I'm not comfortable unless I clap the full thirty-six times, and sometimes when the general applause has died down, I'm left, a lone clapper frantically trying to make up the number, attracting odd looks and giggles.

At school, everyone seems to get ahead of me.

It's not that I don't have friends; I do. David, Andrew, Christopher – I spend whole days with them at weekends or during the holidays. But at some point I seem to get left behind. It's as if I've missed some vital pieces of information about the rules of being human; as though everyone has been to 'how to do life' lessons while I wasn't there. I don't know what this magic knowledge is, only that I feel an increasing sense of isolation from other people; especially in groups and especially at school.

At playtime, everyone runs around the garden, often separating into gangs. There are boy gangs and girl gangs, never mixed – all the boys think the girls are sissy; the girls reciprocate with whatever they feel best describes the boys.

There are inter-gang chases, rough-and-tumbles and the occasional fight. Because the girls tend to stay at school until they're eleven before moving on – most of the boys leave to go to prep school aged eight – the older ones are much bigger than any of the boys and the results are usually one-sided.

I *am* in a gang. David's in it and Christopher and Andrew (the captain) and three others, Charlie, Peter and Philip, who has bright red hair. We lie in wait, hiding behind trees at the edge of the garden.

'Attack!' shouts Andrew.

And we all jump out to ambush our chosen girl-gang.

'Get them! Grab their legs!' shout the others.

'Yeah! Get their legs,' I shout, trying to echo their enthusiasm.

We chase the screaming girls around the lawn, trying to trip them up.

It's meant to be fun.

Except that it's not. I don't feel comfortable being part of the gang. I'm frightened of the older girls and I generally skip around the periphery of the action, trying to look as though I'm enjoying it.

'Go on! Get her!' I shout from the side lines, knowing I'm lying. I don't care. I just want to get away.

Occasionally, attempting to force myself into the spirit of it, I single out the smallest, weediest-looking girl I can see and make a half-hearted effort to 'get her', but it never works.

I hate it. I'm scared of being hurt; frightened of letting go. I imagine my face being trampled in the mud, having my head squashed so that it collapses in on itself and blood and brains leak out all over the grass.

'Just going to the loo,' I say, and I hide away in the darkened, grubby outside lavatories, sniffing nervously and grunting, worried in case I'm discovered, aching for the end-of-playtime bell which means I can re-emerge without losing face.

But although individually they're my friends, the gang as a whole come to see me as a useless appendage, someone who's not pulling his weight in the playground. For a while they tolerate it, but one morning during break they call me to a conference in the sandpit where I am summarily 'bunked'.

It's a relief not to have to pretend any more, and back in the classroom, no longer in gang mode, David and the rest still treat me perfectly normally, bearing no grudges, seemingly unable to connect James the gang wimp with James the classmate.

Now during break, no longer seeking a franchise in the boys' loos, I sit at the edge of the playground idly toying with a stone, tossing it between my hands, watching my ex-gang members rushing about, screaming, laughing, enjoying themselves naturally, instinctively knowing I should be there doing the same but unable to work out why I don't want to and why I'm afraid.

Sometimes I have to count the number of children I can see. This isn't easy because everyone's always moving and I can't be sure I haven't counted the same person twice. If there's any doubt I have to start again. Break-time passes quite quickly like this, but if the bell goes before I've finished, I have to make sure I've accounted for everyone, which means I'm often the last to return to the classroom.

And something's happened to my handwriting. It's got slower and slower and I'm falling behind the rest of the class. Suddenly, each letter has to 'feel' right before I can move on to the next one. It has nothing to do with neatness; in my mind a perfect 'd' can cheerfully resemble the meanderings of an ink-saturated maggot, but as long as it 'looks' right it doesn't matter. It's all about 'rightness', whether the letters – and thus, the words – feel comfortable. My finished stories always look far longer than they are because of all the space taken up with crossings-out and holes where I've had to go over a letter again and again and again until the pen nib punctures the paper.

Very occasionally I get a whole word absolutely perfect first time and in my excitement I shout out something like 'Look! I've done a *really* good word!' Whereupon, probably from the tone of my voice rather than from what I've said, everyone jumps up from their seats to come and examine my masterpiece. There's the odd 'Oh yeah' and 'Cor' and 'That's good' from those who probably don't have a clue what I'm on about but are either being generous or think they ought to be seen to have an opinion, before the teacher claps her hands, signalling everybody to return to their seats.

Miss Paget interprets this as laziness and slapdashery and during certain lessons I'm put into a semi-remedial section of the class to practise my handwriting by copying out single letters and phrases from a textbook: 'Mrs Potts likes flowers' and 'Mr Potts likes to wash his car.'

But it works.

At least Miss Paget *thinks* it's worked.

It hasn't really.

My writing does improve, yes, but only because the Controller has moved on.

By the end of my final term at primary school, those first sniffs at the carol service have developed into a whole army of urges and compulsions.

These include:

Sniffs (only sporadically).

Grunts (a little more often than the sniffs, but still fairly infrequent).

Short coughs.

Fast blinks.

Face-making.

Counting almost anything.

Touching and tapping.

Terror of the dark (I'm convinced a man wearing a blue workman's jacket – not unlike Bert's – is hiding somewhere in my bedroom waiting to attack me and I can't go to sleep unless the passage light is on and the door is wide open).

Shouts (rare, but always guaranteed to cause a stir, especially among the older generation).

Like cells viewed through a microscope, the urges are a constantly moving mass, shifting, evolving and adapting, and although the physical, outwardly visible movements have lessened in their intensity and therefore go largely unnoticed by all but Jane and my parents, it's the counting, the touching and the mental obsessions that continually interrupt, crashing in on my thought processes.

Only two areas in my life are urge-free: during sleep when my mind shuts down, and while I'm playing either the recorder or the piano.

Piano-playing in particular seems to soothe the Controller into non-existence, freeing me, allowing me to experience calm, absolute 'rightness' without the need to pay for it. I spend almost every free moment at the piano, developing an untrained technique based entirely on experimentation.

The End

Fuck!
　　The chair's wet!
　　'What the hell?'
　　And my trousers.
　　'Jesus!'
　　White jeans.
　　'Bugger!'
　　Jump up quick.
　　What did I spill?
　　'Oh, Christ! No!'
　　Turn and look at the cushion.
　　Too late now. It's soaked in.
　　Damp patch.
　　'Fuck!'
　　'Fuck!'
　　Stained.
　　Hit it! Poke the stain! Hard as you can.

Have to go and change.
Need a bath.
Walk slowly to the stairs.
Stamp on the waste-paper basket.
Kill it!
Then gently stroke it once with my big toe.
Then up the stairs.

Chapter 3
Words and Music

'What's your name?' *Huge* boy, table captain.

'Warboys,' he replies, and he shoves a couple of thick chips into his mouth, having not so much as glanced at me.

I stare at him, confused. Is he teasing me? Didn't he understand the question?

'But . . . what's your name?' I ask, internally flinching at having to repeat myself.

He looks at me as though I'd said, 'Your mother's a camel!'

'Warboys!' More than a hint of impatience in his voice.

I realise I'm making a fool of myself, that maybe he's talking in some kind of elaborate prep school code which the new boys aren't yet party to, but I can't help myself, I press on.

'Yes . . . but what's your name?'

He looks at me sharply, impatience no longer just hinted

at, and in a voice which matches his expression says, 'Warboys! My *name* . . . is Warboys!'

I'm silent. I don't understand.

Warboys *isn't* a name. It doesn't mean *anything*. It's just a word which spontaneously conjures up an image of grey, storm-tossed battleships.

Not daring to say anything more, and feeling like an idiot, I turn my attention back to my plate.

A few moments later, in a gentler tone, he says, 'Look . . . what's *your* name?'

'James.'

'No, what's your *surname*?'

'McConnel.'

'Well, at school we call each other by our last names. Didn't anyone tell you?'

I shake my head.

'I'm Warboys, you're McConnel, that chap over there's Barratt. Do you understand now?'

Of course; but I wish I hadn't asked. His name won't leave me. It goes round and round and round for days. Warboys, Warboys, Warboys, War . . . boys, Boyswar, Woysboar, Oarsbwyo, bwyo, bwyo, War . . . ships, Boats . . . war, Wugga-lugga-flugga . . . pooka-mucker . . . on and on and on and on and on until Warboys doesn't sound like Warboys any more. Walking along passageways or running on the games field, my legs move to an unwanted insistent rhythm: War! Boys! War! Boys! War! Boys! The water spewing from the bath taps seems to be reciting warboyswarboyswarboyswarboys at high speed. Everything I do is Warboys.

The Controller is having a field day.

*   *   *   *   *

Boarding school is a daunting new experience. The thought of being away from home for at least four weeks is sick-making. Like many of the other new boys I spend the first day or two in semi-tearful misery, feeling as if I'm being punished.

Everything's so big; like watching life through a magnifying glass. The building itself is enormous; its formal façade is forbidding and impersonal and its huge, high-ceilinged rooms pulse with severe formality. I find myself hugging the walls of corridors to avoid being run over by groups of dangerously large boys clumping past, hard leather soles clacking noisily, almost threateningly, against the stone or dark, polished wooden floors.

I hate it.

For about week . . . after which I settle in quite nicely.

My piano teacher, Mr Llewellyn, is an excitable man with long sideburns and a Welsh accent. What I notice immediately, though, are his fingertips. They are a rich, dark yellow, the result of years of chain-smoking, which he does throughout my first lesson, lighting each new cigarette from the glowing end of the previous one, inhaling deeply with all the desperation of a half-drowned man. In thirty minutes he gets through six; I know, because I count them.

Sitting me down at the piano, he begins: 'Have you had lessons before?'

'No . . . sir.' I keep forgetting my 'sirs'.

'Well, no matter. Can you play anything?'

'Yes, sir.'

'Show me then.'

Prepared for this, I play him 'Puff the Magic Dragon', my latest favourite, courtesy of Jane, who has the record, now almost worn out with overuse.

When I've finished there's a brief silence, then: 'How did you learn that?'

'I've got the record, sir.'

'So you learned it by ear, did you?'

I remain silent, not understanding.

'I mean you learned it by hearing it, not from the music.'

'Yes, sir.'

'Can you read music at all?'

'No, sir. My father can.'

'Well, you've obviously got some talent, but I think we need to start you from scratch so you can learn to read.'

Sprinkling ash on to his rough tweed jacket, he gets up from his chair, cigarette in mouth, head up, eyes half closed against the smoke, and rummages around in a chaotic cupboard across the room. He returns with a thin floppy book.

'Right,' he says, 'have a look at this.'

Easy Piano Pieces by Edmund Gibbons, Part One is printed on the front in flowery orange script, around which cavort several happy-looking pixies in various jaunty poses. He opens it at page one: *Exercise 1 – Pixie Dance*.

I've not had much contact with pixies, but if I had, I'm sure the music they dance to couldn't possibly be less interesting than the eight long, slow, identical notes that make up the piece Mr Llewellyn now plays.

I've seen music before, of course, on the piano at home. Daddy has *Preludes and Fugues by J.S. Bach*, a thick book, each page covered in what looks like a mass of tiny tadpoles frozen in mid-swim, attached to rows and rows of closely grouped straight lines running across the page. I've never paid it much attention, happy just to work out my favourite tunes by trial and error.

Edmund Gibbons's music is different. It's much bigger and simpler-looking.

'The important thing,' he says, glancing at me, 'is counting.'

My ears prick up.

'Once you learn how many counts each note is worth, you can start playing rhythms. This first note –' he points at an egg-shaped, tailless tadpole with a hole in it – 'is a semibreve.'

I nod.

'It's worth four beats, which means that when you play, you count to four before moving on to the next note.' He looks at me questioningly, eyebrows raised.

I nod, pleased at the four-ness of it.

'Good,' he says. 'Now these lines –' he indicates the five straight lines across the page – 'are called the stave. Okay?'

I nod.

'Each line and space tells you which notes to play.'

I nod.

'So this note attached to the bottom line of the stave is a D.'

I nod.

'And this –' he points to a note near the middle of the keyboard – 'is D on the piano.'

I nod.

'So the first note of "Pixie Dance" is a semibreve on D. Clear?'

I nod . . . even though he lost me after the word 'stave'. I nod partly because I feel I ought to have understood, and partly because the brusqueness of his manner suggests that if I admit defeat he might be cross. However, the piece is so simple I pick it up immediately, and though I haven't a clue how it relates to what's printed on the page, playing it back from memory instead, Mr Llewellyn seems pleased that I appear to have grasped the fundamentals of musical notation.

But from that day on, Edmund Gibbons and I are at war.

Every week I am set new pieces to learn and I sit baffled in a practice room, poring over a seemingly inexhaustible supply of pixie activities: parachuting pixies, sailing pixies, pixies who swim, slide, climb, jump, dress up as Red Indians and cowboys; slave pixies, farmyard pixies, Chinese pixies, French revolutionary pixies. No area of pixie life is left unserenaded by Gibbons the pixie bard.

None of it makes sense. It's easy enough to identify the actual notes but I can't work out the rhythms. Am I supposed to start counting when I press the note, or wait until I've pressed it and *then* start? And if I'm supposed to wait until I've pressed it, how *long* do I wait? This is not music, it's maths. I spend a lot of time adding things up in my mind, but it's usually clear-cut and precise. There are *exactly* eight people sitting at the table. Before I start eating, I tap my knife against the plate *exactly* four times – or sixteen or thirty-six, depending on how the Controller feels. Reading music is 'counting with pre-conditions'. It's frustrating and boring, so I spend more and more time doing what I like best: improvising and playing by ear.

Each of my lessons is a facsimile of the previous one. I sit at the piano, able to play most of the notes, but quite unable to play in time. Mr Llewellyn starts shouting at me, his voice rising a notch both in pitch and strength of Welsh accent. 'Wretched boy! You haven't done any practice *again*, have you?' Finally shoving me off the piano stool to show me how it should sound. And each time I memorise what he plays and when I sit down again I duplicate it, and by the end of the lesson he calms down, satisfied that I've made at least *some* progress.

But at the end of six months I still can't make head or tail of it . . .

Until, during choir practice one afternoon, I quiz Dixon Minor, a fellow treble sitting next to me.

'Don't you understand about bar lines?' he asks, pointing at one of the short vertical lines splitting the stave at various points.

'No,' I say, 'Fagbreath Llewellyn just starts shouting at me if I tell him I don't understand something.'

'It's easy,' he says. 'When you get to the end of a bar you just start counting at one again. They're like little boxes. Look . . . one two three four, barline. One two three four barline. You see?'

Yes! It's so obvious!

What *I've* been doing until now is counting each note value, adding it to the next and the next and the next and the next, ending up with a huge number, having to do the mental arithmetic as well as playing, losing count and getting in a muddle. Suddenly I understand. It all makes perfect sense at last, no longer a mysterious mathematical puzzle; and all unlocked for me by another eight-year-old boy.

We have group music lessons with Fagbreath as well, and one day he decides we should listen to a piece of music called Pomp and Circumstance March No 1, by a man called El Gar. Stupid names, both of them. Pomp and Circumstance doesn't mean anything – how can you call a piece of music

Pomp and Circumstance? Pomp and Circumstance!

PompandCircumstancePompandCircumstancePompand Circumstance!

Poggersagger! Poggersagger! Poggersagger!

Pizar! Pizar! Pizar!

El . . . Gar . . . It makes me think of a tomato; maybe he's Spanish.

El Gar! El Gar! ElGarElGarElGar!

Mr Llewellyn puts on a record, and lively music starts up. It's fast and energetic, and because the word 'march' makes me think of the guards at Buckingham Palace, I find myself visualising them. The trouble is, although the basic beat is very marchable to, all the other stuff El Gar has written around it sounds like cartoon music. Suddenly there are 150 Charlie Chaplins in red uniforms and tall black furry hats tripping and falling all over each other in that big road that leads up to the Palace. Each time they try to get up again, they trip over one of their neighbours. It's chaos. There are loud trombones farting with laughter down at the bottom, while up above, the violins and trumpets scream with delight. I can't help giggling.

'What are you laughing at, McConnel?'

'Nothing, sir.'

'Well, don't!'

I look around to see if anyone else thinks it's funny. They all just look bored.

Then something really extraordinary happens. Suddenly, out of the chaos and comic mayhem comes this electrifying tune that sets the hairs at the back of my neck tingling. It's beautiful – the most beautiful thing I've ever heard. It's quiet, so simple and elegant. It seems to yearn for something, yet it has such dignity. It speaks to me.

Da – da – da da da – da – da

Da – da – da da da – daaaaaaaaaaa

I feel as though I've been injected with golden syrup. Pure bliss; I'm almost floating. It's a tune that knows and understands me, fits in with me. Though I've never heard it before, it's a tune I've always known. It completely fills me, takes me away from me.

I'm not me any more, I just am.

But it doesn't last long enough, and infuriatingly, moments later, the Chaplins are back. This time they're not funny. I want to hear that tune again.

After five unendurable minutes of chaos, it returns, huge and proud and grand and honest, and it's me.

And when it's finished, suddenly, I *have* to go to the piano.

'Sit down, McConnel!'

I can't. Mr Llewellyn intercepts me, blocking my way. I try moving around him but he grabs my arm to stop me.

'Didn't you hear me, boy? I said sit *down!*'

But now I *need* to touch the piano, not to play any more, just to touch the wood, the shiny, shiny brown hard wood. I struggle with him, the sense of urgency and panic rising in me at the thought of what will happen if I don't make contact. Finally, I pull away from his grasp and manage it, only fleetingly, but it's enough.

'Right,' he screams, 'get out of my class!'

I go straight to a practice room and spend the rest of the lesson trying to work out the wonderful tune. I play it over and over and over and over again for weeks.

*   *   *   *   *

'Can you play "Food Glorious Food"?'

'"Edelweiss"!'

'"Chitty Chitty Bang Bang"!'

'That's amazing!'

I begin to realise that the other boys like my piano playing. When I play for them, I belong. I know they notice my sniffs and grunts and face-making because sometimes I'll catch one of them staring at me curiously for a moment or two, but they don't seem to mind and no one ever says anything. I get a thrill out of performing, showing off, improvising musical 'jokes' based on tunes from *Oliver* and *The Sound of Music*, which they all know. During break-times I often sit at an out-of-tune 'honky-tonk' piano in one of the practice rooms, surrounded by six or seven of my classmates.

I love all the admiring glances and the laughter, and while I still feel oddly disconnected overall, at these times, as well as on the sports field, I feel 'equal to' instead of 'nearly'.

I enjoy sports. I'm quite good at cricket and I love football. Because it's organised, I don't feel uncomfortable like I did in the playground at Miss Paget's. I find it much easier belonging, being part of the team, when all I have to do is concentrate on scoring goals; when there's no need to interact directly or observe any rules other than the rules of the game. As with music, when the point of it all is so simple and clear-cut that doubts or worries about getting it wrong can't intrude, then it's easy.

But I have one overriding fear. Swimming.

I *hate* swimming. I hate everything associated with it. It frightens me; the smell of chlorine, the painted blue walls and bottom of the pool, the diving board, the silver rail at the top of the steps, the concrete-slabbed edging, even a pair of swimming trunks drying on a rack in the changing rooms. I can't get the hang of swimming. I'm terrified of water. Terrified of drowning.

During the three or four hours leading up to a swimming lesson I feel a sickening, gradually tightening knot of tension in my stomach. Everybody in the school has learned how to swim but me. I can't help it. I panic. Even though I know the strokes, I'm not brave enough to kick my feet off the ground and trust the process. To make matters worse, I'm depriving everyone of a free 'half day', the headmaster's promised treat if the whole school can swim two lengths by the end of term. Early on, those of us who couldn't swim had to take turns putting on a towelling harness attached to a rope, which was tied to a pole at one end and held by the swimming master, supporting us as we flailed around in the water. I'm still at this stage and I hate it more than anything because I'm convinced the rope will break.

And one afternoon I'm struggling along at the deep end when the rope does break and although I don't feel it break, inexplicably I begin to sink and for a split second I do nothing because I can't believe it. But then panic takes over and I thrash about, fighting with the water, trying to get on top of it, all logic and thoughts of breaststroke gone from my mind. As my head dips under completely, I can see the sun rippling through the surface above me like a chaotic kaleidoscope while the outside world slowly retreats and all sound stops and then everything suddenly goes very slowly and I'm terrified and I'm swallowing water. Then I bob briefly to the surface again and I hear the swimming master shouting, 'Grab a hold of the rope!' And among the panic and the fear I think it's rather strange that he says 'grab a hold' and not just 'grab hold', but I can't grab the rope because I can't think what that means. Then I'm under again and I'm swallowing more water, which tastes of chlorine, and I want to cry but I can't and I don't want to die and I know I'm going to die and then I hear a faint splashing sound somewhere. It sounds as if it's coming from the next-door room and then someone's hands grab me under my arms and I'm on the surface again and I'm coughing and crying and being sick all at the same time. I'm so cold and the swimming master is pulling me towards the steps and then I'm out of the pool and a towel is wrapped around me and I'm shaking . . . and I *knew* it would happen.

And as I'm lying in the sickbay resting, I relive the experience again and again and I think about drowning, which seems like such a soft kind of cruelty. Soft, soft soft. The soft water, gentle, but so hard – and I hate it and I curl up when I think of what might have happened. The Controller makes me take hard, sharp breaths and I act out what it feels like to drown, pretending my throat and my lungs are full of water.

Academically, though, things go quite well, to begin with. At the end of my first year I come second overall. However, something changes between years one and two and I go into a dramatic decline. I don't know what it is, but one term the work is challenging and enjoyable, the next my concentration has died and I'm finding it harder and harder to focus on anything for more than a few minutes at a time. This is reflected in my exam results.

At the end of my second year, when the headmaster, Mr Horton, reads out the marks for each pupil, he rounds off his speech: 'Before I finish, I would like to mention three boys who, in my view, are wasting their parents' money at this school.'

A short pause while he looks around the room, making sure he has our full attention. He does, absolutely. I can feel the instant tension as four or eight of the lowest achievers – me among them – stiffen, suddenly nauseous with the terrifying internal question, 'Will it be me?'

'They are Philip Ambrose, James McConnel and Nicholas Lacy.'

Another pause. I don't know about the other two, but I can feel every eye in the room scanning me, examining, judging and rejecting me; the 'loser', the 'thick one', the 'dunce'.

'All three of you are scraping along at the bottom of your respective classes,' he continues. 'None of you appear to have made any effort whatsoever in any of your subjects during the past year, and this will be reflected in your school reports. I suggest you use the summer break to think about how you plan to rectify the situation.'

I cringe. I fold inwardly, head down, arms crossed, knowing what he thinks of me; knowing that everyone else knows; projecting forward to the first day of the holidays when Dad will open my school report, sit me down on the sofa next to him and go through each painful comment – 'could do better', 'consistently lazy', 'cannot seem to operate as part of a group', 'has not made enough effort this year' – and in patient, utterly reasonable tones will ask me why I think I'm doing so badly, reducing me to tears.

When nothing changes and I remain consistently at the bottom of my class, I'm sent to an educational therapist for evaluation. He asks me all kinds of stupid questions, then some not so stupid questions and then some questions I don't understand at all. In his report he says I'm probably a late developer, that I sometimes don't stop to think before answering, but otherwise he can't find much wrong with me.

And then at thirteen:

'Right, gents. Nine o'clock. Please turn over your papers and begin. You have three hours.'

Occasion: Common Entrance Exam.
Intended School: Eton.
Subject: History.
Place: The Library.
Invigilator: Malcolm Carter; fat French teacher and bully (though he likes *me*).
Mood: Worried – hate history.
Thoughts: 'Hargan Way', a nonsensical phrase which has been with me for about a week.

I turn my paper over, remove my hand briefly so that all contact is broken, whisper 'her her' twice, then repeat it until it feels right, flip the paper back over, face down, tap it gently three times, in my mind adding two more 'her hers' to make five, then turn it right-side up again ready to start. At the top I write *James McConnel*, almost the last thing I do with any real confidence for the following two hours and fifty-nine minutes.

PART A General History: You must answer ALL the questions.

Question 1: Which treaty, drawn up in 1713 after the War of Spanish Succession, was named after the Dutch city in which it was signed?

Erm.

Er.

Erm.

Come on, think of all the cities you know in Holland.

Amsterdam.

The treaty of Amsterdam.

Never heard of it, doesn't sound right.

The treaty of The Hague.

The Hague . . . Hague . . . Hague, sounds like Hargan . . .

Hargan Way.

Harganharganharganharganhargan . . . shut up!

Rotterdam . . . the treaty of Rotterdam. No.

Damn!

Damn Damn. The treaty of Damn Dam.

Damdamdamdamdam!

Shut up.

Come back to it.

Question 2: What was the name of Henry VIII's third wife, the mother of Edward VI?

Anne Boleyn – was it?

Or Catherine of Aragon?

Hang on, Mum taught me this: 'Divorced, beheaded, died. Divorced, beheaded, survived.'

So she died . . . not much help.

Anne Boleyn, Catherine of Aragon.

Anne Boleyn, Catherine of Aragon.

What the hell were the others called?

Okay, there was **Anne** Boleyn and **Catherine** of Aragon.

Anne Boleyn and **Catherine** of Aragon . . . and . . .

Move on . . .

Question 3: What was the name of the battle in which Henry V famously defeated the French in 1415?

You're joking.

Question 4: On which island was Napoleon Bonap . . .

Move on.
   And on.
   And on.

Question 12: Who was Prime Minister during World War II?

Aha! Think I know this one.
   Winston Churchill.
   Dad met him once.

'James?'
   'Yes, sir?'
   'Your Common Entrance results have come in; and I have to tell you that with the exception of French, which you passed, I'm afraid your other marks were well below the required fifty-five per cent. So you will not be going to Eton next term. Better luck next time.'
   Half-term, a few days later.
   'Jemmy?'
   'Yes?'
   'Could you come in here a minute? Mum and I would like a word.'
   It had to come sometime. It's been ominously quiet so far, though I've known something was up from the half-

overheard telephone conversations when they speak in that politely official voice reserved for bank managers and headmasters.

Mum's smiling. 'Come and sit down, darling.'

'Yes, come and sit down, old boy.' Dad's smiling too.

Brutus-like.

I sit, Caesar-like.

They took me to see the film *Julius Caesar* but I hated the blood when Caesar was stabbed, so we left early. But I caught the gist of it.

Mum goes first. 'Now listen, darling, I know you must be very disappointed about Eton and obviously we are too, a little, but it's not the end of the world.' She looks as though it might be.

'Not the end of the world at all,' comments Dad, almost absent-mindedly.

'And we still think you'd be happy there,' continues Mum.

'Very happy there.'

'Oh, Adrian, do stop interrupting.'

'I was only saying—'

'Well, I wish you wouldn't! Now the thing is, Jamie, we've had a word with Mr Horton . . . and *he* thinks you'd have a much better chance next year . . .'

Look out, Julius.

'. . . if we moved you to this lovely school in Sussex, which specialises in getting boys through Common Entrance.'

Bloody hell. I hadn't expected *this*.

'But . . .' I protest.

'Darling, I *know* it would mean leaving Westford,' she continues, 'and we have thought about this quite hard.'

'But . . .'

'Shh, darling, listen a minute! There are only about thirty boys. It's very informal, you don't have to wear a uniform and they take you on all sorts of trips at weekends.'

'But . . .'

'We just want what's best for you.'

'I think it *is* the right thing, actually.' Dad still sounds distracted.

Mum carries on regardless. 'And you won't be going alone. Apparently there's another boy from Westford as well . . . Philip Ambrose is going.'

Oh great . . . Thicky Ambrose.

The same thicky Ambrose with whom I topped the bill on Mr Horton's 'least likely' list three years ago. Except *he's* probably sitting shell-shocked on a sofa somewhere thinking, 'Oh great . . . Thicky McConnel.'

The Controller goes fishing and hauls in a couple of coughs, sniffs and a neck jerk.

'But what if I promise to work really hard? Can't I just stay at Westford?'

'Oh, darling . . .'

'And what about the piano?'

'Yes, I know that's important, and they *do* have a piano there, I asked specially.'

'But can I have lessons?'

'That I don't know, darling; we'll have to see.'

'But I *need* lessons.'

'Sweetie, I *know* you do, but the thing is –' she takes a deep breath – 'isn't it more important to get through your Common Entrance first? *Then* you can have piano lessons at Eton.'

Silence – shocked (me), expectant/hopeful (them).

Dad, still sounding preoccupied, says, 'Run by a man called Ryan . . . sounds quite nice . . . Irish, though.'

'Oh *do* shut up, Adrian!'

Silence.

I tap my right knee eight times in a vain attempt to feel better.

I know they're trying to help. I know they care. But I don't care if they care. I feel *awful*: patronised, humiliated and disgusted with myself for having sunk so low.

I'm being sent . . . to a school . . . no, a 'crammer' . . . for idiots.

It won't be twenty-nine idiots and me; it'll be thirty idiots. And I'll be one of them.

I will belong. At last. It'll be official.

James McConnel: IDIOT

I'm determined to hate it.

Absolutely determined.

Even though Mr Ryan, brimming with good humour under his owlish horn-rimmed glasses, and his wife – cuddly and matronly – welcome me like a long-awaited tax rebate into what is essentially their home with added classrooms and dormitories. And even though the other boys, far from being thick and idiotic, seem sensitive and friendly.

The first night, lying in bed, my emotions alternating between misery, then fury at my parents, I ache to be back at Westford – envying those who are – longing for its now-comforting and familiar austerity, its utilitarian decor and hard wooden floors. This place, for all its carpeted cosiness, feels alien, threatening and claustrophobic.

It won't do.

After breakfast the following morning, I decide to run away.

Creeping out of the school gates with 50p in my pocket, I can't help letting a sense of the dramatic sneak in. Now that I'm actually doing something, it may as well be an adventure – with nerves.

On the one hand, I'm the abused child on the run from a Dickensian nightmare, on the other, I'm an escapee, a secret agent, Steve McQueen, as I leap into a ditch at the side of the road to hide when I see the postman's van approaching. I'm Jim Phelps, my Mission Impossible to infiltrate Billingshurst railway station without being detected.

Thirty minutes later I arrive.

It feels similar to Winchester station, from where we go to London on family trips, but it's strange being in this environment by myself without my parents. It's unreal. Even time seems unreal. It's not 'school' time or 'holiday' time. I'm on 'non' time, 'zombie' time. Normal, everyday things like Marks and Spencer and Nescafé don't belong here somehow.

As I study the train timetable, my eyes wander down the list of mostly unrecognisable names until they alight on Portsmouth. I know it's in Hampshire and I'm sure we went there for the day once, so it can't be that far from home. Or was that Bournemouth? I can't remember, so I poke at the word 'Portsmouth' on the timetable several times with my forefinger and then sniff four times to make it right. Yes, it must have been Portsmouth.

There's a newsagent's on the platform.

Armed with a sandwich, a Mars bar, a can of Coke, the *Beano*, my train ticket and the remaining 2p, I board the train and crouch in a seat, nervously looking round, ever watchful for a posse from the school.

Once in Portsmouth, I'll be able to catch a bus to Romsey, then another one to Plaitford. I've got to get home, all the way, by myself; anything less is failure. I want to see their faces when I walk in through the front door. They'll be *so* impressed that I've managed to make it halfway across the country alone, and with only 50p. Mum will cry with relief that I'm safe and they'll realise how desperately unhappy I've been, marvel at the lengths I've gone to and send me straight back to Westford.

'Tickets, please! All tickets, please!'

I hand him mine.

'Thank you, young man.'

Click as he punches it.

'Day off school then?'

'Er, yes.'

'Lucky chap,' and he moves on down the carriage.

The trouble is I've only got 2p left.

Which isn't going to get me very far on a bus.

I didn't realise it was all going to cost so much.

To get only halfway and then have to ring for help . . .

Pathetic.

They'll be furious.

And send me straight back to Sussex.

I push my head against the headrest as hard as I can.

Maybe I could hitch-hike.

No . . . too dangerous.

And Mum would be even more furious.

I could say my money was stolen.

No, that's useless; they'd still be furious.

What if I was *stopped* from getting home?

Could say I had an accident.

Bus crash.

Nah . . .

I gaze out of the window, searching for inspiration.

Sheep.

And chocolate.

Chocolate sheep; sheepandchocolatesheepandchocolate!

Ch-ch-ch-ch-ch-ch-ch-ch-ch-ch-ch! Shut up!

Then I have an idea . . .

An inspiration . . .

Which gets me off the hook . . .

Gets me home . . .

And gets me back to Westford.

But it's a terrible lie.

Portsmouth.

I get off the train and wander round the station, looking for a telephone box.

I'm nervous now, from the anticipation.

There's one! By the entrance.

Just about managing to open the heavy red door, I stagger in.

I lift the receiver and dial.

'Hello?' Mum's voice.

The pips go and I push my 2p into the slot.

'Mum?'

'Hello, darling. How are you getting on?'

'Mum, I've been kidnapped.'

'*What!* What d'you mean!? Darling, where *are* you?'

'Portsmouth.'

'*Portsmouth!*'

I can hear Dad in the background. 'What's happened?'

Mum sounds terrible. 'He says he's been kidnapped!'

Then, to me, 'Oh my God, darling, what's going on, where are—'

Pip pip pip pip pip pip pip . . . out of money.

It's done.

No going back.

I'm feeling awful about having lied.

Mum's voice. Oh God.

I've told my parents I've been kidnapped.

I haven't *been* kidnapped.

But they think I have.

Or maybe they don't, I don't know.

What if I really *had* been kidnapped?

What would happen then?

What would happen if I was murdered because my parents couldn't pay the ransom?

Face face face face, neck jerk jerk jerk jerk jerk.

C-A-L-M D-O-W-N.

You *haven't* been kidnapped. It's fine. And you can't stop now.

What would I do if I'd just been kidnapped and escaped?

It's not enough to have been kidnapped; I have to have *escaped* as well.

It's obvious. How else would I have got here otherwise?

Unless the kidnapper got cold feet . . .

That's possible.

The police.

That's what I'd do. I'd ring the police.

But I haven't got any money left.

In that case I'd try to find a police station.

I'd be in a rush, upset, crying probably, or too shocked to cry.

I don't know.

I start walking.

Damn the paving stones! Not now! One-two-three-four. Stop it!

How many lamp-posts before I can ask?

Sixteen. That means it'll be okay.

Middle-aged woman with a pram; grandmother maybe.

'Excuse me,' I say, acting breathless, traumatised, 'I need to find a police station and fast!'

This sounds acceptably like something one of the Avengers might say.

I long for her to reciprocate with something equally dramatic like, 'Oh my God! What's happened? You look terrible!'

But, disappointingly, she just says, 'You're miles away, love; it's right up the other end of town.' She points. 'Just keep walking, far as you can see, then ask again, okay?'

'Oh shit!' I say dramatically, as if it's already too late, and set off again at a fast walk, attempting to convey nail-biting urgency.

I walk and walk and walk. Portsmouth is huge.

About twenty minutes later (sixteen groups of sixteen lamp-posts), I see an old lady with one of those old-ladyish wicker shopping baskets on two wheels. 'Excuse me,' I ask. 'Can you tell me where the police station is, please?'

She doesn't say anything but, frowning, looks up the road in both directions as if deciding where she thinks it ought to be, rather than where it is.

'I think,' she says unhurriedly, 'you've come too far. I'm *sure* it's back that way,' and she points to where I've just come from.

'Oh God,' I mutter, still in character but considering 'shit' a bit much for an old lady, and start retracing my steps.

Ten minutes later, on the point of asking yet again, there's a hoot from behind me. I turn to see a police car containing two policemen pulling into the side of the road, blue light flashing silently. One of them gets out and starts walking towards me.

'Your name James?'

'Yes.'

'James McConnel?'

'Yes.'

'You all right?'

'Yes . . . *No* . . .'

He puts his mouth to his radio. 'Foxtrot four to base, over.'

A crackly voice replies, 'Go ahead, Foxtrot four.'

'Yeah, we've found our missing lad. James McConnel, Goldsmith Avenue. Seems okay, we're bringing him in, over.'

'Roger that.'

'Over and out.'

He turns back to me.

'Been looking for you; we've had your mum on the phone. You've got a lot of people very worried about you, d'you know that?'

I wish he hadn't added 'd'you know that?' It makes it sound as if I'm being told off.

Opening the back door of the car, he says, 'Come on, jump in, we'll give you a lift.'

I climb in, wondering how they found me so quickly, realising I've got to do a lot more acting – and lying. He shuts the door, walks round and gets into the front passenger seat.

'Lucky we found you,' he says as we move off.

'Wanted a day off school, did we?'

I'm stunned. How can *anyone* be so insensitive?

'No, I was kidnapped,' I say, trumping him.

'Kidnapped!'

He and the driver swap glances. Clearly they haven't been told.

'That must have been . . . interesting.'

Interesting!? Terrifying, maybe, or awful, but hardly just interesting.

But I think they believe me.

'It was very frightening,' I say. 'He had a gun.'

I didn't mean to say that. It never even occurred to me. It just slipped out.

'A gun!' More exchanged glances. I can't see their faces, but I can tell they're taking this very seriously now.

'That does sound pretty frightening.'

'It was,' I say.

When we arrive at the police station I'm handed over to another policeman, who introduces himself as Alan. All around me there is officialdom, busy-ness, uniforms, the sound of typewriters clacking, telephones ringing. He installs me in a stark interview room and brings me tea and biscuits.

'Right now, James, your parents are on their way, but why don't you tell me the whole story in your own words from the beginning. Just take your time, there's no hurry; all right?'

He seems sympathetic. I've got to be very careful to get the details right. Time and again I've seen Kojak catching criminals out on the details.

'Well,' I begin, 'I'd just had breakfast, which was cereal – Rice Krispies – a fried egg, some bacon, one sausage and two pieces of toast with marm—'

'It's okay, James, I don't need to know what you had.'

'Oh. Well, after breakfast I went up to the dormitory to clean my teeth – I use Macleans toothpaste . . .'

I wait until he nods.

'Then I came downstairs and went outside to go across to the classroom for lessons.'

'What time was this, roughly?'

'Erm . . . about half past eight.'

He writes it down on a small pad.

'Okay. Then what?'

'Well, I was just near the front gate when I heard a *psst* sound coming from the bushes.'

'A *psst* sound?'

'Yes, like someone trying to get my attention.'

'So what did you do?'

'Well, I thought maybe it was one of the boys having a joke, so I went over to have a look.'

'Yes?'

'And . . . there was this man standing behind the bushes . . . he had something in his hand. It looked to me like it was made of black metal.'

'And did you see what it was?'

'I think it might have been a gun.'

'A gun!?'

His reaction is similar to the car policeman's.

'Yes, and he was sort of . . . pointing it at me.'

'Was he now . . . and what did this man look like? What was he wearing?'

Hadn't *thought* of this. Hadn't thought about the kidnapper at all. Damn, why didn't I think of that?

The Controller throws me a few sniffs and a cough.

'Well,' I say, improvising, 'he had . . . dark hair . . .'

. . . made of chocolate . . . each little strand thin thin thin, so thin it'll break! Crack! Split! Smash!

C-RRRR-ACK!

Stop it!

' . . . and a white mackintosh, brown trousers and black shoes.'

'Black . . . shoes,' he repeats slowly, while writing. He looks up. 'And what about his face?'

'Er . . . it was white.'

'White,' he echoes again. 'Go on.'

'He had blue eyes, I think . . . I can't remember any more.'

'Okay.'

'Well, he pointed the gun at me and signalled me to come over to him. I was frightened he would shoot me if I didn't.'

'So it *was* a gun. You said you weren't sure.'

'Yes . . . when I got closer I could see it.'

'Ah, of course. What did the gun look like?'

'It was black and shiny . . . I think it might have been a Colt .45.'

I shouldn't have said that. I *shouldn't* have said that; but I wanted to impress him.

'Know about guns, do you?'

'Not really . . . but . . . it looked like one of those ones you see in westerns.'

'I . . . see.' The 'I' is long, the 'see' is short.

I move on quickly to distract him.

'So I went over to him and he made me walk to the train station. He put the gun in his pocket so no one could see it, but I knew it was still pointing at me.'

'That must have been frightening.'

'Yes . . . it was *very* frightening.'

Putting his pad and pencil on the desk, leaning back in his chair and crossing his arms, he says, 'And what did this very frightening man with the gun say to you on your walk to the station?'

'He didn't say anything. I think he was worried in case I could identify his voice.'

'Mm hmm.'

I sniff loudly, wrinkle my nose and cough.

'Are you all right? Sounds like you've got a cold.'

'Er, no, it's hay fever.'

'Oh. So what happened then?'

'Well, when we got to the station, he made me buy two tickets to Portsmouth.'

'*He* made *you* buy the tickets?'

'Yes.'

'How did you know where he wanted to go?'

'Erm . . . he told me to buy them.'

'*Did* he? So he wasn't *that* worried about you identifying his voice, then?'

'Er . . . no . . . I s'pose not.'

Damn! Another mistake.

'And how did you pay for these tickets?'

Pause.

'He . . . gave me some money.'

'Oh he did? And were there many people in the station?'

'Er, quite a few, yes.'

'And I don't suppose . . . with all these people around . . . you thought to ask for help?'

'Erm . . . he still had the gun in his pocket, which was pointing at me.'

'Oh I seeee . . . Of course, the gun.'

'And,' I continue, 'he said, "Don't try any funny business, or else," so I was really scared.'

'Yes, I'm sure you were. So what happened then?'

'He made me get on the train and it was really frightening still, and he was watching me all the way until we got to a place called Fratton.'

'Fratton!? It's a long way from Billingshurst to Fratton. What were you doing all that time?'

'He was just sitting, watching me. He didn't say anything.'

'Oh. So he just sat there?'

'Yes, and when we got to Fratton, he suddenly jumped up and got off the train.'

'What, just like that?'

'Yes. I don't know why he did it.'

'No, nor do I. So what did *you* do?'

'I was really frightened and when I got to Portsmouth I rang my parents.'

'And you didn't think to tell someone on the train what had happened?'

'I was too shocked and I didn't think anyone would believe me. It was very frightening.'

'You could've dialled 999.'

'I didn't have any money left.'

'You don't need money for 999 calls.'

'Oh. I didn't know.'

Pause. Alan taps the end of his pen on the table a few times (nine, I count them).

'Mmm . . . you *have* had a busy time, haven't you?'

'I s'pose so.' I try looking as forlorn as I can.

He sighs, a long deep sigh.

'How are you feeling now?'

'All right,' I say; 'a bit scared still.'

Another pause; longer this time.

'Mmm. Well, I have to say, James,' he sniffs, 'I don't think that's quite what happened, is it?'

He looks directly at me, calm, relaxed . . . and intimidating.

Suddenly I'm on edge. 'What—'

'I don't think you were kidnapped at all. I think you decided you'd like a day off school and you made up this story to get yourself out of trouble.'

'What . . . ? I didn't.'

'In fact, James, you've put your parents through a great deal of worry and trouble for nothing, haven't you?'

'No! He stole my 50p!' I say, outraged, as if it'll help.

'You're asking me to believe that a man kidnapped you in Sussex, took you all the way to Fratton on the train – a journey of nearly two hours – and then left you, for no reason at all?'

'I know it seems strange, but it's true.'

'Well, I don't think it *is* true. You've wasted a lot of people's time and energy, young man. Now, I'm going to leave you here for a while; I want you to have a good think about what you've done today. And then I'll come back later and you can tell me what *really* happened. Okay?'

I say nothing, and he leaves the room.

I sit there for what seems like an age.

He knows I lied.

I feel ashamed.

Ashamed and miserable. I can feel prickling behind my eyes.

Made *worse* because he wasn't even cross. It would be so much better if he was cross with me. But he just sounded disappointed, which hurts far more because it feels dismissive, as if I were an irritating little nuisance not worth the effort of full-blown anger.

I'm so angry with myself; for having been found out, for having been so stupid.

And they'll tell my parents, and they *will* be cross. Furious. And I'll be sent back to Sussex. And then all the other boys will know.

'Chitty Chitty Bang Bang,' I murmur under my breath to help ease my embarrassment and discomfort.

Chitty Chitty Bang Bang.

Flitty mitty bitty witty quitty titty.

Tittytittytittytittytttttttttttttttttttttttttttttttttttttt.

Hee hee hee hee hee hee hee hee.

Heeeeeeeeeeeeeeeeeeeeeeeeeeeeeeeee.

Eeeeeeeeeeeee ya! Heeeeeeeeeeeeeeeee ya!

Cough! Cough! Neck stretch.

Five taps on the table.

How can I salvage it?

I go back over my story, trying to work out where I went wrong, searching for a magic phrase, a missed event that will transform their disappointed disbelief into instant, backtracking credulity.

And I sit. Feeling worse and worse as the minute hand on the wall clock creeps through thirty endless minutes.

And then the door opens again, and in walk . . . my parents.

They aren't furious. Just relieved to have me back in one piece.

I never see Alan again.

I never do have to tell the truth.

They drive me home and never once mention the 'kidnapping'. They tell me I have to return to Sussex, but that if I still hate it after a week, they'll take me out and send me back to Westford, assuming Westford has room for me.

And the terrible, awful thing is . . . I enjoy it. The work's hard, but Mr Ryan is a great teacher. I get on with the other boys; there's time to play the piano and show off. At the end of the week, the school bus takes us to a local fair, where I spend the afternoon laughing, having fun with everyone, being happy.

But I can't admit it. I *cannot* . . . admit it.

On Sunday morning I ring my parents and tell them I still hate it.

They pick me up the next day and I go back to Westford.

And I feel terribly guilty.

'Hey! I thought you'd left!'

I grin.

'What are *you* doing back here?'

'I was sent to a crammer. I didn't like it, so I ran away.'

I'm a hero.

'Cor, really!'

And 'Wow!'

And 'Incredible!'

And 'How did you get out?'

And I tell them, loving the attention.

But I'm glad to be back. Fagbreath Llewellyn isn't the best piano teacher in the world, but he's the only one I've got.

All but one of my contemporaries have moved on. Back in the sixth form again, second time around I find the work much easier.

But again, I fail my Common Entrance, and again, I'm not

particularly disappointed. However, my results are a little better this time, and on discovering that not only is a minor public school, Rimmington Hall, prepared to take me on the strength of them, but is particularly interested in my musical abilities, Mr Llewellyn drives me down there one day in May to play to them.

I'm offered a music exhibition, a sub-scholarship. This delights everyone. Suddenly I'm a golden boy. My name miraculously appears up on the wall in gold letters, the hall of fame reserved for scholarship and exhibition winners. At the end of the summer term during the dreaded 'results', my stock has risen from 'waster of his parents' money' to 'outstanding musician'. Crammers and failed Common Entrance exams are now forgotten, blasted into nothingness by the blinding light of my triumph.

I feel good.

Rimmington Hall.

I'm looking forward to it.

The End

Ahh!
> Bath.
> Better.
> Hot as possible.
> Sunburn hot.
> Anaesthetic.
> Stay still, soap.
> Stay *still*!
> Don't you dare . . . move!
> Not a millimetre!
> Not one!
> Not even the tiniest fraction of a millimetre.
> Slippery bloody stuff!
> Lie back . . . slowly.
> Sing 'Pugga mugga lugga wugga **poo man** . . .'
> Very, very slowly . . .
> To the theme tune of the *Batman* TV series.

As low in my voice as I can . . .
Deep breath.
'Oooooooooooooooooooooooooooooooooooooooooo . . .'
One . . . long . . . note.
Then the other vowels, to see what they sound like.
Hold each for as long as possible.
And . . . release.

Chapter 4
The Fabulous Trio

I can sense it coming, even before they do.

The familiar, tiny symptoms, the subtle change of atmosphere.

I can feel it.

There'll be a general lull in activity, a moment of group quiet, boredom even – and then one by one they search for something on which to focus their attention.

Next come the whispering and fidgeting, fingers pointed in my direction, quick glances – and on cue the sickening creeping dread slowly engulfs me, beginning in my stomach, radiating outwards, quickening my heartbeat as adrenaline floods my system. A combination of butterflies, raw fear and hopelessness.

And with the feeling of stark injustice, there's a sneaking suspicion that perhaps I deserve it and the faintest whiff of excitement right at the bottom of the fear.

Sexual. Masochistic. Barely noticeable.

Gradually – as in those Fifties B-movies where aliens have invaded the minds of all the citizens of a Mid-Western American town, except the hero – they turn towards me, as one, synchronised, slow smiles spreading across the ringleaders' faces.

Always the same ringleaders: Thompson, Hargreaves, Carson-Scott.

They want this moment badly.

Particularly Thompson, the leader of leaders. Gleeful, yet drunk with suppressed anger. For him, I think it's revenge. I can see it in his eyes. I don't know why; there's too much cruelty there.

I hate him.

Everything about him disgusts me.

If I was a hate machine, spewing out hatred by the gallon, I could never produce enough to fully express how I feel about him.

I hate his short dark hair, his pointed nose, his perm-anently narrowed 'cool' eyes, the knee-length, high-heeled soft leather boots which are his pride and joy, his perm-anently superior expression and bearing, all of which he hopes will say, 'I'm mysterious and dangerous – don't mess with me.'

At night I sometimes visualise him tied to the floor while I bash and bash and bash at him with a sledgehammer. Bashing until his entire body is as flattened as a minute steak. Beyond dead; not a once-living thing at all: just a nasty mess for the cleaning staff to deal with.

'Mc-Con-nel . . .' Thompson – spoken in a sing-song voice; gently, as if reminding a child it's bathtime again.

'Wanker!' Venomous – Hargreaves; heavy and piggish. He waddles rather than walks. His eyes look Chinese because his fat puffy cheeks push upwards, half closing them.

'Twitch!' Jokey and high – Carson-Scott, short, but athletic and immensely strong.

They jigger like marionettes, jerking their heads and arms, making exaggerated faces, giggling, mentally patting each other on the back for their uncanny, realistic impersonations of me.

Safely united.

The Fabulous Trio.

The Leaders.

Here to rally the troops and boost team spirit. The common-room press gang for those who are not natural predators but who, given the chance, willingly participate.

There are a few who don't get involved, but not many.

It started on my first evening. All the new boys had to go through an initiation test in the junior common room. This consisted of being squeezed into a large black plastic rubbish bin, hoisted up on to a high table, and then pushed off. You were considered to have passed if you could endure it without making a sound, either of complaint or of fear.

I arrived late, by which time all the other new boys had already been initiated. To begin with, I refused to allow them to come near me. I was frightened, outraged and overwhelmed. I misunderstood the situation, thinking that I was being specifically picked on, and though I eventually succumbed, in their minds I was already chicken, a spoilsport, an outsider; so that when they did start noticing my twitches, I already had form upon which they could build.

Sometimes I pretend to get angry, which only encourages them. Sometimes I act nonchalantly, as though I haven't realised what's on the agenda. Or sometimes I appeal to the better nature of one of the lesser bullies with whom I am on reasonable terms when we are alone, but who mysteriously switches personalities, seduced by the need to be part of the pack, and becomes just another of the bastards.

They edge in closer, tentative at first, as one might approach a wounded animal, surrounding me.

'Does little Jamie want his mummy?'

'Mummy, Mummy, help me, Mummy.'

'Bet she twitches as well!'

Laughter; a few more voices, each trying to outdo the previous one-liner.

'Does she twitch like you, TWITCH?'

'Twitch twitch TWITCH!'

'Bitch!'

'Yeah, TWITCH BITCH!'

More laughing, the ringleaders exultant, some of the rest less so.

An image of Mum leaps spontaneously into my mind; a kind, gentle image of home, on which I'm unable to prevent the words TWITCH BITCH being superimposed in large white capital letters. It cuts deep. *They* have caused this image to become degraded. I feel a stab of rage, but it can't yet compete with the fear.

'Surprised the Twitch Bitch didn't kill you at birth!'

'Probably came *out* twitching!'

Hoots of laughter at this. More join in.

'Yeah, probably twitching when he was an embryo!'

'That's what we should call him: Embryo!'

'EMBRYO! EMBRYO! TWITCHY LITTLE EMBRYO!'

This is the worst part. The taunting without touching. The cutting insults. The waiting.

The physical beating when it comes will almost be a release. Adrenaline is a powerful painkiller and the punches and kicks won't hurt much until later; long after it's finished.

'Fuck off!' I say, without the conviction it deserves.

'*What* did you say to me? Embryo! Wanker! You wanker! You FUCKING WANKER!'

And again, that rage in Thompson's voice; rage that seems to come from somewhere else.

'Leave me alone.'

'*Leave me alone*,' they imitate.

More laughter.

'Poor little Embryo!'

More imitative puppetry.

Until first contact is made. By Thompson.

A teasing one-fingered poke, not hard, perhaps on my shoulder or chest, not unlike one might give a friend in a moment of light-hearted, boyish skirmishing; but here it's designed to antagonise.

Then another, from someone else.

'Come on then! Embryo! Twitch! Wanker!'

Daring me to retaliate.

Then another . . . and another . . . and another . . . each one harder than the last, until I say, 'Stop it! Just leave me alone.' And I retreat until I'm backed up against one of the desks. Fear gnaws at my guts, stronger than my anger, so it still doesn't sound convincing.

'*Leave me alone!*' Hargreaves mimics. 'God, you are such a *creep*, McConnel!'

And having treated themselves to the appetiser, the first proper punch of the main course arrives, as if from nowhere, panic having deprived me of the capacity to judge movement and speed.

Another punch; a smile, still daring me to fight back,

giving them the excuse to launch themselves at me in earnest. They drag it out, excited, forming a circle around me like scavenging hyenas, pushing me from one to the other, laughing, jeering, loving it. I have to go with the flow; I have no control.

Time slows, and in passing I recognise a look in one or two peripheral faces, a look that says, 'Thank God this is not happening to me,' and I sense something approaching pity in their eyes.

The pushing becomes more vicious, more determined, punch-pushes now, faster and faster and faster until at some point blind rage overtakes me, outstripping my fear. I drop to my knees and grab Thompson's ankles, trying to trip him. But it *never* works. It's a lesson I seem unable to learn; I do the same thing every time. Instead of collapsing, he manages to keep his balance by grabbing my hair, then he knees me in the face, leans forward and with cold, almost surgical precision, slams his elbow into my back, winding me. Once on the floor, they all move in. I'm pulverised by fists and feet until I curl up like a hedgehog, utterly submissive. I shut down. I feel nothing and wait for it to end.

'Wanker!' Kick.

'Embryo!' Punch.

'Creep!' Knee . . . on and on and on, until, gradually, mirroring the way it began, it tails off as one by one the bastards move away, leaving the fabulous trio to tidy up with a residual 'Creep!' or 'Wanker!' or 'Embryo!' or 'Twitch!'? And as a parting gesture, Thompson makes a hoiking sound deep within him and spits, the resulting gob of phlegm landing on my jumper. Then, chattering among themselves, they too abandon the kill, on a high, their retreating laughter radiating disgust.

I pick myself up and, shaking, make my way as quickly and unobtrusively as I can to the washrooms, desperate to avoid the shame of having to explain to a passing prefect or master why I look as I do – clothes filthy with dust and detritus from the floor, my hair in disarray, lip bleeding.

Inside the washroom, still shaking, I go into a frenzy of twitching: head jerks, kicks, air punches. Then I stop in front of the mirror and smile the widest smile I can, trying to force the corners of my mouth up to my ears (without using my hands). I need to see the opposite of my mood. Not feel it, just see what it looks like.

Smile, smile, smile. Happy face. Happy face. Look as happy as you can.

I stand for a moment studying my reflection, wondering what others would think if they could see me.

Then, jaw aching, anger rising, I lock myself in a cubicle and, without even lifting the lid to check for the snakes as I usually would – 'Screw you, snakes! Kill me if you want, I don't care!' – I sit dry-eyed, waiting until the shaking subsides. Ironically, the same heightened emotional state that produces the aggressive twitching can sometimes banish the compulsions. This is especially true for anger, which often conquers the fear of retribution if I don't give in to the Controller, but not for long.

I never cry. Never. I retreat, withdrawing into myself a little further each time for protection, until I'm not sure what I am any more.

I poke the metal paper dispenser with the tip of my right little finger, which hurts, but I continue anyway until it feels right. I remove two sheets of the thin, coarse paper and sniff it violently many, many times before using it to wipe the blood off my lip and snot off my jersey. Then I scrunch it up and flush it away. Still fuelled by anger, I go through another intense series of face-making, grunts, neck stretches and arm movements, which, as before, are far more aggressive than usual.

Then I'm still for a while, sniffing occasionally, replaying the scene in my mind, creating alternative outcomes in which I emerge triumphant, smashing Thompson full in the face, kicking him in the balls, watching Hargreaves's face creasing in agony as I plunge a knife into his flabby, disgusting stomach.

Finally, back in reality, calming down, I try to think of ways in which I can make it 'right'.

And gradually, very gradually, I find myself justifying their actions.

'They didn't *really* mean it . . .'

'It was just a bit fun . . .'

'Maybe I overreacted . . . '

The Controller interrupts in the guise of an elderly Brigadier: 'I'm rather fond of them actually . . .'

This time a *verbal*, rather than a *visual* 'opposite', rearranging it to suit . . . again and again.

'I'm rather fond of them actually.'

'I'm rather **fond** of them actually.'

'I'm rather fond of **them** actually.'

'Actually I'm rather **fond** of them.'

'Actually I'm rather **fond** of them.'

'**Fond** of them actually I am rather' – in as elderly and Brigadier-like a fashion as possible, until it sounds right . . . as *completely* opposite as I can make it.

The Controller backs off.

Perhaps I *was* being a bit of a creep; and my twitches *can* be annoying.

Maybe if I got Thompson alone and *apologised* to him one-on-one he'd be sympathetic and stop picking on me.

That might work.

By himself he'd be different; he wouldn't feel the need to show off and be the group leader. He might even be a nice chap. A feeling of warmth and hope steals over me as I embrace this possibility. Thompson, the nice chap; my special friend; with whom I have a secret non-aggression pact.

I tidy myself up, finger-brush my hair and walk back along the corridor to the common room. Thompson is sitting by himself at his desk cutting up a piece of leather with a penknife to make a backing for his watchstrap.

I approach him tentatively and lean against his desk, trying to look as carefree and relaxed as I can.

'What do *you* want?' he says, looking up at me briefly before continuing to cut.

'That looks good,' I say, hoping a compliment will get me off on the right note.

'Piss off, Twitch!'

'Yeah, I do twitch a lot, don't I?' I say conversationally, half laughing, desperately nervous. 'It must be quite annoying.' And before he can answer, I say, 'Look, I'm really sorry about what happened just now; can we try and forget it?'

Please don't hurt me again, I plead internally.

He looks up, faintly baffled, as though he simply can't believe what he's just heard, and I hope against hope he's about to say something conciliatory or comforting. But his face hardens.

'Fuck *off*, will you, Twitch! *Em*bryo! Go on, *piss* off, you wanker!'

I slink away, hating him; hating myself for having tried;

for having known all along it was a pointless exercise and yet *still* doing it.

Who could I tell?

No one. Certainly not my parents.

Not in a million years.

During my first week 'Johnny' Clarke, my housemaster, called me into his study for a friendly chat to see how I was settling in. In his precise voice, he finished by saying, 'Now, James, if you ever have any problems or worries, please feel free to come and see me; my door will always be open.'

'Thank you, sir.'

But I can't tell *him*.

I'd feel ashamed and guilty. I *should* be able to stand up for myself, shouldn't I?

In my mind I hear the voice of the Controller Brigadier again; outraged this time.

'**Pull** yourself together, boy! Fight **back**! Give those buggers **What For** and stop being a bloody **pansy**!'

In any case, what could I say?

'Excuse me, sir, I feel isolated and different from other people and I'm being bullied; Thompson, Hargreaves and Carson-Scott are the ringleaders but most of the other boys also hate me because I'm a creep and a wanker who can't stop twitching and making funny noises.'

Besides, what good would it do? As soon as they found out I'd told someone, they'd punish me even more.

I'm on constant alert, watching for the signs. More often than not an attack takes place in the common room or the dormitory before lights-out; but it can happen anywhere. It isn't always a full-blown beating; sometimes just a quick punch and a push in the lunch queue or a jab in the ribs at the beginning of a lesson before the master arrives. Neither is it always physical. In fact, the majority of attacks are psychological: name-calling, hiding my belongings, opening my letters from home and reading them aloud to collected squeals of delight and ridicule, 'accidentally' knocking books off my desk and spitting on them, pissing in my bed.

I try everything I can think of to fit in. I ingratiate myself, suck up, smile, laugh along with them at my own expense. I ignore my own opinions, heartily agreeing with anything anyone says if there's the slightest chance they'll like me, or at least, not reject me. But the more I acquiesce, the more I'm despised.

I've had to work out various strategies to avoid potential confrontations. To begin with, walking down one of the long school corridors – of which there are many – seeing a pair of ringleaders coming towards me, my heart would start racing, and I'd wonder if I would get a quick round of 'Embryo, wanker, and Twitch' as they passed, or – if they weren't in a hurry – whether they would stop for a punch or a trip or a push against the wall. Now, I peer cautiously down the corridor first to see if the coast is clear, before making for the other end as quickly as I can – we're not allowed to run – breathing an inward sigh of relief when I reach it, before choosing one of a number of escape routes down adjoining passages. Walking anywhere, inside or out, is like a game of nail-biting rounders, in which I try to reach designated safe spots without meeting trouble on the way.

Not everyone's foul all the time, though, and occasionally I misread the signals: someone says 'hi' in what I realise too late is a genuine greeting and, thinking they're taking the piss, I tell them to fuck off, earning myself another enemy.

*   *   *   *   *

I first see my new piano teacher, Peter Radcliff, an up-and-coming concert pianist, when he's introduced to the whole school at assembly. A few days after the beginning of term, I half-engineer our first meeting.

I'm sitting at the piano, not in the music block, but in one of the very few practice rooms on the first floor of the main school overlooking the quad. Suddenly, from my vantage point I see him walking across and, determined to attract his attention, I start playing the most complex piece I know – a Rachmaninov Prelude – as loudly as I can.

I'm convinced he'll be wowed by my piano playing. I'm filled with echoes of the blind praise I've received thus far. How many other thirteen-year-olds can play the pieces I can? How many people can play chunks of the classical orchestral repertoire by ear from memory? I wowed them at Westford and I've wowed my way into Rimmington. I'm fully expecting to wow him as well. My imagination soars. He'll probably start me on one of the romantic piano concertos. Before long I'll be entered into the Leeds International Piano Competition, where, at fifteen, I'll become the youngest ever winner. A career on the concert platform will beckon.

Halfway through the most difficult section of the piece there's a knock at the door and in walks Radcliff.

I look up at him, stop playing and attempt surprise.

'Hi,' he says.

'Hello, sir.' I shuffle the chair and half stand.

'S'okay.' He puts out his hand. 'Don't get up.'

I sit again.

'I heard someone playing and just thought I'd introduce myself – Peter Radcliff.'

He reaches out and we shake.

A brief pause.

'And you are . . .?'

'Oh . . . James McConnel, sir. Sorry.'

'Oh, *now* I know who you are. You're the Exhibitioner. I think I'm teaching you, aren't I?'

'Don't know, sir; no one's told me yet.'

'Well, you're on my list so I'm afraid you're stuck with me.'

I smile.

'How are you settling in?' he continues. 'You enjoying it?'

'It's okay. It's all a bit new.'

'Yes, well, I'm new too, so we can both be new together, can't we?'

'Yes, sir.' I like his informality.

'So,' he says, 'Rachmaninov, eh? That's fairly impressive.'

Now I begin to glow inwardly, waiting for the 'wow'.

But instead: 'How about giving me that middle section again.'

I set off at high speed, much faster than Rachmaninov ever intended, just to show him how truly impressive I can be.

Halfway through, he puts up his hand again. 'Okay, hold it there a minute, but keep your hands where they are.'

I freeze and he moves around next to me.

'Right,' he says, 'now look at your elbows.'

I do.

'You see how they're both sticking out?'

'Yes, sir.'

He moves one of them.

'And they're stiff as a board; come on, relax, *relax*!' He jiggles the elbow gently.

I relax them.

'*That's* better. The whole thing about playing the piano is that the weight should come from the shoulders. If you stiffen your elbows then everything else'll stiffen too; your shoulders, your wrists and your fingers. If you relax and let your shoulders do the work, you'll play much better. D'you see what I mean?'

'Yes, sir.' He's obviously not wowed at all.

'Okay, try it again, and not so fast this time. Relax into it. Enjoy it.'

I try, but by the end I realise I still look like a chicken in mid-flap.

'That was a bit better actually,' he says. Then he puts his forefinger to his teeth, holds it there for a few seconds, thinking, then sighs with a long 'mmm' sound, withdraws his finger and says, almost sympathetically, 'I don't know who's been teaching you, but . . . frankly they haven't done a very good job.'

'Oh,' I say, feeling dreadful now.

'But,' he says, changing his tone, seeing the 'I'm a failure' look on my face, 'before you throw yourself out of the window, you've obviously got a lot of talent and we *can* put it right, but it'll take six months and it'll mean a lot of work. D'you think you can manage that?'

'Yes, sir.' At least he thinks I'm talented.

Christ! To have to learn it all again . . .

But Radcliff turns out to be everything I've ever wanted in a piano teacher. We hit it off right away, not least because we both bite our fingernails, discovering – in the course of one early lesson – that our chewing techniques are very similar. Bursting with energy, wearing one of an array of trendy pairs of flared corduroy jeans, he has a wide knowledge of music, infinite patience and a great sense of humour.

He makes me work hard and when he thinks I'm being lazy loses no time in telling me so. Increasingly, he doesn't need to. He has the knack of making my lessons endlessly fascinating, infecting me with his own enthusiasm for the music and my ability to play it.

There are lengthy digressions during which we discuss composers and their music, particularly Ravel and Stravinsky, both of whom he worships. We swap jokes and anecdotes and he never treats me as anything other than his musical equal. He tops up the self-confidence which has all but drained away elsewhere. He never once remarks on my face-making or tapping on the piano lid; he accepts me and the music block becomes my sanctuary. He also suggests I take up an orchestral instrument to broaden my horizons. I settle on the flute.

I join the school choir and, in doing so, I make a friend.

Alex is in my year, my house and my common room. He's one of the few non-bullies; large for his age, quietly secure and not in the least intimidated by Thompson and his gang of three. We have music in common and his reputation as a friend of Embryo doesn't appear to bother him. Neither, for some reason, does it bother me when he occasionally mimics my twitches.

In our second year we both opt for organ lessons with Titus de Groot, the magnificently named choir and organ master, which adds a further bond since we are the only two organists in the school. He's my one friend, and with him beside me, walking down corridors doesn't fill me with as much trepidation as it used to.

In our third year, we share a study/bedroom, and I find

that now that I am out of the common room environment for good, able to retreat to my own room, another safe spot in the rounders field, my life improves still further.

The Controller, however, always on the lookout, creates a new fear: terror of sleeping in a room by myself. Fortunately it's never completely dark – my other fear – as there are always exterior night lights left on in front of the school, over which our window looks. When Alex is there, I'm fine. However, we are allowed to choose which weekends we spend at home and although I try to make sure that ours coincide, occasionally they don't.

On these nights I barely sleep at all, on permanent alert, terrified that either the man wearing the blue workman's jacket or – a new one – a fat Italian taxi driver in a chef's uniform are lurking somewhere in the room. Why a taxi driver? Why Italian? Why a *chef's* uniform? Sometimes I try rationalising it. It's ridiculous! But it doesn't make any difference.

Before I get into bed I have to spend a long, long time checking every conceivable hiding place – behind the furniture, under the beds, in the cupboards – and because both these men could be any size, I have to include my desk drawers, geometry box, wash bag, pillowcase, the basin plughole, waste-paper basket and a myriad other little nooks and crannies. That done, I lie, pulse racing, listening intently, jumping at any sudden, unidentifiable sound.

The Controller, realising it's on to a winner, extends this fear to the daytime, particularly in the music block and the chapel. This curtails my practice time on the organ and I find it impossible to venture into the chapel when I want to practise unless someone else – the Chaplain, one of the Sacristans or a group of visitors – are in there with me. The organ stool is surrounded by a semi-circular curtain for privacy and I can't relax, terrified that at any moment I'll be stabbed in the back by the blue-coated man wielding a hunting knife. The music block is slightly easier. If it's empty, I dash up the stairs, race along the corridor and make for one of the small practice rooms in which I can feel safe, although I always jam a chair against the door handle just in case.

Academically I'm well below average, except in French. Part of the trouble – and it is only part of it – is my handwriting again. There are numerous lessons in which we have to copy out notes that are projected on to a white screen. Because there's always a sense of urgency, having to copy each page quite quickly before it's removed and replaced, I get into a panic because I have to go over certain words again and again until they're right. I get very behind, and not wanting to ask for more time in case I aggravate the rest of the class, I either miss out large chunks of text or scribble so fast and so frantically, the result is illegible.

I'm idle. At least that's what they tell me. There are times when I can't be bothered to revise for a history exam or practise the organ and I have a very low boredom threshold. The problem is that I find it hard to concentrate for sustained periods of time without either the Controller butting in or something else getting in the way. Any kind of exterior noise – a fly buzzing round the classroom, a drill outside or the school maintenance man's radio – infuriates me, attaching itself to my mind, magnifying itself to such an extent that everything else is blocked out.

My name always seems to appear near the bottom of the results sheet and my school reports are littered with familiar phrases: 'could do better', 'finds it hard to concentrate', 'needs to adjust his attitude if he's to pass his O levels', and one in particular: 'is in danger of becoming a gifted dilettante'.

But after four years at Rimmington Hall, with continued encouragement from Mr Radcliff, I realise that more than anything I want to be a pianist. Music is the one area in which I can completely be myself. All the twitches and obsessions disappear when I play the piano. I'm calm and focused. There are no taunts and no bullies. I like myself.

Radcliff is due to leave the school at the end of the summer term to concentrate on his own concert career, but we've discussed various possibilities. I decide to aim for the Royal College of Music and he submits the application form.

During the holidays, aged seventeen, in preparation for my A levels, my parents decide I should spend some time in France brushing up my accent and my vocabulary.

It's a summer that changes everything.

The End

Hate getting *out* of the bath.

    Hate the actual moment of decision.

    Switching from mini escape . . .

    Back to practical reality.

    Steaming pink flesh . . .

    Swelled by the heat.

    Hand on the basin to steady myself.

    Dressing gown, towel . . .

    Wet footprints on the carpet to the bedroom.

    Must remember not to walk on them in my socks.

    I always *fucking* forget.

    Bastard wet socks.

    Niggling, irritating, small-minded annoyance.

    'Footprints footprints foo foo foo foo foo f f f f f f f f f f f f f f f fffff!'

    Fuck off!

    Heart racing even faster now.

Return of the headache.
Like a film sequel.
My mouth tastes horrible.
I'm dehydrated, thirsty.

Chapter 5
A Little Bike Trouble

The South of France is hot and arid. I'm staying with a police inspector and his family – Monsieur and Madame Levigne – in a small village near Avignon. I've no idea how my parents found them. This is not an 'exchange'; I'm a paying guest for three weeks.

They're nice enough. Four children; two grown up and living in Paris, the other two, teenagers, still at home. I go a bundle on their sixteen-year-old daughter Agnès, a name which in English sounds like a bag lady, but when pronounced correctly in French – 'Ann-yes' – lends itself to fantasies in which, finding ourselves alone in the house, we accidentally bump into each other, the touch electric. With a quiet intensity I tell her I love her and she, having ached for me, falls into my arms and we kiss. Then she calls me 'cherie'. I long for her to call me 'cherie'.

I can't get beyond that part, in spite of an extensive pep talk the headmaster gave us in my final term at prep school. I'm still not sure what you're supposed to do in bed, but 'Agnès' becomes an internal mantra – nothing to do with the Controller – gently taking up residence in my head.

I follow her around the house like a devoted puppy, keeping my twitches to an absolute minimum, unloading any really tiresome ones in my bedroom between times. Mrs Police Inspector is friendly and kind, but no one speaks any English. As for Le Monsieur himself, he's my internal Controller Brigadier's notion of what constitutes a 'Bloody Frog'. Short and squat, covered in hair – apart from his head – his sense of personal hygiene redefines the word 'unsanitary'. When he's not manicuring his blue Mercedes or bullying his gendarmes, he ambles topless around the house, his belly trying its best to escape from a pair of tight-fitting, yellow nylon Y-fronts with small telltale stains of past leakage at the crotch.

Almost exclusively we eat cold meat and salad. Fine, except that Monsieur constantly picks at the food during its preparation with hands that only moments before have been intimately acquainted with yellow nylon. Whatever the cause, after only a week I discover to my horror that I have worms.

Utterly mortified and far too ashamed to mention it, I climb on to the 'fut fut' moped that Monsieur has lent me and go in search of a chemist, armed only with schoolroom French and a seventeen-year-old's propensity for embarrassment.

Avignon is beautiful. I've read about it in my travel guide. Best known for its famous 'pont' which straddles the Rhône, it dates back more than two millennia and boasts a fort, a papal palace, churches and various museums. In my present mood, however, wobbling uncertainly from time to time, having not entirely mastered the moped's controls, I couldn't care less; I'm in a panic.

'Chemist' is not a French word.

Nor is 'chemiste' or 'chemis'.

I know because I'm greeted with blank looks from those I ask.

It's only by chance – glancing through a shop window and seeing bottles labelled 'shampooing' – that I realise that a green cross with the word 'pharmacie' above it is what I'm looking for.

I enter – tapping the glass door seven times for good luck on the way in – and wait at the back of the short queue, nerves jangling in anticipation.

Squeezing comprehension from the pharmacist proves almost impossible, and having quite forgotten to bring my Cassell's English-French dictionary with me, I'm stumped. *'Petits serpents blancs'*, the best I can come up with, doesn't compute. We stand, staring at each other in linguistic stalemate. Finally, when I'm on the point of giving up and trying somewhere else, a woman's voice behind me says in perfect Home Counties English, 'Can I help?'

I turn and find myself face to face with the sort of woman who might conceivably know my parents. She's roughly the same age as Mum, wears what Mum might wear on holiday – bright cotton summer dress, sun hat and over-the-shoulder handbag – speaks like Mum in that efficient middle-class accent, and were it not for the fact that she's *not* actually Mum, she *would* be.

'Hello.' I can feel my face reddening.

'Would you like me to translate for you?' I notice her breasts are quite large.

'Erm . . . well . . . I'm trying to get something for . . . my sister . . . she's got . . . worms.'

'Oh I see.' It comes out as 'Oh-ice . . . see' with the 'ice' bit held for a second or two; but years of the very best social training – tailor-made for just this kind of mildly embarrassing scene – kick in and, turning to the pharmacist with the sort of expression one might use when asking for a bottle of aspirin, she rattles off a sentence ending with the word '*vers*'.

The pharmacist looks over at me with sudden understanding: '*Ah, tu as des vers?*'

'*Non, non!*' I protest, waving my hands, doing my best to communicate an appropriate sense of outrage. '*C'est pour ma soeur!*' Triumphantly adding, '*Elle est malade,*' to really hammer the point home.

'*Ah bon,*' he says, fetching a box of pills and slipping them, mercifully quickly, into a paper bag, clearly believing *every* word I've said. '*Dix-sept francs, monsieur.*'

I hand him the money, take the bag and make for the door with a quick 'Thanks very much' to my interpreter. But she isn't finished with me.

'So, are you on holiday?'

Actually, her breasts are *huge*; squidgy and flumpy.

'Yes . . . I . . . and my sister . . . are staying with a French family.'

'Oh really, near here?'

'Quite near, about four miles away.'

God, I want to **touch** them! Go on! Give them a squeeze! **Stop it!**

'Heavens! You don't play tennis, do you? It's just that my son Guy is *desperate* to have a game with someone and you must be about his age.'

'Well, it's very kind of you . . . but we're going home

tomorrow morning . . . very early . . . so I don't think we'll have time . . . and we've been invited to a bullfight this afternoon.'

Look at her breasts! Look at her breasts! Look at them! Look at them! DON'T . . . look . . . at . . . the . . . squidge . . . Okay, just a quick one! **NO!** Dammit! Not right. One more, just one more . . . Oh **God** I want to *squidge* them! Just once! Bore your eyes into them, like Superman! Melt them! Become them! No **DON'T!** Yes. Lookatthem! Lookatthem lookathemlookathemlookatthem!

STOP IT!

'What a shame. Never mind. Where are you heading back to?'

Christ!

'Hampshire.'

'Oh really? Where?'

'Quite near Romsey?' I say it as a question, but in my head it's a plea – *please* don't tell me you live there!

'Oh no, don't know it. No, we have friends in Petersfield, that's all – the Scotts?'

Relief surges through me. God *bless* the Scotts! Never heard of them.

'Er, no I don't think so' – as if I'd *admit* it!

'Oh well. Have a good trip home; I hope your sister feels better.'

'Thanks. Bye.'

Outside the shop.

'Oh, my God, how awful! Christ! God, bloody hell – TitsTitsTits**TitsTits!**'

'Bugger, bugger! Shit! (Violent twitch, shoulders, neck, left leg.)

Bugger bugger shit shit.
Bugger bugger shit shit.
Bugger bugger shit shit, we love you.
And in.
Bugger bugger shit shit.
Bugger bugger shit shit what we'll do . . .'
(To the tune of 'Chitty Chitty Bang Bang')

Thirty minutes later I'm on my way back to the house. I'm wearing a light blue long-sleeved shirt, unbuttoned, flip-flops and a pair of light blue jeans, my worm pills squished tightly in my pocket. The breeze blows the shirt backwards like a parachute as the moped hurtles along the uneven French B-road, occasionally reaching the dizzying speed of forty kph.

Crossroads ahead. Stop.

Look *droit*, look *gauche*, look *droit* again. Twitch right, twitch left, and once more to the right to make three; add two *droits* and the *gauche* to make six, and one upward look (neither *gauche* nor *droit*) to make seven. Safe to go.

Damn! Car coming.

Wait, but twitch-rev the engine in an aggressive Hell's Angels sort of way. Twitch rev, twitch rev . . .

NOTE: A fully grown motorbike has gears, a clutch and therefore a neutral setting which allows an aggressive Hell's Angel type to rev to his heart's content, before changing up and roaring off. Unfortunately, these features are not installed on my 49cc Mobylette, which cannot distinguish between the instruction to rev and the instruction to accelerate.

Almost at once, it seems, I'm being gently raised up on an

invisible, adjustable bed. I don't actually *know* it's a bed, but something is supporting me. Everything around me is grey, in shadow. Somehow I can see this, even though my eyes are shut. I don't question where I am; all is calm; all feels natural. I can hear a loud, high-pitched whistling in my ears, but it's not really distressing. I accept everything.

Gradually, I can make out distant voices through the audible fog and suddenly there's excruciating pain in my left upper arm. I panic and start thrashing about but something holds me down firmly and I hear a man's voice telling me to stop struggling. I know what he's saying from the tone of his voice, even though I don't understand the words. Then the grey bed sinks down again, a long way down, hundreds of metres, and at some time during the descent I seem to part company with my grey body and watch it disappearing into the bottomless depths. Then I too disappear.

The next time I surface, I hear and feel the repetitive rasp of a razor as someone shaves my head; then more pain, this time on my right ear, followed almost immediately by intense pins and needles halfway up my right arm. Again I struggle, but opening my eyes briefly, I catch a glimpse of bright lights and blood. There's no surprise; and in spite of the discomfort it still feels quite natural to be here.

'What is your name?' a male voice asks in heavily accented English. It calms me.

'James,' I murmur.

He says something else but I can't make it out because the grey bed does its stuff once more, and down we go into oblivion.

Next time it's my left leg. Not so painful this and I'm more aware of what's going on around me. I can hear the noise of quietly humming machinery. The whistling noise has gone.

Then nothing.

Then more nothing . . .

But I know time is passing.

I'm tired.

But I feel terrific.

Then a room.

Brighter, but still with shadows.

People. I can see them – sort of; shadowy and vague.

'Hello James.' A man's voice. French accent.

'Hello.' A croak.

'How do you feel?'

'Okay.'

'Do you know where you are?'

'No.' Never thought about it.

'You had an accident. Do you remember?'

'No.' I can't. I really can't. The only image I have is of revving the moped.

'Well, your parents are coming to see you. They will be here in the morning.'

Then nothing . . .

Until: 'Hello, darling.' Mum's voice. She sounds so *calm*.

'Hello, old boy.' Dad.

'Hi, Mum.' Still a croak.

'How are you feeling?'

I want to say, 'Great!' But it doesn't seem appropriate.

'Okay,' I say.

Trouble is, I feel fantastic! *Why* have they come? Honestly! They needn't have bothered. I feel like a terrible fraud. If I sound too happy they'll think they've wasted their time and be cross.

'Polly sends her love,' Mum says.

Pause.

'Who's Polly?' I try to sound confused.

Much, much longer pause.

Then, quietly, as though to a child, 'You know who Polly is, darling, don't you?'

Well, of *course* I know who Polly is! But it doesn't seem fair if I don't at least *pretend* there's something wrong with me!

And I hear tears in her voice as she moves away to my father and whispers, 'For God's sake! He doesn't even know who Polly is!'

Shit. Now I feel guilty.

After the hazy awareness of my parents' first visit, life seems to consist of a series of short waking moments interspersed with much, much longer periods of sleep.

Later, I discover I've been under sedation for nearly a week. I know I've had some kind of accident, but I still don't really care. My body feels as though it's suspended in the centre of a soothing cloud. From time to time I catch glimpses of young, softly spoken girls in purple and white uniforms hovering over me. I can feel someone removing a tube from my penis, washing me and replacing it. I'm not embarrassed but I'm desperate for a pee. I can't seem to go at all, which is the only discomfort.

The next time I wake, I'm more aware of what's going on. I can see clearly when I open my eyes now; the sense of looking through a misted window is gone. My parents are in the room and there's a doctor with them. They're wearing conspiratorial looks which say, 'We've been talking about you, but you're far too ill for us to tell you what's been said.'

'Hello, darling,' Mum says. 'How do you feel?' She leans

towards me and kisses my forehead the way she used to when I was ill and she wanted to gauge whether or not I had a temperature before resorting to the thermometer. Worry and bravery do battle in her expression.

'Okay,' I say, surprised at how weak my voice still sounds.

'Hello, old boy,' Dad says. 'How are you getting on?'

'Okay,' I say again.

I know he's as worried as Mum is, but his tone of voice is exactly the same as if he were asking how I was getting on with painting the garden fence or mowing the lawn.

'Darling,' Mum says, 'this is Monsieur Letranc. He's the doctor who operated on your arm.'

This is news to me. So far, I haven't a clue what's wrong with me. I know there's been an accident but that's all. From my limited vantage point I try looking around me and see that my right arm, bandaged from armpit to fingertips, is suspended about nine inches above the bed. My left arm's in an open plaster, also suspended. My left leg's in an open plaster as well and my right leg appears undamaged except for a few cuts and bruises.

'Hello, James. So what have you been doing to yourself, uh?' His English is pretty good.

'I had an accident?' It's half a question.

'You did have an accident, my friend. Quite a big accident. You were in a car, yes?'

He must have known I wasn't in a car. He's testing me.

'No, I was riding a moped.'

'Ah, a moped. And did you wear a . . .' he cups his head with both hands, 'hat, on this moped?'

'No, I didn't.'

'Oh darling, why not?'

'Please, madame, let *me* talk to him.'

'Sorry.' As he turns back, Mum mouths 'Why not?' to Dad.

'And what happened on the moped? Do you know?'

I don't. All I *can* remember is getting to the crossroads and revving the engine, then nothing. I tell him.

'Okay, you don't remember the car hitting you, no?'

'No, I don't, but I think I remember *seeing* a car.'

'Okay. So what do you do in England?'

'I'm still at school.'

'Uh huh. And you have any brothers and sisters?'

'Yes, I've got one sister.'

'Oh, thank God,' says Mum.

'And what is her name?' he asks.

'Polly,' I say, suddenly realising the point of the question.

'Good,' he says. 'And what you like to do at your school?'

'I play the piano.'

'Ah, I like piano! You know Keith Jarrett?"

'No, I don't.'

'What you like then?'

'Classical music.'

'Oh, Beethove! Bach! Yes?' (Why do the French miss out the 'n' of Beethoven?)

'Yes.'

'What music you like to play?'

'Erm, Chopin, Rachmaninov . . . and Beethoven.'

'Good! Very good.'

He looks over at my parents and in an aside which suggests the continuance of a previous conversation, says, 'Apart from the concussion, I don't think there is any damage to the head.'

'Thank God,' Mum says again, eyes closing.

He turns back to me and, satisfied that I'm not a moron after all, adopts a conversational tone.

'Okay, young man, you are lucky to be still with us.' And as though he were a tour guide pointing out the more curious architectural features at Versailles, he continues, 'Now, you 'ave broken your leg 'ere.' He points to my left leg. 'And your arm 'ere.' He gestures to my left arm. 'Yes?'

'Yes,' I say, baffled because I can't remember having done it.

'This,' he gestures dismissively, 'is not serious. But,' he continues, grabbing an invisible pumpkin, 'we 'ave two problems.'

This sounds horribly like understatement.

'When the car hit you, you go over the engine and through the front window, okay?'

'Yes,' I say.

'The glass . . . it 'ave cut your right arm and sever . . . the radial . . . nerve.' He demonstrates this on his own arm.

Mum's eyebrows furrow and she breathes in sharply.

'Okay . . . so this is the first problem. When the car stop, you fall back *out* of the window and hit the road. This, I think, is when you break your left leg and your left arm. When the left arm break, the broken bones pinch the radial nerve in *this* arm and make more damage. This is the second problem. You understand?'

'Yes.' But I don't know what it means.

'Okay, so you have the *same* injury in *both* arms. This is coincidence, no? Now,' he continues, 'I need to look at your hands. Please relax.'

He reaches up and unties the strings holding up my right arm, lowering it gently on to the bed.

'Okay. James, can you raise your wrist for me? Just your wrist.'

116

I try, but nothing happens. I'm more puzzled than anything else. My brain's telling my wrist to lift, but it won't move. There's no pain, though.

'I can't,' I say.

'Oh my God!' Mum whispers.

'Try it again.'

I still can't. Moving around the bed, he asks me to do the same thing for my left hand. Again, I can't.

'I don't understand,' I say. 'What's the matter with me?'

He stretches out his hands.

'Your hands, for the moment, they are *paralysées* – paralysed. This is because the radial nerves are not working. In your right arm, the nerve was cut. Now; I 'ave stitch the two ends of the nerves together, and they may grow back. Only time can say, but I must tell you, James, there is no guarantee.'

He gesticulates with his left hand to put the point across. He pauses for me to digest this.

'In two days I will operate and put a metal plate in your *left* arm to hold the bones together and protect the nerve from more damage. You understand?'

I nod as best I can.

'But, monsieur,' Mum says, her face contorted with worry, 'will he be able to play the piano again?' Her whole being is focused on Letranc, her demeanour utterly submissive, her attitude that of a defeated Christian pleading for mercy in the gladiatorial arena.

'I don't know, madame. In the left arm, probably yes. Although the damage is near the shoulder, the nerve casing, it is not cut, but the inside pieces must grow all the way down to the fingers. This will take between four and six months.'

117

Six months!

''Ere,' he points to my right elbow, 'it is less distance, but the nerve casing is cut. I hope it will grow, but I cannot be sure. We must wait to see.'

They leave, to let me rest.

The first thought that zooms unbidden into my mind is how the hell you masturbate with paralysed hands.

The second thought is that at least I won't have to practise the piano any more.

At all.

Thank God.

Why would I think that?

Why do I want to shout 'Yippee!' at the thought?

Shouldn't I be stunned or something?

People are always shocked in films. Or they burst into tears.

I don't feel shocked or anything!

I'm quite *enjoying* myself.

Cautiously, I check out what hurts.

By flexing my jaw muscles I can tell that my head and my right ear are bandaged.

Then I try bending my right leg, just to get used to moving it again. It's a little stiff, but there's no pain.

I raise my left leg. Once is enough; sharp pain . . .

I lift my right arm very gingerly, resisting the urge to smash it down hard on to the bed. The wrist flops down, but the arm itself moves okay, though I can't feel anything.

Raising my left arm is painful, but not unbearable.

I relax.

And then, suddenly I'm struck by the incredible

coincidence of it. Of all the things I could have done to myself; of the virtually limitless array of muscles, nerves and bones I could have injured, why is it my *hands*? *One* of them being paralysed, maybe (although for a pianist that's quite a coincidence in itself). But *both* of them!? That seems beyond coincidence, somehow; almost as if it was planned that way.

It's so *weird*.

Over the following days, my returning strength allows me – among other things – to appreciate just how good the French health service is. From the look of them, all French nurses are required by law to be stunningly beautiful. For breakfast, in my spotless private room, I'm hand-fed fresh croissants dipped in hot chocolate by Angélique or Anna, both of whom have the (combined) bedside manner of Julie Christie and Florence Nightingale. Brutally casting Agnès aside in my affections, I fall hopelessly in love with Anna.

For lunch I'm offered an à la carte menu (with wine) which would shame Maxim's in Paris; likewise dinner. The only blot on this cosseted landscape is when both nurses come to remove my catheter. Try as I might to focus every fibre of my being on dead nuns in black plastic bin liners, blood flow triumphs over my stiffening resolve.

After two weeks, I'm (regretfully) flown home – in a private jet, no less, because the airlines won't risk taking me in my condition – and back in England, I'm transferred to hospital in Salisbury for a further three weeks. After the dreamy luxury of France, where reality was a blur thanks to Angélique and Anna, the NHS is a bit of a come-down.

But at least I have visitors, although I must look terrible, because one of them faints dead away when she sees me. My torso is so covered with cuts, scrapes and bruises, some bandaged, some not, that I can't wear a pyjama top. My head's been half shaved to get access to the cuts on my scalp. My face is deathly pale; it too is covered with bruises, cuts and stitches. My ear, badly sliced in the accident, is healing nicely, but still wouldn't look out of place in a butcher's window.

I eat a lot of fruit.

Everyone brings fruit.

Well, not quite everyone.

One afternoon my housemaster Johnny Clarke and his wife come to visit. Johnny's brandishing an enormous, home-made, thickly iced chocolate cake with cherries on top. It's beautiful and a welcome change.

Johnny sits at the end of the bed holding the cake, looking a little uncomfortable, as if he'd rather be anywhere else than in a hospital, while Mrs Johnny takes the bedside chair.

'How are you, James?' Johnny asks.

'I'm fine.' Which seems a stupid thing to say.

'Poor you; *horrible* thing to happen.' His wife.

'Yes, awful,' says Johnny.

Silence.

Johnny really does look very uncomfortable. I'm not used to having to make small talk with my housemaster. Usually we have common ground. Things like: 'James, I think we need to have a chat about your exam results. They're not very impressive, are they?' Or: 'McConnel, you were seen wandering round the school grounds at midnight last night by the Bursar. Would you please tell me what you were doing?'

So I point out how tanned they both look.

They tell me they've been sailing during the holidays. Then where they've been, what their boat's called, how many nights they stayed, who they saw, what they ate.

Silence.

Finally, Mrs J plucks up her courage. 'James, what happened?'

And the ice breaks.

I tell them. I *love* telling people and with so much recent practice, plus a natural tendency to over-dramatise, I set to with enthusiasm, leaving nothing to the imagination. I've always found it hard to restrict myself when it comes to details, in any case. The Controller always urges me to add things that I myself would normally omit.

I describe my journey to Avignon on the moped (though I omit the worms); my arrival at the crossroads; how I can't really remember what happened; what it feels like to be in and out of consciousness; how much I liked the food and (feigning sheepishness) the nurses. Finally, I give them a run-down of my injuries. During the early part of the story Johnny's face registers concern and sympathy, but as I go into more detail he looks increasingly uncomfortable.

Undaunted, I backtrack to my second operation when my left arm was plated, describing how, having been wheeled fully conscious into the operating theatre before I was anaesthetised, I looked over to a bench beside me and saw what looked like a misshapen napkin ring lying beside six stainless-steel screws and a common-or-garden screwdriver. I describe the process by which they cut deep into my arm with a scalpel, stretched back the skin, one surgeon holding the broken bones together while Monsieur Letranc fitted the napkin ring-shaped plate around them before drilling holes, inserting the screws and tightening them to make sure everything was kept firmly in place.

Johnny's complexion suddenly turns the deathly, sweaty colour of tapioca. His hands rise in slow motion and the chocolate cake lifts off like a cherry-topped, slowly spinning spacecraft, rising majestically towards the ceiling, while Johnny, fainting, falls backwards, his head hitting my right ankle – fracturing the bone. The cake then surrenders to gravity and lands on the floor with a 'plumph', exploding. Johnny slides slowly off the bed, out cold, to join it.

With a horrified gasp, Mrs J kneels beside him. 'Johnny! Darling!' she moans, patting his face frantically, ignoring the disembowelled chocolate cake now carpeting the floor.

Johnny groans feebly.

Someone shouts, 'Nurse! Nurse! I think he's fainted!'

A flurry of nurses arrive ... well, two of them ... and between them, with Mrs J helping, they manage to lift Johnny – who's already coming round – on to the bedside chair.

It's so *odd* – shocking actually – watching someone like that so completely out of context. I've never experienced Johnny being anything other than a schoolmaster; I only ever see him in his study or the classroom. Like Miss Paget at primary school, I can't even imagine him doing *normal* things like eating cornflakes or putting on his socks – let alone fainting.

I don't know how to react. I'm hemmed in, somewhere between wanting to laugh from the sight of Mr and Mrs J behaving so uncharacteristically, wanting to shout 'fuck' because of the excruciating pain in my ankle and just looking concerned.

'I'm so sorry, James,' Johnny mutters, having recovered a little but still white as a sheet.

'It's all right, darling.' Mrs J strokes his head and looks up at me as she would a doctor, worried for her child. 'I'm afraid Johnny's never been a great one for hospitals, although I have to say, *this* has never happened before.'

She turns back to him. 'Feeling better?'

He nods, accepting the tea brought by Nurse One, while Nurse Two scrabbles about on the floor with dustpan and cake.

What worries me is that they might want to keep him in overnight for observation, thereby making it impossible for me to smoke, which by this time I've managed to do, with difficulty, using my left hand. A friend smuggled in two packets of twenty for me and they're hidden surreptitiously at the back of my bedside cupboard. Fortunately, Johnny seems as keen to leave as I am to see him go, at which point, to spare him further humiliation, I report my latest injury to the ward matron.

I have physiotherapy, occupational therapy, exercises and x-rays. I eat custard with rhubarb, custard with prunes, apples, pears and gooseberries. I eat stodgy stews, bangers and mash and cabbage and cabbage and cabbage; and when the three weeks are up, I come home to recuperate for a few days to build up my strength.

Six weeks after the accident and a couple of weeks into the winter term, I'm back at school. Accustomed to being treated as a punchbag, I can't get used to the fact that I'm now something of a heroic curiosity. Everything has miraculously changed. The smallest twitch of the wrist on a moped throttle in France and, thanks to the Controller, I seem – finally – to have passed my initiation test.

Many of the chief bullies – including Thompson, Hargreaves and Carson-Scott – left at the end of the previous term, hopefully to spend lives in misery and great pain, but the remaining ones – now ex-bullies – couldn't be nicer. There is nothing so disconcerting as seeing a face that hitherto has only ever scowled at you suddenly break into a sheepish grin, especially when the sheepishness is guilt-based.

And I forgive them.

Instantly.

I don't even think about it.

Don't consider all the hits, pushes and insults over the years.

One smile and the slate is wiped clean.

I'm just . . . so . . . grateful.

They like me and that's all that matters.

Especially when I go into the gorier details of the accident and treatment, not to mention Johnny Clarke's fainting episode. We have common ground at last. I'm 'one of the lads', guest speaker at the cheap-thrills society.

Even my twitches don't attract attention any more; they're greeted with polite tolerance, conveniently bracketed in with my other injuries.

This makes me very uncomfortable and I do my best to repress the Controller. I imagine somehow that everyone's tolerance is wafer thin; that I'm on trial; that if I overdo it or take advantage of their patience, the ice'll break and once again I'll become an object of ridicule. Having hobbled my way on to the nursery slopes of popularity, I'm desperately anxious to maintain it. It's unnerving; I never know how I'm supposed to act – or react – to someone I used to hate, being nice to me.

The Hammer House of Horror look helps. With my left leg still in plaster, my largest accessories are two heavy wooden crutches, as seen in black and white World War II films. My hands, which would otherwise droop down in an effeminate flop, are kept level with my wrists by means of removable sprung splints made of wire and leather. Since they're quite bulky I have to roll my sleeves up to accommodate them, which means they're permanently on display. My hair's very short, the local barber having done his best to match the embryonic growth in the area of my scalp that was shaved in France. My right ear is still a livid red and badly scarred; I have another scar to the right of my nose, and my right eyebrow's missing altogether.

I continue daily physiotherapy with – of all people – Johnny-the-Fainter's wife, who's a qualified physiotherapist. It's an exhausting process as, endlessly patient, she tries to cajole my lifeless wrists into action; but there's an almost limitless supply of tea and biscuits, which, to a schoolboy on a 50p-a-week tuck budget, is a nice perk.

Gradually I learn to *use* all the attention.

Time and again I go through my story, honing it, adding self-deprecatory jokes to make myself appear immensely brave in the face of this 'awful tragedy'. I talk about the sexy nurses and the amazing food and the operations and the blood and the private jet.

And they never seem to tire of it!

I love explaining to a small, riveted gathering that it now takes me a full five minutes to get my one sock on – I even demonstrate.

It gets a laugh.

I *love* the laughs and gradually I realise that with a little work, I can get more of them.

I do silly tricks with my crutches.

They're impressed.

I flap my limp-wristed hands around like a performing seal.

They're amazed!

'God, he's so *brave* and so funny!'

'He's probably really miserable underneath, but look how positive he is!'

'What a great bloke!'

Who cares if I can't play the piano any more!

They like me – in the same way that I've spent years watching *others* being accepted and liked but not knowing how to do it myself.

But now I can; through laughter, through joking. No more do I have to ingratiate myself, or agonise or avoid. I can hobble down a corridor with confidence. No one's going to hit me or bully me.

I'm king.

I don't have anything to prove. I don't have to do *anything*.

I'm the centre of attention in an effortless, comfortable time warp.

On my occasional visits to the music block, hearing others fumble their way through pieces I used to be able to play, all I feel is amused irony that now they're actually better pianists than I am.

I still play sometimes. I have to. If I don't for any length of time, my whole body misses it and I find myself humming and singing or whistling all day long. Even with my limitations, by judicial use of the sustain pedal and using one limp finger on each hand I can still produce a reasonable sound, picking out tunes in the same way I used to as a child.

I mess about, not feeling any great sense of loss, just enjoying being twitch-free for a while.

I have immense power. Do I fancy missing a couple of irksome lessons in the morning? No problem; I send a message to the classroom pleading tiredness or pain. I'm supposed to be doing A level Music and French and although I've got textbooks to read, written work is impossible because I can't hold a pen properly.

I'm given my own bedsit/study. People are always dropping in to ask if I need anything: cups of coffee? Something from the tuck shop? Nothing's too much trouble. Everybody, it seems, wants to be *in* with the school Comedy Frankenstein. At mealtimes, my food's brought to me; cleared away afterwards.

I'm given a prefect's badge under the misguided assumption that serious injury and self-deprecating bravery must somehow go hand in hand with a growing sense of responsibility.

In short, I take every possible opportunity to milk my condition for all it's worth, because they love me.

From the vantage point of prefect-hood, I'm well placed to observe up-and-coming bullies – and bullied – in the years below me. Watching the little victims, I see myself in them; I see their fatal mistakes, their insecurities, their lack of self-belief as they desperately try – and fail – to fit in. There's not much I can do. I can see they're as ashamed as I was, and in offering a kind word or sympathy I'm only contributing to their sense of their own failure. When I *do* encounter the guarded aftermath of a bullying session – the near tears of the tormented, the self-important 'butter-wouldn't-melt-in-my-mouth' looks from his tormentors – I long to punch the little fuckers full in their smug little faces.

*   *   *   *   *

'See you after half-term, Mac.'

'Yeah, bye, Mac, have a good time.'

'See ya, Mac.'

'Hope you feel better.'

'Good luck, Mac.'

Mac, my new 'he's a nice bloke' nickname and image. Not an Embryo or Twitch to be heard. And so, home for the long, two-week half-term, the conquering hero.

But what I get is grown-up, genuine concern and, worst of all, pity. I don't want all this crap! I *want* the hero worship. I want admiration. I want the 'Cors!' and 'Reallys!' and the 'Bloody amazings!' I want the laughs.

Mum, well-meaning, hovers round me like a butterfly, scattering nuggets of comfort, eternally wanting up-to-the-minute progress reports. 'How are your hands this morning?' 'Are you very depressed, darling?' 'I'm sure it'll all be all right in the end, my love, don't worry too much.'

How do I tell her I'm not worried?

Not at all.

Quite the opposite.

I'm perfectly happy being an invalid. I enjoy it. At least, I enjoy it at school.

I don't need – or want – their worry.

I'd be fine if they'd just leave me alone and stop going *on* about it.

But *everyone* thinks I'm suffering. All their friends, Mr and Mrs Flint, Bert . . . they all think I'm being so bloody brave . . . when really I couldn't care less!

At this moment I wouldn't care if I was paralysed for life!

I'm sure Mum thinks that if I'm left alone for too long I'll sink into a morass of depression. I won't . . . at least I *might* if they don't stop being so bloody *nice* to me.

I'm quite happy sitting in my room listening to Puccini.

But it's a vicious circle. The more irritated I get with all the understanding and patronising, the more understanding and patronising people get, until I explode and become aggressive and say something I later regret.

Which makes me feel awful. I know they think I'm being rude because I'm upset about my hands.

I'm *not*. But they keep *on* making allowances for me.

It's intolerable.

I can't wait to get back to school again.

The End

Clean trousers, clean T-shirt.
    Check my watch again: 8 p.m.
    I'm hungry.
    Walk downstairs.
    Thank **Christ!**
    Thumping's stopped.
    'About bloody time too!'
    They must have gone out.
    Into the kitchen.
    Open the fridge.
    Nothing.
    Close it.
    Check again.
    And again.
    And again.
    Once more.
    Doesn't matter.

Need to go to the off-licence anyway.
I fancy a crisps sandwich.
Cheese and onion.
Softness versus crunch.
Complete opposites.
I love that.

Chapter 6
The Digital Challenge

I'm old news. No longer the school hero-cum-cabaret. I look relatively normal now. Two short weeks and the leg plaster and crutches have gone, my hair's growing fast and the scars on my face and ear are beginning to fade. My new slim-line, sleeve-friendly splints are barely visible. I simply don't stand out any more.

There's no bullying; nothing like that. Everyone's just as friendly, but the interest, the fascination I inspired during the first half of term, has all but disappeared. Without the visual injuries that make up my comedy/tragedy routine, I've reverted to type. I am who I was before the accident.

My parents have lent me a walking stick to help with my ankle – Johnny's little gift, the only injury apart from my hands that gives me any trouble; it still aches occasionally. One afternoon, I'm walking along a corridor carrying the stick but not using it, when I hear a group of boys about to come into view. Slowing to a hobble and leaning heavily on the stick for full effect, I move to the centre of the corridor and smile with pained bravery as they approach, hoping for some kind of acknowledgement of my heroism.

But like ants encountering an obstacle, they peel apart and walk around me, barely noticing.

Three weeks ago they'd have made a bit of a fuss.

'How are you getting on?'

'Anything you need?'

'How are the hands?'

'Christ! Did Johnny *really* faint when he saw you?'

The irony's not lost on me. When I was injured, when I became a cripple, I was a success. I was an imaginative cripple. I was a *brilliant* cripple. An entertaining cripple. That's it! I was an entertainer. A *show*-cripple. Fuck it! I was a *great* cripple.

CrippleCrippleCrippleCrippleCripple! Damn it! **Bugger** of a tongue-twister.

I had comedy crutches, comedy bandages, plaster, scars; the works. And my audience loved me.

'Ladies and gennelmen! Right now! Just for you! Before your very eyes! James, the happy cripple will perform his world famous "DRINK THE GLASS OF WATER TRICK"!! This he will do using BOTH HANDS! Yes, ladies and gennelmen, you heard me correctly, I said BOTH HANDS!!! And what's more, ladies and gennelmen, he will perform this trick without spilling a SINGLE DROP!!!'

I was a riot in the dining hall. Now I'm recovering, I'm just . . . normal again. A normal cripple. Nothing special. Because even though my hands are still dead, without the comedy props the act doesn't work. And all that's left is sympathy. Pity.

The voices of two outraged Controller Brigadiers invade my mind.

'Terrible thing! What a tragedy! Frightful irony! Such a great show-cripple; the *one* thing he loved doing and he can't do it any more! Such a shame!'

'Brilliant though, wasn't he?'

'Lord, *yes*! One of the best!'

'Bloody funny! Loved the flapping seal trick! Ha!'

'Christ, yes, that was a scream!'

'Oh well, can't be helped.'

'That's what comes of recovery.'

'Certainly does, old boy.'

'Yes, poor chap; what's he fit for now, eh? I mean, really, what's he *fit* for?'

'Dunno . . . normality, I suppose . . .'

'Fancy a brandy?'

'Yes. Why not!'

Except I'm *not* normal again. Not at all. All the comedy features have recovered. Except for my hands. But hands aren't funny; not by themselves. Yes, the flapping seal routine *was* great. They loved it. But without the crutches and the plaster – they're not enough. What can you *do* with just hands? After all, I can't play the piano any more . . .

I can't play the piano . . .

I . . . can't . . . play . . . the . . . piano . . .

And finally . . .

Finally . . .

It dawns.

And gradually, during the following days, the questions I've never really considered, never worried about enough to consider, burn their way into my consciousness.

What if they *don't* recover?

What if I'm stuck wearing these stupid splints for the rest of my life?

What's the point of being a show-cripple if no one's interested?

And yet, if I don't recover, I still won't have to *do* anything. I could actually fail quite successfully. But that would mean sympathy. I *hate* fucking sympathy! *Admiration*, yes. Admiration for being cool and heroic. But not sympathy. Who the fuck wants sympathy?

Christ . . .

And what about the music?

How would I get on if couldn't ever play the piano again? Or the organ? Or even the flute? Anything?

Did I *really* think it was that funny? Taking fifteen minutes to get dressed? Or taking ten minutes to clean my teeth because I couldn't hold the toothbrush properly? *They* thought it was. And yes, I did, because *they* did. It made me feel great!

It *was* bloody funny.

And all the spreading, cutting, scooping, pouring, drinking and eating that I've had to find alternative ways to manage? The comedy versions were hysterical. But without an audience they're nothing. Just tedious, clumsy, everyday necessities.

Now at mealtimes I find myself watching all the intricate little hand movements that others take for granted – holding up a knife and fork, spontaneously raising and curling a little finger to lift a cup, buttering a piece of toast . . . effortlessly.

The number of ways we communicate with our hands is amazing. We shake them in greeting, we wave goodbye, we clap in appreciation, we point, we use them to say 'stop', to say 'go', 'this big', 'this small', 'louder', 'softer', 'up', 'down', 'round', 'shh!', 'go away!'

I can't do any of them.

I can't do *anything* properly!

And *my* hands look disgusting. The muscles have become flaccid and puffy from lack of use. I have fat person's hands and because I can't even open them they're permanently bunched in a semi-fist; they get sweaty and start smelling like my feet, which means I have to wash them at least three times a day.

Where's the comedy in that?

Late November. I'm sitting by the open window in my study. It's a bright, unusually warm afternoon, and I'm watching the world go by: boys running around on the rugger pitch, the traffic in and out of the tuck shop . . .

From nowhere comes the thought: I could always kill myself.

Don't be *stupid*. That only happens in films.

I lean out of the window and look down at the concrete, grey and moss-stained. What would happen if I did? Jump, I mean. No, not *even* jump. I could just *fall*, tumble out of the window headfirst.

That would do it.

But would I die because my head hit the concrete? Or would the momentum of my body force my head to twist, which would break my neck?

Both probably.

Would I feel it?

Would it hurt?

Would there be *time* for it to hurt?

And what kind of *noise* would I make?

What *does* a falling body sound like?

Maybe it'd be an amplified 'plumph' like Johnny's chocolate cake.

Plumph! Plumph!

Or a sack of potatoes.

Presumably there'd be a few cracks as the bones broke.

Maybe a sort of 'Plumph Crack'?

Or 'Crack Plumph'?

No . . .

It'd be simultaneous, wouldn't it?

'CrackleUmph!'

Yes . . .

CrackleUmph! CrackleUmph! CrackleUmph! Cr-cr-cr-**cr-cr-cr-cr-cr-cr-cr-cr**!

I'd go out with a . . . CrackleUmph!

'And turning to local news,' the radio announcer would say, 'James McConnel went out with a CrackleUmph!'

Like a Heffalump!

CrackleUmph! Heffalump!

So . . . I'm dead. Lying awkwardly on the concrete, lifeless eyes staring skywards.

What happens then?

Well, I wouldn't have to be a failed cripple, for a start.

Except suicides go to hell, don't they?

And it's illegal . . .

Stupid law . . .

I lean out a little further for a proper look.

Concrete . . .

The Controller urges me to smile; to do the absolute opposite of what I feel.

And I smile and I smile, lifting my arms from the windowsill, forcing it, trying to get the corners of my mouth up to my eyes, and I lean a little further still.

Now jump . . .

Come on! Jump!

Think! They'd all understand! 'Poor James! He was so devastated at the thought of never being able to play the piano again that he jumped.'

Go on. Jump.

Ha, ha, very funny!

Because I really don't mean it, it's a game. I'm playing at suicide. In a way, I wish it wasn't a game. I wish I could feel it for real.

You can stop all this shit once and for all . . . you can start again.

Rewind, begin again . . .

Rewind, begin again . . .

Rewind.

Rewind.

No more pity . . .

No more sympathy . . .

No more piano . . .

FUCK OFF!

But I still lean . . . even though I know it's a game . . . and I stare at the concrete. And suddenly I *need* to, *have* to . . .

And the thoughts crowd in like locusts . . . the *real* thoughts.

Go on!

Do it!

For fuck's sake, just *do* it!

Jump!

And I lean . . .

Who'll get my stereo system?

Push yourself towards the concrete!

Go on, **push! push! push!**

I'll miss the dogs . . .

Meld with the mould on the concrete.

Meld meld **meld** with it.

My velvet jacket . . .

Mould with the meld.

Each grain of the concrete.

Each microscopic miasmic fiasmic tiny black *hole* in the concrete.

Who'd miss me?

Push push PUSH towards the concrete!

Hit the concrete!

From up here . . .

My parents would miss me.

Reach out and hit it . . .

Of *course* they'd bloody miss me.

Go on, **hit** it!

Hit it!

Hit it with your whole body!

Become the concrete!

You **are** concrete!

Come On!

DO IT! DO IT! DO IT! DO IT! DO IT! STOP!

For God's sake, **STOP!**

Just **STOP!**

Stop! Stop! Stop it! Now!

What the **fuck** are you **doing?!**

My heart's racing, pounding, shouting.

I never meant to . . .

But then I did.

Christ! *Why?*

I pull back inside.

And the sun is still shining.

And they're still playing rugger.

And they're still coming and going from the tuck shop.

And nothing seems to have changed.

And I close the window and sit on the bed shaking, feeling exactly like I used to after a bullying session.

But this time . . . for the first time . . . in years . . .

I'm crying.

I'm sitting with Mrs Johnny in her kitchen when under the skin on my right wrist a tendon suddenly flickers into life. The tiniest of movements, barely noticeable; but to me – and Mrs J – I might as well have climbed Everest. If anything, she is more excited than I am; she claps her hands in delight, clasps me in her arms and gives me a kiss. Despite this un-housemaster's-wifely behaviour, I find it touching that she cares so much. I didn't realise. After a celebratory cup of tea and a biscuit, I ring my parents.

Mum's reaction: 'Oh Jamie! Thank God!'

Dad's: 'Well done, old boy; that's marvellous!'

Over the next few weeks, miraculously, other little muscles emerge from hibernation and during the Christmas holidays, like an ancient but lovingly restored engine, my right hand gradually coughs and splutters its way back to life.

Recovery quickly gathers momentum, but there are problems. Some of the tiny revitalised nerve tendrils, having grown the length of my forearm, mistakenly attach themselves to different muscles, which means that, like a

141

faulty telephone exchange, various messages get wrongly routed. If my brain tells my thumb to move, for instance, my third finger now twitches instead. I have to re-educate my brain to issue new sets of instructions to compensate. The best therapy for this, I'm told, is playing the piano.

Back at school in early January for the spring term, and spurred on by the almost daily improvements, I weld myself to the piano in the ornate King's Gallery, silently scrutinised by a series of full-length portraits of British monarchs, and try to boost the embryonic life in my hands. Pressing *down* the keys has never been the problem. What I've been robbed of, but what is now slowly improving, is the ability to lift the fingers up again. They still resemble puffy sausages, as the muscles themselves need to regenerate. Gradually, with the exercise, my fingers begin to differ in appearance, the ones on my left hand, as ever, resembling loose-skinned chipolatas, the ones on the right starting to look as they once did.

It's an exhausting process and when I rest, I sit back in the chair and gaze at the faces in the portraits. In the midst of such august company, I imagine myself fully recovered, playing to the crowned heads of Europe, lionised by fan-wielding duchesses, admired and respected by princes, hailed as the greatest pianist of all time; or at least, of a time when they didn't have fucking mopeds.

About seven weeks after that first flicker of life, my left hand also begins to awaken. Since the nerves in this arm weren't severed, merely sent to sleep, none of the instructions have altered and within a matter of weeks it overtakes my right hand dramatically. Within a month and a half it's almost as good as new. I can start playing the organ again; and the flute.

By the end of February my left hand has recovered about

ninety-five per cent. My right hand, however, seems to come to a grinding halt at about seventy-five per cent. Part of the damaged nerve simply hasn't revived and certain crucial movements, such as the ability to twist my wrist from side to side or lift my outstretched palm, never return. In addition, the surface of my arm remains completely numb.

So it's obvious that if I want to be a musician I'm going to have to find some means other than the piano. My flute playing is only average and I doubt if the Controller will allow me to become a conductor without throwing an orchestra into complete disarray.

Which leaves the organ.

Which at first glance might not seem very different from the piano. But it's quite different in a number of ways, not least because the foot-pedal keyboard adds greatly to the number of notes you can play simultaneously.

If you press a note gently on the piano, it'll play quietly. Hit the note hard and it'll sound loud. My right hand remains clumsy so, to begin with, I find it hard to play sensitively. I'm still re-educating the fingers to behave in the way I want them to, but the sound I produce is uneven and amateurish.

On the organ, however, it doesn't matter how hard (or soft) you hit the notes; it sounds exactly the same, which means that as long as I can play the notes themselves – 'lending' some to my left hand when necessary – it doesn't matter how loud or soft I play them.

Auditions for the Royal College were held in December and after the accident I naturally assumed I wouldn't be going. However, in late January, when my left hand begins to recover, my organ teacher Titus de Groot rings the Royal College, explains the situation and asks if they would be prepared to see me after all. They say they would.

I set to work.

Four months later I travel to London for the audition and, two weeks after that, a letter arrives from the Royal College congratulating me, saying they will expect me in September. At last I feel as though I'm back on track.

The End

It's strange when you go outside . . .
And it's suddenly night.
When you haven't experienced the transition from day.
Makes me feel guilty.
Only for a second, though.
Amber street lamps reflected off parked cars.
Other people.
Man late home from work.
Girl on her way out somewhere.
Normality.
I'm off to see the Wizard
The wonderful Wizard of . . .
What rhymes with 'Oz'?
Boz, coz, doz, foz, goz, hoz, joz, koz, loz, moz, noz, poz,
quoz, roz, soz . . .
Nothing much.
The off-licence is filthy and utilitarian.

No frills, just booze and basic food.

Scan the shelves . . .

So much choice, so many yummy colours.

Like a toy shop.

And tonight . . . I think we might try something . . . exotic.

How about some . . . Cointreau!

Or Chartreuse. Haven't had that in ages.

Damn, they haven't got it.

All right. Cointreau, then.

Plus the crisps and a loaf of bread.

Chapter 7
A Twitch in Time

'Now you will be careful, won't you?'

'Yes, Mum.'

'And promise me you won't get mugged?'

'Yes, Mum . . .' faintly exasperated.

'Train's coming.' My father.

'Oh Lord, so it is! Bye, darling, good luck, have a *lovely* time; look after yourself and we'll see you on Friday.'

'Bye, Mum.' I give her a kiss and a brief hug.

'Bye, old boy; be good.' Manly shoulder pats.

'Bye, Poll.' Quick, slightly sheepish brotherly/sisterly kisses.

London means freedom. Eighteen years under a microscope and finally I'm a grown-up. I can do anything I want. To ease me gently into independence, some cousins have rented me a room in their South Kensington house as a paying guest, a shortish walk from the Royal College of Music.

I'm excited. I'm expecting music students to be different from other people. I imagine them as erudite and elevated, mildly eccentric but colourful and humorous; gentle, understanding souls who'll take me to their collective bosom. I have visions of a group of us going regularly to concerts at the Albert or Queen Elizabeth Halls, opera at Covent Garden, theatres and cabarets; discussing music endlessly, laughing, chatting . . . enjoying.

Approaching the college on my first morning, music case in hand, the building seems alive with the sounds of countless students practising in un-soundproofed rooms – violins, trumpets, pianos, singers, clarinets, horns – a concert of chaos – Charles Ives-like, each impervious to and independent of all the others.

The Controller has been playing havoc with the paving stones along Queen's Gate and Prince Consort Road.

1, 2, 3, 4, 5, 6, 7 – crack.

1, 2, 3, 4, 5, 6, 7 – crack.

1, 2, 3, 4, 5, 6, 7 – crack.

Neck jerks and head taps.

'Stop it!' I say this out loud. I never usually do but I'm nervous.

Odd look from a man getting out of his car. Christ! Didn't see him.

Front steps, Royal College of Music.

Pause before the double doors for a series of violent staccato double-sniffs, then an 'mm mm'. Tap the highly polished handle seven times for luck and push into the large entrance hall, mosaic floor and pillars. God, it's noisy: added percussive clicks and clacks and voices.

To my right, just inside, a hall porter-cum-doorman is seated behind a desk, looking like what I imagine an Italian traffic warden looks like, in a dark blue uniform with brass buttons, red sash and soft blue and white peaked cap.

'Morning, young man.'

'Good morning.' Normally, I'd just say 'Morning,' but nerves seem to breed formality.

'What can I do for you?'

'This is my first day here.'

'Righty-oh. First thing you need to do: sign in . . . just . . . here,' and he points to an open book on the desk in front of him.

While I pick up the string-attached biro and sign my name, he 'pom poms' to himself briefly before commenting, 'Bit colder out there today.'

'Yes, it is,' I reply, glancing out of the window for politeness's sake before replacing the biro and gathering up my music case.

'Thank you, young man!'

I wish he wouldn't call me that. I pull out my weekly schedule.

'Erm . . . could you tell me where Room A2 is, please?'

He points. 'Up the stairs, first floor, turn left, it's on your right.'

'Thank you.' I turn to walk away.

'Good luck, young man.'

'Oh . . . thanks.'

First year, first term, first day, first lesson: 'aural training'. Up the stairs, threading my way past rushing students, instruments and music cases. There it is, Room A2, white letters on the door. I must be nearly the last to arrive. Most of the fifteen or so seats are taken, but I spot an empty place at the back.

'Morning,' I say cheerfully, belying my nerves.

One or two noncommittal grunts in reply, but mostly they ignore me.

Ashamed of my disgraceful outburst, I walk over and sit down. Then I look around, still feeling stupid, struggling with this for a while before I can focus fully on my surroundings.

A couple of the men are whispering to each other, clearly friends already, but everyone else is silent; there's a definite tension in the air. Surreptitious little looks, sizing each other up, wondering who's going to be the star of the class or if we're good enough to be here at all. It's faintly hostile.

The room, dingy and well-used, could be straight out of Rimmington Hall, apart from some stray percussion instruments on a side table and the two black grand pianos side by side next to it.

A mixed bunch of people.

And no uniforms.

Feels odd.

Odd . . . dod . . . dod . . . dod, dod, dod . . . where does the 'd' stop and the 'o' begin, I wonder? If I start with the 'd' and go 'do' (as in 'dot') do do do do do and get faster and faster; at some point the 'o' takes over and it becomes 'odd' again.

Mustn't forget I'm a grown-up now.

I don't feel very grown up.

Two pretty girls next to each other at the front – one blonde, the other brunette – sitting like statues. Carefully dressed, somehow 'minxish'.

Another girl: small, studious-looking, pale, thick-lensed glasses, 'knit-it-yourself-but-haven't-quite-got-the-hang-of-it-yet' woollen jumper, black nylon trousers, fat legs and sandals.

Small chap in the corner, dead centre parting, glasses,

acne, tweed jacket, purple shirt, check trousers. Not sure *what* you'd call those things on his feet: shoe-dals? Boot-flops?

Next to him, rock-star type, shoulder-length auburn hair, beard, moustache, pinstripe suit jacket, white T-shirt, blue jeans and cowboy boots; cool and unapproachable, I should think.

The door opens.

'Morning, everyone.'

Sporadic 'mornings' in reply. I have to stop myself adding 'sir' out of habit.

My first music professor.

Doesn't *look* especially professorial. In my mind the word conjures up white-haired, semi-geniuses with German accents. This man looks like a maths teacher. Maths jacket, maths shirt, maths trousers and shoes.

He walks over and stands by one of the pianos with an open book. 'I'm Dennis Ashcroft. Hello. Let's see who you all are. When I read out your name, could you please raise your hand.'

He studies the book.

'Kevin Barratt?'

'Here.' Mr Purple Shirt raises his hand.

'Right. Samantha Clusky?

'Here.' Sing-song Scots accent straight out of *Brigadoon*, long dark hair, directly in front of me.

'Okay. Jason Hedley?'

'Here.' Mr Rock Star, who smiles unexpectedly. His fingers are nicotine-stained.

'James McConnel.'

'Here,' I say.

'Catherine Millwood?'

151

'Here.' One of the Minxes.

The list goes on.

Having finished, he snaps the book shut and produces some sheets of blank manuscript paper from his briefcase, which he starts handing round.

'Right, I just want to get an idea of what you can all do; so for today I'm going to give you a few exercises and we'll see how you get on. Okay?'

More sporadic grunts.

'Pencils out, please.'

There's a lot of scrabbling about in music cases while Dennis moves to one of the pianos. He starts with rhythmic dictation, playing a phrase on the piano which we have to write down, rhythm only, not the notes. He plays it once. Then again, and we all set to work in the following silence.

I find this relatively easy, and see that both the Minxes, Kevin Purple Shirt, Rock Star Jason and a few others do, too. Samantha from *Brigadoon*, however, seems to be struggling and finishes last.

Dennis stands up. 'Right, are you all done?'

More grunts.

'Good. Okay, let's see what you've got.' He scans the class. 'Er . . . Kevin, can you clap what you've written, please?'

My heart sinks.

Christ!

I can feel the Controller licking its lips.

It's music, for God's sake; you never twitch when you play music. Just imagine it's the piano.

Kevin looks down at his paper and claps the rhythm confidently and effortlessly. I notice his hands. They're strong, elegant, with beautifully manicured fingernails which put my chewed, savaged ones to shame.

'Good,' says Dennis, 'spot on, well done. Samantha, why don't you have a go?'

'Em, hope I've got this right,' she says nervously. I love her lilting Scots accent. Can't see her face, though.

She starts tentatively, claps for a few seconds, then jiggles her hands wildly in a fluster. 'Oh no, that's wrong; can I start again?'

'It's all right, take your time,' Dennis says gently.

She tries again, getting about three-quarters of the way through – with mistakes – before stopping abruptly. 'I couldn't quite get the last bit.' She looks up at Dennis apologetically.

'Never mind. Not bad. Er . . . James, how about you?'

Nervous, I launch into it at high speed, just to get it over with, racing against the Controller in case it decides to try and force me to add extra notes in the middle or at the end.

I get through it.

'Good,' says Dennis, 'a bit fast, but well done. Jason, how about you?'

But before Jason can begin, the Controller ambushes me, grabs my hands and I start clapping like a psychotic machine gun, on and on and on, unable to stop until it's right . . . there's always . . . one . . . more . . . sodding . . . note . . . to make it . . . **RIGHT!**

Shit . . .

Silence.

Dreadful . . . heavy . . . absolute.

Twenty eyes shoot in my direction, followed almost immediately by two more – Samantha's, who has to turn her head 180 degrees to look at me properly. I only caught a brief glimpse of her face when I came in, but it's a lovely face . . . gentle.

Astonished.

Time slows . . . then stops.

Sometimes in a film, often at the beginning, the action freezes, the camera pulls back and back and back . . . until the image becomes a framed photograph on a piano or a side table in a different scene altogether.

This is one of those photographs; a snapshot which will be added to my internal 'life photograph album'. Unforgettable and indelible, along with Thompson's boots, Mrs Ferguson's make-up, the moped, Polly's bleeding head, Warboys, the bearded lady . . . incalculable others.

Bugger bugger shit shit.

Chugger Pitty Chang Bang.

I realise they're waiting for me to say something.

'Sorry,' I mutter, putting both culprits to my mouth, 'I was just trying something . . .'

For a beat, nothing changes, the world remains frozen; but then, slowly, like a film projector cranking up, time resumes.

Dennis, frowning in puzzlement, turns his head slowly away; but for a moment his eyes won't follow. He clears his throat. 'Right, okay . . . so, Catherine, how did you do?'

She claps gently and accurately, and as the lesson moves on, gradually, I allow myself to settle back, enjoying it. But the occasional after-looks of curiosity are unmistakable.

Or is it just my imagination?

I become friendly with Jason the Rock Star, whose performance I interrupted and whose personality is nothing like his appearance. Initially we have smoking in common – the majority of the students don't seem to smoke – and since we're only allowed to light up in the canteen, much of our casual friendship is conducted there or outside in the street.

The Controller, incidentally, ensures I spend far more money on cigarettes than the amount I actually smoke, forcing me – once lit and in my mouth – to tap each one violently downwards with my forefinger seven times. Invariably they snap in half, which, if repairable, I mend with the Sellotape I now carry in my music case for the purpose. More often they're ruined, which means lighting another. Even then, the ones which do somehow hold together, hanging at odd angles, creased and bent, still have to survive the urge I have to crush them or bash them whenever I take a drag or flick off the ash. Cigarettes – like so many other things – are too soft; too indecisive. I have to resist the urge to squish each new packet or punch it, to make it *do* something or *be* something resolute and strong.

Jason has a broad Yorkshire accent, is desperately short of money and lives in a squat in Crouch End with his girlfriend, existing entirely on his student grant and any part-time evening jobs he can find as barman or waiter. It takes him an hour and a half to get into college on the bus each morning, and comparing his life with mine, I feel horribly guilty, increasing my journey time to half an hour and shrinking my cousins' house to a small flat when he asks where I live.

In terms of our backgrounds we're as different as Handel and handle and yet we get on very well, even without the music – like me, he's an organist. He's laid-back, quiet and plays both the piano and the organ fiendishly well – far better than me, and not just because of the limitations in my right hand.

And Jason has a twitch.

Which is fascinating. I've never *met* anyone else who twitches.

It's not a very big twitch – a few faces and some Groucho Marx eyebrow business – but it looks so weird seeing someone do what I do and it doesn't fit with his otherwise calm exterior.

When I bring up the subject he's reticent and unwilling to discuss it in any detail, but I never feel the need to hold back in his company and he always seems quite comfortable, leaning lackadaisically against a wall, puffing away himself, watching in detached amusement at my attempts to smoke a cigarette without annihilating it first.

As for the other students, I veer more towards the girls than the men. During lunch breaks in the crowded canteen, we naturally sit with our regular classmates, which in my case means the three or four girls with whom I feel most at ease.

I always play it safe. With the exception of Samantha, who I get to know because she's also an organist, I steer away from the prettier girls, feeling they're too good for me, worried that if I approach them I'll be laughed at or ridiculed. It's probably my imagination, since both the Minxes, especially Catherine, always smile and say hello whenever we see each other. Nonetheless, the prettier the girl, the more tongue-tied I become. Consequently, my lunch companions, though perfectly friendly, are among the plainest in my year. I don't think Stella likes me very much.

With the exception of Jason, the other men are the real problem. I still can't work out why I don't fit in. I try analysing *my* behaviour versus *theirs*. They have a hidden bond which I'm not party to; like a technique I've never learned. I watch them day after day, studying their expressions, listening to

what they say, how they say it and trying to imitate it –
without success.

At Rimmington I thought it might have been because I
was a musician, that if I was in an environment with other
musicians then all would be well and I would belong. But it's
not. I'm not actively disliked; I just feel excluded. I've tried all
the old tricks I've tried before. If I find myself in the canteen
with a couple of the lads, I listen enthusiastically to their
exploits in the student bar, doing my utmost to get into the
spirit of it.

'Je-sus! I was wrecked last night!' says Tony, a trumpeter.
'Nearly didn't make it in for the Beethoven this morning.' He
sniffs loudly. It strikes me how mismatched 'Beethoven' and
'wrecked' sound in close proximity.

'Yeah, me too,' Terry, a horn player replies. 'Must've put
away about ten pints, I reckon. Completely screwed up the
trio in the third movement.'

'Which Beethoven?' I ask.

'Eroica,' says Terry, barely glancing at me.

'Great piece,' I say, nodding, hoping we can talk about
music.

'Good night, though, eh?' says Tony, grinning.

Obviously not.

'Yeah, not bad!' Terry grins too.

'Sounds great!' I say, determined to get in on the act.
'Wish I'd been there. I love getting wrecked!' And in turn, I
grin, emulating theirs.

Odd look from Terry.

Odd look from Tony.

'Missed *Match of the Day*, though,' adds Terry finally,
ignoring me.

'Oh shit!' says Tony. 'Who was it?'

'Chelsea–Liverpool.'

'No! Fuck! Who won?'

'Dunno,' says Terry, 'but Chelsea haven't been the same since Osgood and Hutchinson.'

'Too right!' Tony says.

'But they—'

'So what were you guys drinking?' I ask, interrupting Terry and backtracking so that at least there's a *chance* I can contribute something. (Who's Hutchinson!?)

'Bitter,' says Tony distractedly.

'Yeah? What's it like here?' I ask, still grinning laddishly as though I'm a connoisseur. I hate bitter; it tastes revolting and it's never fizzy enough.

'I dunno.' Tony shrugs, looking faintly annoyed now. 'What do you think? It's just bitter!'

'Yeah, I s'pose so.' I nod again, as though seeing his point, but feeling like an idiot.

Terry continues, 'Hutchinson and Houseman; they were a great team, but at least they've still got Harris.'

'Yeah, but is it enough? If only Hudson hadn't gone to Stoke, they'd be all right.' Tony looks worried. I try to 'feel' for him.

'Yeah,' says Terry, 'what they need is another Osgood.'

'*And* another Dave Sexton,' adds Tony.

'So are you both Chelsea supporters then?' I ask, realising that booze is probably best left.

'Yeah,' says Terry, as if it was a stupid question, which of course it was. I *know* it was. I knew before I asked, but I couldn't think of anything else to say.

The final humiliation comes a few days later when I take completely seriously their assertion that the government is considering the decimalisation of time. I sit like an idiot, wanting so much to fit in, that the idea of there being a hundred seconds in a minute and ten hours in a day seems utterly plausible. Only later does it dawn on me that they were taking the piss.

I've given up trying now.

At weekends I go home to my parents, partly because I feel I ought to, but mainly because my cousins don't want me hanging around. My relationship with my parents has sunk to an all-time low. It usually starts well enough. I arrive at Winchester station, where one or other of them is waiting. We drive home in semi-companionable silence. I greet and am greeted by whichever one hasn't picked me up – and Polly, if she's at home – then we all sit down, them with stiff G and Ts, me with a glass of beer – and then the trouble starts.

It's always the same and I sit, dreading that first question: 'So, darling, what've you been up to? How's college?'

A perfectly reasonable thing to ask; but I feel badgered; questions about London, who my friends are, what I get up to in the evenings, if I'm having fun, am I eating enough?

How do I tell them I've got no friends at all, other than a long-haired chain-smoking Yorkshireman who lives in a Crouch End squat? That I mostly go out alone – and then hardly ever – and that I'm not particularly enjoying college life in any case. I clam up, I get irritable and argumentative, and by the time Sunday night comes round again, we all breathe a silent sigh of relief.

Meanwhile, the Controller, ever vigilant and on top form, has come up with a new addition to the obsessional fold, whereby I have to breathe in as deeply as possible with the force of a vacuum cleaner, hold it until my face goes red, then breathe slowly out again without making *any* noise . . . at all. Even the tiniest sound of air coming up from my lungs or the faintest click of saliva on my tongue means repeating the process until I get it right.

I sit in class after class like an angina patient getting completely out of breath, panting with the exertion. I daresay it increases my lung capacity, which is probably good for my flute embouchure, but quite apart from the strange looks I get from my immediate neighbours, it's embarrassing if I'm asked a question in mid-hold and have to expel my breath suddenly in order to answer.

Then something happens by complete chance; a tiny, almost insignificant event; something which changes the way I see myself, but more importantly, changes the way *others* see me.

And it all has to do with my dog.

I don't actually have a dog.

But that's not the point.

The End

Cointreau, neatly wrapped and bagged.
  I feel safe now, walking home.
  Like I'm carrying a gun.
  Liquid protection.
  To ward off evil.
  My internal security system.
  Slightly impatient now.
  In through the front door.
  Formalities out of the way first.
  Throw the worst of the mess into the bin.
  Make the sandwich.
  Unwrap the Cointreau.
  Fetch a glass.
  Put all three by the chair.
  Then cigarettes and lighter.
  Phone off the hook.
  Find the TV remote again.

Good. Organised.
Comfortable.
And finally.
Sit.
Ahh!

Chapter 8
The Rescue Dog

Damn! Five past two.

Late . . . again! Hate being late.

I just popped out for some cigarettes. There was a long queue.

Dammit!

Musical 'form and structure' with Mr Gunton, and the whole year'll be there too, not split into groups. They'll all turn in their seats to look at me. Embarrassing.

Come on, run! Down the stairs, along the corridor . . . and in.

Out of breath.

Gunton's in the middle of a sentence, something about Tartini and the Devil's Trill Sonata.

Jason's there, and Stella, and Samantha, and Kevin and Terry and Tony . . . all of them.

Everyone looks round. But only briefly.

Not so embarrassing after all; it'll be fine . . . but Gunton stops.

'Good lunch, James?' he says good-humouredly, not descending to sarcasm, genuinely interested almost.

'Erm, yes thanks. Sorry I'm late. I had to –' I nearly say, 'get some cigarettes', but this sounds feeble, so without thinking I fib – 'go and feed the dog.'

An image of our family black Labrador suddenly appears in my mind. Can't *think* what made me say that. However, it's an interesting enough excuse to raise a small titter in the ranks.

'Oh,' he says, faintly intrigued. 'What kind of dog d'you *have*?'

'Erm, black Labrador,' I say, borrowing from reality, adding, 'Milly; she's very sweet.'

Another titter.

'Oh,' he says again, 'and you had to feed her.'

'Yes, Winalot biscuits and Pedigree Chum,' I say, straight-faced, improvising madly.

The specificity of this, plus, possibly, my matter-of-fact expression, gets a big laugh, and suddenly I realise I'm enjoying myself. They think I'm funny. They're laughing; I don't really *care* whether it's at me or with me. It's a positive reaction, the same positive reaction I used to get when I was on crutches, and I start tingling all over, a combination of nerves and excitement.

'Really?' he says.

'Yes,' I say, getting into my stride, though still not entirely sure what's coming next. 'Yes, I always find it's much better to soak the biscuits in boiling water first, let them cool for a while and then add the meat, don't you?'

I got the 'don't you?' from either my mother or Fanny Cradock – I can't remember which – but it's the sort of thing people say when they're discussing tiny variations in a recipe.

Things like 'I prefer to put the butter in *before* the lemon juice, don't you?' It's a cosy expression which helps to include the other person. Here, though, it sounds slightly cheeky without being overtly rude, which is why it gets the biggest laugh so far.

Gunton takes it very well, and laughs along with the rest.

'I don't have a dog, I'm afraid. Perhaps you'd like to bring Milly *along* with you next time and we can all meet her . . . then you wouldn't have to be late.'

Another laugh, as he puts me gently back in my place. Touché, Mr Gunton. But I seem to have started something.

The following week Gunton asks, 'How's Milly today? Properly nourished, I hope?'

Inevitable laugh.

'She's fine, thanks; sends her love,' I reply jovially, which gets a good laugh. I've prepared this in advance, going through several different responses just in case.

The next week he settles for 'Fed the dog?'

Gentle titter.

'Yes, thanks.'

Shorter titter this time.

Clearly the joke's beginning to wear a little thin, because he doesn't mention it again. But what sticks is the laughter. Being noticed. I don't *need* to be a cripple. I can get a warm reaction from the group just by saying something stupid or inappropriate.

Sometimes we have to demonstrate our skills in front of the class, sight-reading music on the piano or showing off our conducting techniques. Rather than just *doing* it, I purposely make 'funny' mistakes, play wrong notes or conduct erratically, anything to get a laugh, to be noticed, to be appreciated. I can feel they're laughing *at* me rather than with me but it doesn't matter; I don't care, I have an audience, I can belong by being a clown. I find it increasingly hard to take anything seriously, always on the lookout for a joke, paranoid that I may lose the edge and revert to my old self in their eyes.

Being the class clown is a positive thing.

Just being tolerated is intolerable.

What works in the lecture halls also works in the canteen. I know I'm lying to myself, but I maintain my pretend interest in Hutchinson and his friends, football in general and the nightly goings-on in the student bar; but by injecting a stupid remark or feigning ignorance – 'what does offside mean?' – I'm rewarded with attention that gives me the impression of being included, if not the reality.

And I work quite hard. I do what's required, turning in essays, practising the organ and flute, learning harmony and counterpoint, going to concerts and singing in the college choir. At the end of my first year I pass my exams . . . but I'm still not enjoying it.

A week or two before the start of the second year, I move into an upmarket student hostel even nearer the college. Of the fifty residents, forty-four are girls, most of whom, I discover, are fresh from boarding schools in Ascot, Wantage and Sherborne. The girls share but we boys/men have our own rooms. I manage to persuade the caretaker to let me install a piano in mine, which gives me a distinct advantage almost immediately.

Up till now, my social life has been virtually nonexistent. During my first year I did go to concerts most weeks, either by myself or sometimes with Samantha. She started the ball rolling by asking me to the Festival Hall one evening, but she made it quite clear that our relationship was to be strictly confined to college and concerts and though we became quite friendly, I never saw her at other times.

Installed in the hostel, desperate to meet any of what seems like a limitless supply of pretty girls, I plan my assault quite carefully. Far too nervous simply to introduce myself – apart from the odd 'hello' on the stairs in passing – which would be far easier, I take the long way round and decide to become 'the tortured genius in room B2' instead, hoping they'll come to me. Every day at about half past five, when I hear the increasing foot traffic at the front door, I make sure I'm at the piano, bashing away, playing the most elaborate things I can think of in order to impress them. They're not to know that I'm missing out the notes that my right hand can't manage. I've learned to fudge things so convincingly by now that although my limitations are very noticeable when I'm playing 'fiddly' music by Bach or Mozart particularly, I can get away with murder when it comes to the sweeping romanticism of Rachmaninov or Brahms, which I think sounds more impressive in any case.

It takes a couple of weeks, during which I sit alone at the breakfast table, as twitch-free as possible – attempting to suppress the urge to whack my knife against the infuriatingly delicate teapots – not quite brave enough yet to make the first move. But finally, as I walk into the dining room one morning, a girl with frizzy hair, sitting with another girl, asks me, 'Excuse me, is it you who plays the piano?'

'Er, yes it is,' I say, being deliberately coy and unassuming.

She looks at her friend briefly as if to say, 'See! I told you so.'

'Gosh, you're very good.'

Genuine compliments make me uncomfortable and I want to say something stupid like 'pickled tomatoes' to disarm it, but I rein in the urge, blush slightly and say instead, 'Oh . . . thanks . . . hope it's not too loud.'

'No, it's lovely. Are you a musician?'

'Yes, I'm at the Royal College of Music . . . up the road.'

'Oh, whereabouts?'

'Just up Queen's Gate.'

She glances at her friend, then back at me. 'That's where we are.'

'Where are you?' I ask.

'Queen's Gate, sixth form; we're doing our A levels.' She smiles.

I've got this overwhelming urge to punch her – just to see what would happen – no other reason. Would she scream? Would she run away? Sit looking shocked? Maybe she'd throw the teapot at me. I don't suppose she'd want to talk to me again. I could ruin the whole thing, right now.

She continues, 'I'm Lizzie, by the way; this is Caroline.'

'Hello,' says her friend, who has dark hair and a set of pearls.

'James,' I say, pointing to my chest, and we all shake hands well-bredly. Summoning courage, I ask, 'Do you mind if I sit with you?'

''Course not,' says Caroline, and she smiles.

With a song in my heart and nervous excitement in my milk-pouring, I grab my cereal from the side table and rush to join them, in case they suddenly decide to leave.

'How long have you two been here?' I ask, wrestling with the Controller, which still seems hell-bent on GBH.

'Couple of weeks,' Lizzy replies.

'Same here,' I say. 'How come you don't live at school?'

'Mummy thought I'd have more fun here.'

'Yes, so did mine,' adds Caroline.

They look at each other conspiratorially and then Lizzie says, faintly sheepishly, 'We're doing the season. There are quite a few debs here.'

'Really? What do you have to do?' I ask, a little awed.

'Oh,' says Lizzie, 'we go to drinks parties and dinner parties and charity balls and the Berkeley Dress Show – I didn't really want to do it, but Mummy insisted. It's quite fun actually; we've met a lot of nice people, haven't we?' She glances at Caroline.

'Yes we have,' Caroline says, 'but the men are pretty ghastly.'

'In what way?' I ask, as if I wasn't one.

'Oh, you know: army bores, Lloyd's brokers, that sort of thing; only want to talk about themselves.'

'How annoying!' I say, nodding sagely – then, pressing my advantage, 'So what do you both want to do when you've finished your As?'

'Well, I want to study opera,' says Lizzie.

Bash the teapot! Go on! **Hit** the fucking thing! **Hard** as you can!

Shut up!

'Really?' I say, excited at the prospect of a common interest. 'Do you sing?'

'Not very well . . . yet, but I'm having lessons.'

'What sort of things?'

'Mozart mostly, I love Mozart.'

'So do I; who wouldn't? What about Wagner?'

I ask this because during the holidays I bought the boxed set of Wagner's *Das Rheingold* and fell in love with it, playing it on my record player almost non-stop.

'Urgh!' says Lizzie, disgusted. 'Can't bear Wagner! Nothing but screaming German sopranos with silly names! Urgh! Hate it!'

'So do I! Couldn't agree more,' I say enthusiastically. 'Give me *Don Giovanni* any day!'

'Ah! I love *Don Giovanni*,' she says and, toast in hand, she starts humming gently.

'Come on, we're going to be late,' Caroline says, looking at her watch, clearly feeling left out.

Ignoring her and not wanting to lose momentum, I chip in quickly with, 'Look, why don't we do a duet? You sing, I'll play.'

'Would you mind?' says Lizzie.

'No, 'course not; it'd be fun.'

'Okay.'

'How about this evening?'

'All right, but it'll have to be fairly quick.' She gestures to Caroline. 'We've got to go to a dinner party.'

'Well, I'll be here.'

'Okay. Sixish?'

'Fine. See you then.'

They both get up, and with a soft 'bye', they leave.

And that's the start. Things just seem to flow. Lizzie introduces me to her friends, both within the house and outside. They in turn introduce me to their friends, and before long my social calendar emerges from hibernation and slowly begins to fill.

First it's drinks, then it's dinner parties, then charity balls, sometimes a combination of all three. I frequent wine bars, restaurants, and nightclubs – usually cheap places; most of us are on a tight budget, even the debs – and more and more faces become familiar each time I walk into a crowded room.

After that it's weekends in the country staying at large comfortable houses run by large comfortable mothers, desperate for their daughters to meet the right people and ultimately marry one of them. I am willingly sucked in and whether or not I'm considered one of the 'right' people, I don't know, but barely a week goes by without the satisfying slap of an 'At Home' invitation hitting the doormat.

It's all very shallow. My Mozart relationship with Lizzie proves to be a one-off, although we spend some fairly rowdy evenings around the piano in my room. Conversations tend to revolve around who was at the last party, who will be at the next, and 'Did you hear about poor Amelia, who got soooo drunk, she was sick all over the Maitre d' and was sent home in disgrace! Ha ha! Such fun!'

I'm enjoying myself. But as always, I avoid the men. I'm still nervous in their company; I can't think what to say and whatever I do say I feel prejudged.

'So what do you do?' This is practically always the opening gambit.

'I'm a music student.'

'Oh . . . really . . .' slightly bored; and already he's looking past me, dismissing me out of hand, scanning the room to see if there's anyone better on the horizon.

Even if I was the German Ambassador I'd still get the same reaction. From the moment we're introduced, from that first look, a subconscious conversation has already taken place and he's registered my discomfort.

'What about you?' I ask.

'Army. Sandhurst.'

'Gosh, is that fun?'

I don't know what else to say. 'Is it good? Does it satisfy you? Do you like being soldier? Are you a fine, fine, fine fine

fine **fine fine fine fine fine fine fine** army officer?'

Or investment banker or insurance broker or venture capitalist – it doesn't matter which.

Whatever I say, his eyes glaze over and he moves on as quickly as possible – more so if I let slip a fast blink, tap my head or abuse my cigarette. But I don't think it's the twitching that's the problem, any more than it is at the Royal College. In fact I find that in social situations I can control the Controller for short periods in the way I've always been able to, and strangely, in a party atmosphere they decrease dramatically as the evening wears on, only to reappear with full force the next morning. I've never been able to work out why.

These males, like those at school and at the Royal College, all seem to have cracked the 'how to do life' thing, and though I try the by now well-rehearsed routine of 'genuine fascination' with all things military or financial, I *still* can't get the hang of it. The sensation of being 'less than' dominates any interaction I have with them. I feel dull. I dread the moment at the end of more conservative weekend dinner parties when the 'ladies' retire, leaving the 'gentlemen' to their port and cigars, wishing to God I could go with the 'ladies' so I won't have to make the huge effort to be 'one of the brotherhood' and pretend to be comfortable speaking a language I can't understand.

Eventually, because outright rejection feels somehow preferable to the unresolved tension of attempting to belong, I revert to my Royal College trick and seek to antagonise in order to get it over with, or at least to get some kind of reaction.

'What do you do?'

'Army.'

'Oh really! Which regiment?'

'Life Guards.'

'Oh yes? Beach or swimming pool? Sorry, just joking!'

He doesn't appreciate it and moves off, but I feel as though I've got the upper hand. I've managed to affect him, even through annoyance.

Fortunately, the ratio of boys to girls is heavily in my favour and I avoid men whenever I can. The girls are more interesting, more interested and on the whole – though not always – prettier.

What really helps is the piano; it never lets me down. Not once. Occasionally I come across one or two people at art school, but I never meet another music student and being one sometimes gives me a certain cachet, which I milk shamelessly.

When I'm invited away for the weekend, I can almost guarantee there'll be a piano lurking somewhere, and having spotted it – if I'm not asked outright – I wait until after dinner when everyone's nicely tanked up and then make my way nonchalantly over and strum a couple of chords in an 'I can take it or leave it' kind of a way. You can almost hear the 'ding' as 'music student' and 'piano' connect in people's minds (it's amazing how often it doesn't until this moment) and then it's just a case of waiting until someone says something like: 'Of course! You play the piano, don't you! Oh, *do* play something. Please!'

Whereupon I try to look modest and flustered and reply, as if I was nervous, 'Oh, all right . . . w-what would you like?'

It's always the same.

'Can you play the theme from *Love Story*?'

Or *Midnight Express*.

Or *Match of the Day*.

And when I can and people gather round the piano to watch, I'm in my element. This is when I'm happiest; I love showing off. And then more television and film themes follow, which I spice up by playing in different styles and before long I'm singing Flanders and Swann and improvising. I only know about three pop songs, so I try confining any requests to film or television music.

Even the men seem impressed, and while I'm at the piano, suddenly I can talk quite happily with them on what feels like an equal level. I don't know what it is, but sitting there makes me feel as if I'm plugged into humanity. As soon as I get up from the piano stool and become just another guest, I feel as though I've been unplugged again.

I lost my virginity just over a month ago. Either I came to it late, or the few people I've sounded out since are lying. Her name was Kate and she seduced me. At least I *think* that's what she did; I don't have much else to compare it with, except what I've seen in films. At the time, she was living in the hostel but she left shortly afterwards.

I don't *think* the two events were connected.

We had shared a table at breakfast once or twice and all I knew about her was that she came from Wales, had short auburn hair, smiled a lot and was at secretarial college.

That was it . . . until one evening, quite late, there was a tentative knock at my door, which I opened to reveal Kate standing in the doorway smiling, blushing faintly, holding a bottle of white wine.

'Kate,' I said, a little surprised.

'Can I come in?' She held the bottle out to me. 'Thought you might be lonely.'

'Erm . . . 'course you can.'

I thought it was a bit odd and I could tell she'd already been drinking; not that she was staggering exactly, just walking 'attentively'. But I didn't see it coming.

She sat on the end of my bed. I played the piano, we talked, drank the wine and, about an hour after she arrived, when I was in the middle of trying to impress her by playing the music from the Fairy Liquid advert, she suddenly came across to me, took my head in her hands, bent over and kissed me . . . hard . . . on the lips.

Which, after the initial shock, I rather enjoyed.

'So um . . . er . . . what brought this on?' I asked when we came up for air, trying to sound unfazed, as though this sort of thing happened all the time.

She blushed again. 'I just . . . sort of . . . felt like it.'

'Oh.'

I thought I should add 'great' or 'very nice' or something appreciative, but I couldn't think what, so I left it.

Then she sat on my lap and we kissed again.

I'd never been alone with a girl in complete privacy before – other than kissing behind the bushes at a weekend party where discovery was always a risk – and although I knew what I *wanted* to do, I couldn't quite summon up the courage to move things on to a different level, because I was frightened of where it might ultimately lead; because if it *did* ultimately lead where it promised to, I was worried I wouldn't be up to the task.

I didn't have to summon up anything.

After about ten minutes, Kate got off my lap and stood by the bed, looking expectant.

'Come on then,' she said, when I didn't move.

'What d'you mean?'

'Come on; undress me.'

'Undress you?' I was suddenly gripped with panic, twitching faintly, beginning to shake. I don't know how I'd envisaged having sexual intercourse, but it wasn't this clinical.

'Yes, stop making faces and undress me.' Which, the way she said it, sounded somewhere between a telling-off from Nanny and a dare.

So I did as I was told, vaguely surprised that, far from questioning it, she seemed to be dismissing my face-making as a mild irritant.

And then she undressed me and I let myself be guided by her, not really knowing what to do. I mean, I *did* know what to do, obviously, but only in theory.

It happened alarmingly quickly (my fault) and I was so nervous I can't remember if I enjoyed it or not. What I do remember is her look of disappointment and frustration afterwards, followed by her suddenly turning alarmingly pale, leaping up off the bed and being aggressively sick in the basin.

But then I meet Jenny.

The End

It's very sophisticated, Cointreau.

Chic.

Sitting here, I could be the French Ambassador . . .

His Exellency Monsieur Jean-Jacques de Bouvier-Flouvier-Mouvier.

At a state dinner.

White tablecloths and waiters.

That first sip is so very civilised.

A strong, thick, biting sweetness . . .

That slices through everything . . .

Promising that everything after it will be wonderful . . .

Because at this point it still feels special.

It still feels like an exception to the rule.

A treat for the palate.

And my spirits soar . . .

Because there is only *now* . . .

Only this second in time . . .

When nothing else matters.
And tomorrow doesn't exist.
And the second sip.
And the third and the fourth . . .
Are just as special.
But then . . .
The second glass *isn't* that special.
Which is a shame.
But it doesn't really matter.

Chapter 9
The Beast

Turning away from the bowl of mashed potato on the sideboard at supper one evening, I notice her immediately.

Smiling.

God, how she smiles . . .

With her eyes . . .

Her whole face . . .

Which lights up, and suddenly you know everything'll be all right.

Who is she?

Pretty face; not beautiful in a classic sense.

I suppose if you were coldly analytical, scrutinising each individual feature, nothing would stand out as stunning. Her nose is a little large. She has a tiny dimple in her chin. Her hair is unremarkable mousy. But that's not what I see.

Taken together . . . as a whole . . . the effect is beautiful . . . really beautiful.

A face greater than the sum of its parts.

The smile – warm. And that laugh – infectious, joyous.

I'm going to know her. It's inevitable. Anything else is unthinkable.

It's true; something really does go 'thud'.

Like a breeze block falling on a lawn.

She's sitting with Leyna, presumably Leyna's new room-mate, the two of them laughing, comfortable. I know Leyna; not well, but sometimes I've sat with her at breakfast. She's Austrian, friendly. There are two spare seats at the table. I approach.

'Hi, Leyna.'

'Hello, Jems,' she says in her gentle accent.

'Can I sit?'

'Of course.'

I'm shaking very slightly. Thuds are thudding everywhere in anticipation.

'Thud, pudd, fudd, budd, cludd,' says the Controller in my mind.

Maybe it should be a 'ping'. In the theme music from the film *Midnight Express* there's an electronic drum riff that 'pings' between each line of the tune. I think of it as a 'ping', but in reality, it sounds more like a 'pong'.

Funny.

Don't!

Twitch!

Sit down carefully, don't rush, take your time. And ignore the urge to smash your knee upwards into the irritatingly unstable table top. All the table tops are loose. They creak and they squeak and they rock.

Break it! **Destroy** the moment!

Watch as the plates, knives, forks and glasses smash on the floor!

Make her think you're a weirdo!

Go on!

Shout **'penis'**!

Hit her!

Stop it!

'Jems, please vould you permit me to introduce you to Jenny,' Leyna says, clearly recalling her school textbook English.

I look straight into the eyes. Hazel.

'Hello.'

'Hello.' She blushes. God, she's blushing! Only a bit. And she smiles.

She knows. We both know. There's an attraction.

It begins slowly, carefully, but never awkward. Becoming a gentle joust with words, expressions, humour . . .

Leyna fades. And the room with her.

And then it's a race, a free-for-all as the barriers come tumbling down and the gates open.

I hear snatches of conversation, but I'm not really listening. It doesn't matter . . .

'Music student . . . Royal College . . . Hampshire . . . parents . . .'

'Hampshire . . . me too . . . Winchester . . . very close . . .'

'Do you know . . . ?'

'Yes . . . haven't seen her for ages . . . coincidence . . .'

'Polly . . . farm . . . school . . .'

'My brother . . . Dad . . . business . . . school . . .'

'Piano . . . organ . . .'

'French Lycée . . . South Ken . . .'

'Accident . . . hands . . . hospital . . .'

'Sounds terrible . . . only tonsils . . .'

'France . . . Avignon . . .'

'Lived in Paris . . . French boyfriend . . . (ouch) . . . broke up . . . (oh good)'

'Tennis . . .'

'Tennis . . . hardly know anyone . . . London very new . . .'

'London very new . . . hardly knew anyone . . .'

'Seventeen . . . June 12th . . .'

'Nineteen . . . January 15th . . .'

'Gemini . . .'

'Capricorn . . .'

But I'm watching her. Drinking her in.

We finish each other's sentences, laughing when it happens. They flow into each other with barely a break.

'Yes! God, I didn't know other people felt like that.'

It's effortless; autopilot.

Her smile has a hint of mischief in it. Even her voice 'smiles' when she's talking. And when she talks she uses trademark phrases and words: 'Oh my God!' and 'Amazing!' And when she's listening – she really knows *how* to listen – she gently strokes her left earlobe with the tips of her fingers, lips parted a little, as she concentrates on what I'm saying, eyebrows raised slightly, expectant, as though I'm the wisest, most interesting person in the world.

Her enthusiasm for life – her energy – is addictive and I watch spellbound as she gestures expansively with her arms and hands to illustrate a point. I talk and I laugh and I smile and there's *such* a connection.

And I want to kiss her neck; not even kiss it; just rest my lips in the warm cleft between neck and jaw, just below her ear . . . where peace resides.

A pause.

Leyna's gone.

Actually, everybody's gone.

I look around. 'Where is everyone?'

'I don't know.'

We stare at each other, and laugh, quietly, awkwardly, knowing; and again she blushes.

I blush.

'What's the time?'

'Nine fifteen. God, we've been here . . .'

'For two hours; I know.'

She smiles.

I smile.

We have a secret, a conspiracy; and it's exciting and warm; our own bubble. Nothing can intrude, not even the Controller.

I'm shaking again.

There's no reason to be nervous, but I am, in spite of everything. Maybe I've misread the signs completely.

I tense.

The next stage . . .

'Shall we . . . have lunch tomorrow?'

Another pause.

'Okay . . . yes, I'd love to.' And she looks straight *at* me.

Her answer is a commitment; which feels *far* beyond lunch. The birth of something.

We both know it.

Silence, for an instant; and we glance at each other, just for a moment, unsmiling.

As if on cue, we get up from the table. I see *all* of her for the first time: slim, four or five inches shorter than me, medium-length skirt, jersey – intensely feminine. She creates a faint breeze as she brushes past me on the way to the door and I get a brief scent of her, fresh, natural, hint of soap; and pings and tingles and thuds and fuds trip over themselves on their way to my stomach.

'Are you okay?' she whispers, taking my hand.

We're watching the Goldie Hawn film *Foul Play*. We've seen each other almost constantly for a week. Seeking any excuse to touch 'accidentally'; hands, arms, shoulders, still physical strangers . . . still tentative . . . excited.

'Yes, fine . . . sorry.'

Shit.

I've been grunting, sniffing and making faces; trying to control it; able to mostly, but in the cinema or theatre or at a concert – anywhere formal – I can't, not completely.

She was bound to notice sometime.

A little later, in the middle of the film: 'Are you *sure* you're okay?' And again she takes my hand, squeezing it, this time not letting go.

'Yes, I'm fine . . . sorry.' Gritting my teeth. 'I need to . . . explain it to you.'

'Explain what?'

'Can I tell you later?'

Pause.

''Course.' She smiles at me, squeezes my hand again and looks back at the screen.

Shit . . .

Now, standing on the Fulham Road, I say, 'I've got some kind of . . . nervous habit.'

'Have you?' She looks up at me, frowning, puzzled, digesting it. Then: 'What kind of habit?'

'Well . . . coughs . . . and sniffs . . . and twitches.'

'Really!'

I'm convinced she's going to say something like 'Right! That's it! Take me home! I'm not going to be seen going out with a loony! Go on, bugger off!' But suddenly her face breaks into a huge smile.

'I think that's *so* sweet.'

Thud. Relief . . . gratitude.

'Really! Doesn't it annoy you?'

'God, no! I think it's *adorable*.'

And for that, I love her.

Fuck you, Thompson! Fuck you, Hargreaves! Fuck you, Carson-Scott!

'Come on,' she says, taking my arm. 'Let's go and get something to eat; I want to *hear* about this.'

Fifteen minutes later, we're sitting in an Italian restaurant.

'You must have noticed,' I say.

'Sort of. I've seen you wrinkling your nose a couple of times; I thought you had a cold or something. Was that a twitch?' She looks at me shyly, as though she shouldn't really be asking, then sips her wine.

'Yes,' I say, adding sheepishly, 'I usually say it's hay fever if anyone asks.'

She laughs. 'Do you?'

'Well, it must look a bit weird. Making faces and sniffing? Are you *sure* it doesn't bother you?'

'No, of course it doesn't. I told you, I think it's adorable.' And again, she takes my hand. Thud. 'What about *you*, though?'

'*God*, it drives me mad! It wastes so much *time*, apart from anything else, because I have to stop what I'm doing. But I don't care who sees me doing it.'

I'm lying. I cringe whenever I get caught twitching in the

street or in a shop; but it feels stupid and weak to admit it to Jenny.

'But why d'you *do* it?'

She's doing that thing with her left earlobe, pulling at it gently, concentrating. Bloody hell, I want to kiss her; she looks so wonderful.

'I don't know. I can't help it. I've *always* done it; coughing, sniffing, making faces and odd noises; not *just* that either.'

'What d'you mean?'

I take a deep breath. 'God . . . it sounds so *stupid*,' I half laugh nervously.

'Well, *go* on.'

I sigh. Where to begin?

'I have to count things . . . touch things . . . I dunno; tap things like . . . tables or . . . teaspoons . . . seven times.'

'You're joking.' And she laughs.

'No I'm not.' I laugh as well. 'I count words and paving stones and . . . cat's-eyes; and I have to imitate things people say and . . . put my shoes in a funny position at night. It's all numbers and counting . . . it's ridiculous.'

'What d'you mean, you *have* to do it?'

'I dunno. I just *have* to. It's like . . . an interruption, controlling me, telling me what to do. If I *don't* check under the bed seven times or clap thirty-seven times at a concert or repeat something I hear like, I dunno, "would you like a cup of tea" until it sounds the same as the person who said it, I keep thinking something ghastly'll happen.'

'What kind of thing?'

'I dunno . . . I'll get run over by a bus or I'll . . . swallow a piece of glass by mistake . . . anything.'

Pause.

'But you *can* stop it, can't you?'

'Yes I can; sometimes for hours. But sooner or later I have to let it out. It feels really uncomfortable if I don't.'

'How bizarre.'

'God, I don't know. I've never really told anyone before, apart from this bloke at college.'

'What bloke?'

'Oh, chap called Jason. He blinks very fast and makes faces. I asked him about it once but he didn't want to talk about it much. It was very strange seeing somebody else doing it.'

She pauses again, then sighs in mock exasperation. 'Oh well, maybe all musicians are just weird.'

'Could be, I s'pose,' and we laugh.

'I don't think you're *that* weird,' she says, adding, with a grin, 'well, maybe a *bit*.'

Another pause and she looks at me, serious now. 'You mustn't worry, you know . . . I think you're lovely.' She takes my hand in both of hers and we sit like that, staring at each other; and I feel the last barriers tumbling down.

We amble slowly home, my arm around her shoulders, no longer needing to touch accidentally. I put my lips to her hair as we walk, breathing in the smell of her. It's out in the open now; something's shifted. And above and beyond the pings and thuds, nerves and my pounding heart, insulated in our bubble from passing taxis, distant police sirens and the general hubbub, I feel a deep, deep calm which, for the moment, even the Controller can't penetrate.

We don't speak.

But we both know.

And as natural as life, or breath, when we reach home, I take her hand and she follows me up the stairs and into my room. And when I turn to her, gently framing her face with my hands, the collective thuds of a thousand books, films and poems come roaring into my mind as if to say, '*This* is what we were talking about,' disappearing instantly in a moment of absolute stillness . . . when our eyes lock.

We kiss. Gentle. Long. Instinctive. We fit. And in the kissing I let go, abandon myself to her, lose myself in her; trust her; something I've never done with anyone.

We break off and, as I've wanted to almost from the first moment, I rest my lips against her neck, kiss her forehead, her cheeks, her nose, her lips again.

'Are you nervous?' she whispers.

'Yes,' I say. 'You?'

'Terrified.'

'We don't have to—'

'Shh!' She puts her finger over my lips. 'I want to.'

'So do I,' I say, which sounds stupid. My heart's still pounding, and with her confirmation that we're actually going to make love, *actually* going to take off our clothes and get into bed together, so completely different from Kate, a fresh wave of nerves and butterflies takes control.

She stands there, looking up at me; allowing me. She's offering herself and I feel like crying. I reach out to undo the top button of her dress, but my hands are shaking so much I fumble with it, and smiling slightly in sympathy, she helps me, putting her hand on mine, then bypassing it. She seems calmer now, far calmer than me, as if having made the decision she can now relax. I feel like a pupil or apprentice, her the teacher.

She reaches for my shirt, and very, very slowly we undress each other, the light bleeding in from the street lamps.

I'm still shaking. I want Jenny to enjoy it.

I want to be a *good* lover.

Lover. Lover . . . it sounds so nineteenth century, doesn't it? Old-fashioned and operatic . . .

Is that what I am? Jenny's lover?

I don't *feel* like a lover.

Or is she *my* lover?

Or are we both each other's lover?

I'm about to make love to my lover.

'I **say**, old boy! I'm about to make love to my luvva! Luvva! **Luvva!**'

The Controller Brigadier interrupting.

'I **say**, ex**cuse** me; would you mind **awfully** if I made love to my luvva?'

'Going to make love to my new **luvva** now, what!! Care to watch, eh? Ha! Jolly good! Carry on, Number One!'

Fuck off!

Or girlfriend?

I'm about to make love to my girlfriend.

Me girlfriend! Me bird!

Gonna **do** 'er! Gonna **do** me bird!

Gonna make love to me bird! **Bird! Bird! Bird!**

Gonna make love to me **bird!**

Fuck . . . OFF!

Jenny.

Jenny, Jenny, Jenny, Jenny . . .

I'm going to make love to Jenny.

I'm about to make love . . . to Jenny.

Shhh . . . yes . . .

I'm making love to Jenny . . .

And calm returns.

God, she looks beautiful. Naked . . . smooth . . . pale in the dim light.

I'd be happy just to watch her; to sit in a chair and gaze at her . . . to *learn* her.

But I reach out and she nestles in close, her hair against my shoulder and we stand together like that for a long, long time, gently hugging, in no hurry, rocking quietly from side to side, dancing almost. The sensation of flesh against flesh, nothing else, body against body, her against me . . . feels . . . I don't know . . . wonderful yes, and new . . . but more than that . . . it's unreserved . . . unconditional . . . defenceless . . .

With our eyes closed we suddenly lose our balance and I have to prevent her from falling on to the bed. It's such an unexpected and mundane interruption we both start giggling. For a few seconds it helps . . . but we revert . . .

Kissing her again, and tentative now, feeling somehow as though I should still ask her permission, I brush my lips against the warm skin of her neck and move slowly downwards . . . hardly believing it yet.

And I *do* learn her; we learn each other; by touch and by smell and by unforeseen instinct. And it's soft, and it's considerate, and it's understanding and forgiving of the tiny mistakes; and it's so much more than I could ever have imagined.

We do everything together, meeting in the evenings and lunchtimes, when I hurtle down Queen's Gate and wait for her to emerge from the French Lycée, my heart racing when I see her multicoloured quilted jacket in the distance.

I'm often late for my after-lunch music classes, arriving out of breath, blaming it on either the poor old dog or seeing my tutor or some other excuse. No one seems to mind much, but I don't care anyway; even though we're practically living together, I would do anything just to squeeze in one more precious minute with Jenny.

I give myself utterly to her, holding back nothing – even the Controller – telling her everything about me, my darkest secrets, my fears, my hopes, constantly telling her how much I love her, need her. In return, she is lavishly affectionate, calling me 'so sweet', 'adorable' and 'gorgeous', though taking a little longer than me to be truly comfortable with the words 'I love you'.

For three months I'm as happy as I can ever remember. We talk incessantly, sit quietly together. I play the piano for her, we laugh, go out, make love. We spend weekends away together, either with her parents or mine or with friends.

I grow to love her little idiosyncrasies: the puzzled frown on her face when she doesn't fully understand something; the way she sits on the edge of the bed when she's getting dressed – which I love to watch – legs crossed as she reaches down to put on her tights, rubbing the tips of her fingernails against the material to check for a ladder, saying 'damn' under her breath if she finds one; the way she sits in front of the mirror as she applies her mascara, eyes wide, mouth in a silent 'o'; the way she looks sitting opposite me at a table, chin on hand, listening – really *listening* – to what I'm saying. I love all these things and more besides.

If we're out with other people – in a restaurant, at a party – I love the secrecy and intrigue of the quick glances or little looks of reassurance we exchange if we aren't next to each other. Sometimes, watching her talk to another man, I wait for these magic signals, only comfortable looking away when she's turned her head slightly to wink at me or blow me a silent kiss.

191

I love her. She's my obsession.

In the mornings I sit through lectures, wanting to smash the clock on the wall, to punish it for being so slow, unable to focus on Schoenberg's fucking tone rows, aching for the moment when I can dash out of the lecture hall, negotiate my way frantically through an assault course of lunchtime students and run down to meet her at the Lycée.

Each evening I race back down Queen's Gate to be ready waiting for her when she gets in. I'm in a permanent state of alertness. There's barely a moment when I'm not consciously thinking of her or feeling a sensation in my body that isn't in some way related to her.

My favourite evenings are spent alone with her, either in my room, at the cinema or at a restaurant. I crave the touch and feel of her all the time, holding her hand, arms round her shoulders, anything. I begin resenting it if we have to go out in a group, wanting to keep her to myself.

Her natural gregariousness and her sunny personality make her increasingly popular; she seems to attract friends and admirers with effortless ease. More and more, our quiet evenings in are peppered with frustrating interruptions.

'Jenny, phone call!'

'Jenny, there's someone to see you!'

At first they seem to annoy her as much they do me. But slowly her attitude changes and what used to be 'Oh God, I'd better see who it is; I won't be long, I promise . . .' (quick kiss) becomes 'Ooh, I wonder who that is; hang on a sec . . .' and she rushes out excitedly.

I become possessive and quietly jealous.

The first time she is asked out for dinner by another man, she consults me, to check if it'll be all right.

'It'll just be dinner,' she says, adding in that cosy,

conspiratorial, slightly suggestive tone that only lovers share, 'and I'll try and get rid of him early.'

'Fine,' I say, as lightly as I can, but inside I'm volcanic and when the evening arrives, like a General, impatient for news from the front, I pace up and down my room, eaten up with an explosive combination of jealousy, anger and panic, unable to stop the nightmarish visions that flood my imagination.

She's in bed with him!

She only *pretended* she was going out for dinner . . .

They haven't gone at all . . .

They've probably driven straight round to his flat . . .

And she's there now . . .

Giving herself to him . . .

They're standing by the bed and she's gazing into his eyes as he slowly undresses her.

Pale, defenceless, exposed, trusting . . .

He's running his hand up her leg – **my** leg . . .

And the **fucking** Controller Brigadier interrupts again, imposing its parody:

'I **say**, old boy! I think you'll find that's my leg you've got there!'

My leg. **My** leg. **My** leg. My **leg**. My **leg**.

I think you'll find that's my **leg!**

I think **you'll** . . . find that's my **leg!**

Leg! Leg! Leg! Leg! My **leg!**

Fuck off!

Fucking bastard, **fucking** willy.

Why's he got a willy?

He shouldn't **have** one!

Shouldn't be **allowed** one.

And I tap my head viciously and repeatedly with tip of my forefinger, jerking my head violently back and forth.

And now she's lying underneath him; naked; submissive . . .

Gazing into his eyes . . .

And they're fucking . . . slowly . . . and her eyes close . . . blissful . . .

And I feel a hideous, shameful combination of disgust and lust at the thought.

He has no knowledge of me. He doesn't know I exist. She hasn't told him. He's doing this because he thinks he has the right.

It should be me . . . I want to stab him . . . stab her!

Soft knocks on the door and in she comes, all smiles.

'God, what an evening!' she says. 'Never again! He was so *boring*. Kept on telling me about his conquests – it was pathetic. He went on and on and on; I think he thought I was impressed. Anyway, I said I had to get up early tomorrow, so he dropped me back.'

And, God, the relief! The release; the forgiveness, the guilt and the shame sweep simultaneously through me.

She kisses me lightly on the lips and gives me a hug. 'Anyway, what've *you* been up to?'

'Oh I dunno' I say; 'this and that; bit of practice; worked on an essay; nothing much really.'

For a while it runs smoothly again – sort of. She's making new friends all the time, some of them with me, some independent of me. Once in a while she goes to a party to which I'm not invited, and each time, as I stand by my window watching her leave the house, the same acidic jealousy wells up in me, and again I pace my room, imagining all kinds of graphic sexual scenes, longing for her to get back and prove me wrong.

When we're out together, I need more reassurance: a

squeeze of the hand, a peck on the cheek, just so I know we're still 'together'. I can't help myself. I cling to her. This has nothing to do with the Controller; it's a different kind of obsession entirely.

And then she's invited away for a whole weekend without me and I let my resentment and jealousy show for the first time. We sit in her room arguing, getting more and more heated, and because I'm on edge, the Controller is going at me hammer and tongs. I'm coughing, sniffing, making faces, tapping and grunting – and finally it gets too much for her.

'For God's sake, stop that *bloody* noise, it's driving me mad!'

She goes; and on Sunday night when she returns, she bounds into my room, all arguments forgotten, affectionate as always, telling me what an 'incredible' weekend it was and how much I would have enjoyed it.

But gradually I sense her drifting away and there's nothing I can do to stop it.

On the surface we're still together; . . . but we're not . . . not really.

Suddenly, she can't meet me in the middle of the day because she's having lunch with an old school friend 'who I haven't seen in yonks'. One by one our evenings together diminish, and time spent apart gradually increases. When we *are* together, it feels like I'm being done a favour. My jealousy becomes all-consuming. I obsess about her; cry over her. My days consist of dreaming up ways to reverse the process and get her back.

I miss more classes, unable to summon the energy or enthusiasm to bother turning up.

But after the Christmas holidays, during which we talk on

the phone but see each other only once, she tells me she wants a break.

'Not permanent; just to see how we feel about each other.'

'But I know *exactly* how I feel about you,' I say, my stomach churning. 'I love you. Let's get married.'

'We *can't* get married,' she says. 'We're too young to get married. *I'm* too young to get married. It's ridiculous!'

A pause.

'In any case,' as if it were even an option, 'I don't honestly think I could cope with your twitching.'

There's a long, long silence.

And in that moment . . . I hate . . .

I hate *her* . . .

I hate myself . . .

I hate the Controller. No longer just an irksome, inconvenient presence. In my mind it shifts, changes and becomes the enemy.

Rechristened as the Beast . . . the **fucking** . . . **fucking** . . . Beast.

And we're at war.

The End

Awake again.
>This time it's a western, Glenn Ford . . .
>Click it off with the remote.
>Feel a bit drunk.
>My watch says 2 a.m.
>Sit for a few seconds and listen.
>God, it's so quiet!
>Nothing.
>Only the ringing in my ears . . .
>Which, if I concentrate . . .
>Grows louder and louder and louder . . .
>Until it's an almost unbearable cacophony.
>High-pitched whistling . . .
>E natural.
>But way, *way* higher than any E natural on the piano.
>So *absolute* silence must be impossible.
>I yawn. I'm exhausted.

And I leak self-disgust.
'What a bastard!' I say, under my breath.
I stand up shakily and go to bed.
'Fuck the Beast!' I think.
'And fuck the blue man!'
'Fuck all of you!'
And I switch the light off . . .
Only once.

Chapter 10
A Tip From Mr Hardy

'*Dear Mr McConnel . . . Your tutors inform me . . . continued absence . . . please contact me . . . may be withdrawn . . . Yours faithfully . . .*'

Eventually, I throw the letters away unopened and stop going to the Royal College altogether. I'm not interested. Nor do I tell my parents. Instead, I sit at the piano, lethargically improvising mournful, tragic music or pacing around my room, restless and miserable. The mere mention of Jenny's name, a fleeting glimpse of her or worse, seeing her at breakfast, produces a violent lurching sensation. She dominates my world. Asleep, I'm at peace, but when I wake, after the few seconds of semi-conscious calm, the familiar butterflies resume their fluttering.

Yet our break-up doesn't appear to have affected her at all. She is as outgoing and happy as she's always been and I watch bitterly from the sidelines as her popularity increases, lurking at my window when she goes out with other men, sitting up late into the night waiting desperately for her to return, dreading the sickening alternative.

Worse still, she keeps alive the idea that the door to our relationship is never entirely closed.

'Oh, James,' she says, 'it's such a pity we're so young. You know, if I met you in about ten years' time, I'd probably marry you; but I can't commit to anyone at the moment, I need to have some fun first.'

Dangling this kind of emotional carrot over me keeps up the agonising hope. If I can just hang on, I think to myself, one day she will marry me; she just needs time. I lose all pride. I don't care. I'm her slave. She is my drug and I'm hopelessly addicted.

In this mood, the Beast is more or less uncontrollable. Fuelled by limitless nervous energy and rage, it mounts a retrospective twitch exhibition, magnifying my current urges and recalling older ones, some of which I haven't performed since I was at school. Back, for instance, comes the need to smile in the mirror to see what the opposite of how I'm feeling looks like. My magic numbers – which usually switch from odd to even on a regular basis – now remain stubbornly odd and stay that way.

My parents, still thinking they have a music student for a son, buy a small flat in Earl's Court as an investment, and I move in, feeling desperately guilty at not having told them, as well as being torn between the miserable prospect of seeing even less of Jenny and the novelty of starting afresh.

Finally, when the guilt becomes intolerable, I visit the college and appeal to the registrar for forgiveness, citing personal problems and promising to be a model student for the remaining six weeks of the summer term if he'll give me another chance. He offers no guarantees, since my attendance record has been abysmal, but agrees to let me try and 'pull myself together' and I return to my classes.

I also install a flatmate, Sophie, but a week after she's moved in, Jenny rings in a fury.

'You cannot live with that girl!' She's almost screaming.

'Why not? What's wrong with her?'

'What's *wrong* with her?! She's a little tart! She's slept with half of London, for God's sake! She'll go after anything in trousers – including you! Everyone hates her! Didn't you know that?'

'No. She seems all right to me.' I'm defensive. 'Are you sure you've got the right person?'

'Yes! 'Course I'm sure! Sophie Smith, blonde hair, works at an estate agents or something.'

'Oh.'

I'm trying to see Sophie as a tart, but I can't. She's never been flirtatious with me, anyway; just . . . normal. Though for an instant I get a frisson of excitement as I visualise her naked body on the single bed in her room, her face ecstatic, so different from how I see her in reality.

Is that how she'd be?

Is that how everyone is?

'You've *got* to get her out of there!'

'I can't,' I say; 'she's only just moved *in*.'

'Well, I'm telling you, James, I will *not* come round while *she's* there.'

She hangs up.

And because I can't bear the thought of not seeing Jenny, I ask a hurt and confused Sophie to leave.

Libby, who I find through an agency, replaces her. She's ideal, cheerful and meets with Jenny's telephone approval. Then one day in late May, Jenny turns up unannounced, checking to make sure I'm still pining after her, serving up a dollop of hope if I don't appear quite as lovesick as she would like.

'I've had a brilliant idea,' she says. 'What are you doing in August?'

Heart thudding, I say, 'Nothing, why?'

'What do you think about doing Inter-Rail?'

'Inter-Rail? What's that?'

'It's fantastic; you buy one ticket – about a hundred quid, I think – and then you can travel on any train in Europe for a whole month; anywhere you like, as often as you want.'

'That sounds fantastic,' I say enthusiastically, not caring a jot about the travelling, just transfixed by the idea of spending an uninterrupted month with her.

'Who else is going?'

'No one. It'd just be us.'

In my head, like a Busby Berkeley line-up, choirs of gold-haloed angels dressed in their best white frocks suddenly burst into a cacophony of rejoicing; bells jangle wildly and the weeks of misery evaporate, replaced by thuds and tingles as my hope tank instantly refills.

It'd just . . . be . . . us!

Just **us!**

Just **us!**

When she's gone I dance around the flat.

Even the Beast rejoices internally.

Us! Us! **Us! Us! Us! Suss! Susssusssusss usssusssusssusssusss!**

Her and me!

Alone!

Together!

Two! Two! Two . . . tu tu tu tu tu . . . French . . . **tu**tu

tutu **tu**tu **tu**tu **tu**tu . . . ballet dress . . . angels in **tu**tus . . . angelic **tu**tus . . .

The Brigadier again:

'I *say*, Mr Angel, do you tutu?'

'I'm sure I saw you tutuing, Mr Angel.'

'Tu tutu?'

'Tutu tu, Monsieur Ange?'

'Tutu toi?'

'Je tutu, mais tu tutu too? Tu too, tu too, tu too!'

Bloody 'tu' and 'too'. Infuriatingly similar; just a small movement of the jaw and lips and I *still* can't say them together fast enough!

Tonguetwister**tonguetwister**tongue twister**tuntuntuntun tundadadadadadada!**

Plinky **Floo**cle!

Kermuggama**aaaaa!**

Enough!

For a whole *month*! How can I possibly *not* get her back!

Miraculously restored to emotional health, I throw myself back into my studies and at the end of my second year, thoroughly unprepared, I sit my exams at the Royal College.

On 1 August I meet Jenny in London. By 31 August we've been to Paris and Lyons and Lake Como and Venice and Florence and Rome and Naples and Brindisi and Athens and Belgrade and Vienna and Salzburg and Mainz and Cologne and Brussels and Amsterdam.

We've seen paintings, frescos, statues, carvings, opera houses, concert halls, churches, palaces, towers, monuments, fountains, Greek temples, Roman ruins, parks, gardens, markets, funfairs, orchestras, buskers, boats, trams, fish, snakes, horses, camels, canals, rivers, lakes, seas, mountains, harbours, beaches. We've eaten in restaurants, bars, cafés and fields, and stayed in hotels, guest houses and youth hostels. We've swum, danced, laughed, argued, spoken French (quite well), German (badly), Italian (very badly), Greek (three words), rowed on rivers (fell in), *rowed* on rivers (screaming at each other), made love (three times), spoken to strangers and walked and walked and walked . . .

And, living at such close quarters, the Beast drove Jenny mad.

Apart from this, she was fascinated by everything and everyone. Truly fascinated. Like a child discovering a new toy, her enthusiasm was boundless.

I *pretended* to be fascinated by everything.

In reality, all I could think about was the next opportunity to hold her hand, stroke her hair, hug her or make love to her. Sometimes I thought I was winning: having lunch overlooking the Grand Canal in Venice, sipping retsina outside a taverna on the beach at twilight, walking hand in hand down the Champs-Elysées, moments when the romantic setting and atmosphere were wildly in my favour. At those times she was affectionate and happy.

One evening, I rang home and spoke to my mother.

'Hello, darling, where *are* you?'

'Rome,' I said.

'Rome! I thought you were still in Naples.'

'We were, but it wasn't that exciting so we left a couple of days early.'

'Oh, darling, you will be careful, won't you? The Italians are such dreadful drivers.'

'Mum!'

'Sorry, darling, but you know I worry. Anyway, how are you getting on? How's Jenny?'

'She's fine.'

'Good.'

A pause.

'Now listen, darling,' she said, 'I've got something to say to you.'

'What?'

'Well, frankly, we're both a little annoyed, actually. We've had a letter from the Royal College.'

'Oh,' I said, tensing, 'what does it say?'

'It says they don't want you back in September. You've failed your exams.'

'Ah.' I was half-expecting it.

'Jamie, what on earth happened? How could you have failed? It's what you always wanted to do!'

'I know. I just . . . didn't enjoy it.'

'Well, aren't you *upset*?' She sounded far more upset than I was.

'To be honest, Mum, not really, no.'

'Aren't you! Well, I think you might be a *bit* upset, really I do!'

'Sorry.'

'Darling, we *have* put quite a lot of money into your education, you know.'

'Yes, I know you have and I'm sorry.'

'And what's all this about you not going to your lectures?'

I paused, embarrassed, guilty.

'Mum, I just couldn't get *on* there.'

'Well, it's no wonder you failed; it says here you missed most of last term! What were you doing, for goodness sake?'

'I wasn't happy, Mum.'

'Why not?'

'Oh I don't know; it's too difficult to explain.'

'Well, I hope you're going to explain when you come back!'

'Please, Mum!'

'Oh well.' She sighed a long sigh. 'Anyway, Dad and I think it's a *great* shame; but I suppose you're old enough to make your own decisions. What on earth are you going to do?'

'I'm not sure. I haven't decided yet.'

When she rang off, I turned to Jenny and smiled.

'Ha!' I said. 'Just been kicked out of the Royal College!'

I wanted her to be impressed; I wanted to show her that I was a rebel, a sexy, single-minded renegade! What did I care for authority! I was just too *big* for them! Too *much* talent – and they couldn't deal with it!

And instead of awe, instead of a laughing 'James, you're mad!' with the subtext 'You crazy, talented, gorgeous, lovable romantic fool; come and undress me at once!' – instead of this, her eyes narrowed. 'Don't you care?'

'No,' I said, shrugging. 'Why should I?'

'Be*cause* . . . it's your career! You're throwing it away!'

'Oh, come on!' This wasn't turning out the way I'd hoped. 'It's *funny*!'

'It's not *funny*. How can you *say* that?! It's pathetic! For God's sake, James, grow up!' Now there was disgust in there somewhere.

I felt rising embarrassment. Forget the romantic stuff, this was becoming a battle to save face.

'It's not pathetic; I hated the place, that's all.'

'How d'you know you hated it? You never *went*! You just

sat in your room doing bugger all, twitching and feeling sorry for yourself!'

That really stung.

She was the reason I'd been sitting in my room doing bugger all; I was pining for *her*. She showed no sympathy, merely impatience. In her mind she had reduced my sufferings to self-pity.

'Oh fuck off!' I said, and stormed out of the room, overcome with rage, guilt, shame and misery.

Later, frantic to make it right at any cost, I apologised for telling her to fuck off and, coldly, she allowed me to hug her.

Back in England I know I've failed.

I've got no idea what to do next and, to make matters worse, now that I'm no longer a student, my father decides it's high time I started supporting myself and withdraws my monthly allowance. Fortunately, they allow me to continue living at the flat. But I desperately need to earn some money.

My first job, working in the storeroom of a gift shop, is short-lived. My task is to unpack boxes containing everything from scented candles to battery-operated vibrating eggs and price them up before putting them on display in the shop. I'm given a price gun, an infuriating machine with a trigger that clicks once to eject a sticky price label and clicks again to load the next label when it's released.

It's a horrible thing. As well as making sure every individual label is in exactly the 'right' place on the candle or egg, the Beast hates the delay between the clicks and forces me to try to speed the process up. Rather than going 'click' . . . pause . . . 'click', I *need* to make the clicks almost simultaneous and I pull the trigger again and again as fast as I can, so that either the mouth of the gun becomes jammed with labels, which means taking the whole thing to bits to clear it, or I finish up with about eight price tags on one item, which means removing seven of them; difficult with bitten fingernails.

When I do eventually have a box ready to take into the shop, I need to place them exactly 'right' on the shelves, which slows me up even further, and once I have a perfectly positioned, neat stack of candles in their flimsy plastic boxes, I hate the delicate balance of it all and sometimes bash the stack hard with the palm of my hand, crushing it. My slowness is interpreted as laziness, and after only three weeks I'm summoned by the manageress.

'I'm sorry, James, you're just not pulling your weight. I'm afraid I'm going to have to let you go.'

My second job, in the run-up to Christmas, is in a stationery shop, working behind the counter and stocking the shelves. If I thought scented candles and vibrating eggs were a challenge, the flimsy weightlessness and 'indecisiveness' of paper and card is a joke. The Beast has almost unlimited gratification with the single multi-coloured sheets of A4, biros, pens, pencils and rubbers. But somehow I manage to hold the job down.

I hate the fact that I'm now like everyone else. I'm just another commuter travelling to and from work on the crushed, rush-hour tube, for instance. Mr Nine-to-five. I'm not even successful; I'm low end on the commuter scale. Dressed in a jersey and jeans, I'm a salt-of-the-earth worker, in a necessary but unremarkable job supplying stationery to all the visibly more successful men in suits surrounding me in the carriage. I find myself fantasising to try and appear special. I choose a character that could account for my appearance and act accordingly.

Sometimes I'm a member of the SAS and I stand stock still while the train's moving, without holding on to the support rail, creating the impression of toughness, as though a little thing like keeping one's balance on a rocking train, though difficult for normal mortals, is child's play to a highly trained killing machine, veteran of covert operations behind enemy lines, where the risk of instant death is a constant companion. In my mind, I imagine the other passengers regarding me with awed respect. I look for the signs of it in their faces.

Sometimes, when I can get a seat, I'm a famous pianist on his way to give a concert at the Royal Festival Hall and I sit gazing dreamily into the middle distance, eyes wide open, supposedly in deep concentration, and perform 'virtual' piano pieces on my knees. Now and again, I pretend I've made a mistake, shake my head in frustration and supposedly go over a phrase, repeating it again and again.

And sometimes, if I'm carrying a pen and paper, I pretend I'm a tortured composer who has just had THE MOST BRILLIANT idea, whereupon I hurriedly scribble a treble clef and five lines and fiendishly jot down random notes, pausing dramatically halfway through, eyes narrowed (SAS-like), pencil raised, conducting faintly to myself as though thinking of what comes next, then returning to fiend mode, finishing with a flourish and smiling to myself, satisfied that the future of the musical masterpiece is secure.

But just because I'm working in a stationery shop during the day, why shouldn't I be a great musician at night?

In my *mind* I'm still a musician. I've *always* been a musician, ever since the day I first struggled with 'Baa baa black sheep' on the piano at home. It's all I've ever wanted to be, despite blowing several chances along the way. Deep down, I know I'll end *up* being a musician; it's just a matter of time.

But what sort of musician? Not a concert pianist, certainly. And not a conductor; the Beast still wouldn't allow that.

So why *not* a composer? I can improvise. I *love* improvising; which is only a jump away from composing. Composing is merely organised improvisation, surely? I spend enough time on the tube pretending to be a composer. Why not try it for real? In terms of 'specialness', composing is about as great as it gets. Who, excepting perhaps an Afghan goatherd, *hasn't* heard of Mozart or Beethoven or Brahms or Bach? No one. So why not me? But what *kind* of composer? What kind of music do I write? I hate so-called 'modern' classical music, most of which sounds like a squeaky gate hinge or polystyrene rubbed against glass. And I don't understand or like pop music. I find the drums threatening.

I need to write something huge and dramatic. Like a piano concerto. But a piano concerto that I myself can play, which means taking the limitations of my hands into consideration. That way, it could be *me* giving the triumphant, first performance at the Festival Hall with the London Symphony Orchestra.

A piano concerto. Not a squeaky, incomprehensible, polystyrene concerto; a concerto with tunes and a heart.

But if I am going to be a composer, I need to be a composer with a difference. A tragic composer, a tortured genius.

The idea appeals and now I have the perfect opportunity. Not only have I been spurned in love – a *must* for tragic, tortured geniuses – but I'm alone (more or less), in misery, with a piano, in a (nearly) top-floor garret – albeit a carpeted, electrified and heated one. I'm not quite penniless, but I can't help that.

Tragic geniuses of the past, I imagine, generally sat in their garrets and suffered with consumption, syphilis or alcoholism. The first two sound horrible. The French Impressionists got it just right: sitting in smoky cafés, dressed in loose-fitting clothes, drinking bottle after bottle of absinthe, surrounded by adoring whores, dismissive of their bourgeois detractors yet still managing to produce seminal works of art. If they could do it, why can't I? Now I'm actually going to put pen to paper, my legacy will be the masterpieces I write.

I prepare myself.

I buy manuscript paper from a music shop, plus pencils, rubber and pencil sharpener (which I get at a discount from work), and at the top of the first page, in flowing, nineteenth-century script – as I interpret it – I write '*Piano Concerto No. 1 by James McConnel*'.

And I decide to start drinking.

Not because I crave alcohol, and not because I want to drown my sorrows. It's purely theatrical. I need something to suit my new status as love-spurned, tragic, tortured genius.

The problem is, I'm not much of a drinker. I got drunk at school once and vandalised the swimming pool with a disused telegraph pole, but apart from that and a few mild hangovers after late nights, I'm an amateur. Not for me the gins and whiskys, though, I want an exotic tipple, as absinthe-like as possible. What I find is Green Chartreuse. Thick, syrupy, sweet and strong, in a suitably exotic bottle, brewed by French monks, which gives it an added mystique.

It's filthy stuff, but I grow to love it.

Then, night after night, after a Jekyll to Hyde trans-formation, I sit at the piano in a white, loose-fitting collarless dress shirt, sleeves rolled up, delicately sipping my absinthe substitute, first from a glass, later from the bottle because it seems more in keeping with Montmartre. I play romantic, slushy music, often into the early hours, jotting down ideas in pencil as they come, sometimes singing along at the top of my voice, increasingly dazzled by my own brilliance.

Occasionally I take a break from being the world's greatest composer and, notwithstanding the Beast's inclinations, become the world's most celebrated conductor, by putting the last movement of Brahms' 2nd Symphony on the record player full blast and leaping all over the sitting-room furniture in a Bernstein-ian frenzy.

Fortunately, this doesn't affect Libby, as she spends most of the time with her boyfriend, increasingly using the flat as a dumping ground for her clothes. However, irate notes from the neighbours start appearing through my door.

Dear Mr McConnel
It might interest you to know that my wife and I were kept awake until well after one o'clock this morning because of your loud piano playing and Hitler-like stamping on the floor.

Mr McConnel
In spite of my previous complaints, you seem to have no notion of neighbourly consideration. I shall therefore be forced to bring up your continued late-night activities at the next Residents' Association meeting.

I make a startling discovery, however. I find a way to tame the Beast – at least temporarily. I would have found it in the end, and in some ways I can't believe I haven't tumbled to it earlier. I've always noticed that when I go to a party, the twitching lessens – or appears to – as the evening wears on. I used to put this down either to the fact that people didn't really notice when they'd had a few drinks, or that because I was dancing or talking animatedly, the twitches naturally decreased on their own.

Being alone is the key.

I've never drunk by myself before and what hits me is that at a certain point the alcohol sends the Beast to sleep. The physical twitches gradually vanish completely and the compulsions diminish. A few remain – bashing the piano lid shut seven times and stabbing the yellow sink sponge with a fork – but even they are less frenetic, less urgent. The feeling that I'll be punished or that something dreadful will happen if I don't twitch decreases dramatically.

It's so simple. So obvious. Booze is the cure; just two or three small liqueur-sized glasses or five or six sips directly from the bottle is enough. It's freedom. It's how I imagine a soldier in Northern Ireland must feel after coming off duty. Time off; peace from being constantly on the alert. Which makes me feel fantastic.

Other people must feel like this all the time.

One Saturday afternoon, feeling tragic, I'm watching television, something I do a lot – my concentration levels when it comes to writing music are pitifully short and I take frequent long breaks – when a Laurel and Hardy film comes on. In this one, Ollie falls passionately in love with a blonde bombshell who strings him along for a while, then dumps him for someone else. In his misery, dragging Stan Laurel along with him, he joins the Foreign Legion and sticks a photograph of his lost love on the inside of his locker door.

When he's hauled up for insubordination a couple of days later, he notices the same photograph on the Commandant's office wall, later discovering that every soldier in the fort has her picture stuck in *their* lockers. They've all been jilted by the same woman.

The Foreign Legion is hardly a realistic option, but it gives me the idea of getting away. There's nothing to keep me in London: Jenny's a lost cause, I hate my job and as long as I take plenty of music paper I can still be a tragic composer-genius. I've never struck out on my own before and done something new. Many people I knew at school took a year off and went abroad, but I never did. Everything I've ever done has always been prearranged and ordered.

It's a snap decision. Having trawled the press for 'situations abroad' and been to a cursory interview, exactly five days later I'm on a coach, bound for the south of France to be supermarket manager on an English campsite.

The End

Birds.

Fucking sparrows.

Noisy little bastards.

Always wake me up.

9.30 a.m.

Terrible hangover.

Stagger downstairs to the kitchen.

Strong cup of coffee.

Always think it's going to make me feel better.

It never does. Nothing does.

Except another drink.

Not now! No fucking way!

I have standards.

I'll *never* drink first thing in the morning.

Traffic's hectic outside.

Everyone buzzing off to work.

Thank God I don't have to.

Might have some toast today.
Swallow a couple of paracetamol.
Another bath.
Then I *must* do some work.

Chapter 11
French Leave

'Get your arse out of bed! C'mon, you're half an hour late, for fuck's sake!'

Shit!

'Coming,' I mutter. Hot and sweaty, half asleep still, scratching at fresh mosquito bites on my legs, I unzip the tent flap and peer out, shielding my eyes against the streaming sunlight.

I'm *not* the supermarket manager at all.

This I discovered last night when I arrived after a gruelling, almost twenty-four-hour journey from England.

Phil – a blond-haired Abba-clone, complete with gold watch, gold medallion, gold earring and various gold hand and wrist accessories – *is*, however.

He's standing there idly scratching his balls, his expression Abba-irritated.

'Right,' he says, pointing a finger at me. 'Shop! Two minutes! Do it again and you're on the bus home, yeah?'

'Sorry,' I say as he stalks off, not quite awake enough yet to feel anything, but somewhere at the back of my mind outraged at his shameful treatment of a twenty-two-year-old tortured genius.

I dress hurriedly, then pick my way through the sea of tents, which extends almost to the beach.

They lied to me in London. What I am, in fact, is a shelf stacker and assistant till operator. Neither is it a supermarket. Not really. A large corner shop best describes it.

My first morning is spent with co-shelf stacker Steve – a bona fide Cockney – who, as he's showing me the stockroom at the back of the shop, asks, 'You go to public school or wot?'

'Yes I did,' I say, nodding, trying to make it sound as if a private education was cruelly thrust upon me and that, given the choice, I'd have preferred to be nailed to the floor.

'Yeah,' he sighs, 'I went to Eton.'

'Did you *really*?' I say with sudden enthusiasm, amazed, then embarrassed at having been so surprised. Surely they take all sorts at Eton these days. Maybe he got a scholarship.

'Yeah,' he sighs again, 'didn't *like* it much, though. Fulla toffs!'

'Yeah!' I say, echoing him, in an 'I hate the bastards too' kind of voice, not sure how else to respond. Is he serious?

A pause, and then: 'You're a toff, aincha?'

'Well,' I say expansively, 'not really.' I laugh nervously, sensing trouble.

'Go on, you are, aincha?'

'Well,' I shrug defensively, 'it . . . depends.'

'Nah, come on; you . . . are . . . a . . . toff! Aincha!?'

'Yes, maybe . . . a little,' I say, defeated.

A pause while he grabs a boxful of sweets.

'Fort so.' He laughs, friendly now, and suddenly it's all right. A wave of relief and gratitude sweeps through me.

'Nah, didn't go to Eton,' he says, indicating another box for me to carry. 'Moorgate Comprehensive, me!'

'Did you enjoy it?' I ask, conscious of the fact that he's a man, hoping it's not a stupid question and still trying to play down my accent.

'S'oright,' he says. 'Left when I was fifteen. You?'

'No, hated my school.'

'Woss wrong wiv it?'

Inspiration strikes. 'Full of toffs,' I say, and he laughs out loud.

I rediscover shelf stacking; or rather, the Beast does. Never have tins of cassoulet and couscous or the awkwardly shaped plethora of cheeses and cold meats in the fridge section been arranged with such fanatical attention to detail. Each circular 'Vache qui rit' rests exactly on top of the one below it; no overlaps, nothing; perfect – except the very top one, which *has* to overlap to the left just a smidgen. Foodstuffs are heavier than scented candles or vibrating eggs and the urge to smash them, once arranged, isn't as strong.

What bugs me is when the customers arrive. Powerless to intervene, I watch them disrupting my tins, thoughtlessly rearranging my cheeses and shuffling through my flat-packs of salami and Parma ham like playing cards, oblivious to the fact that when they've gone, I have to go and set everything straight again.

There are about thirty members of staff on the camp site, half-and-half women and men. Of the men, there are a core of eight Londoners; tough, physical 'blokes' – Steve among them – heavy-drinking, raucous and rowdy, inclined to 'patriotic' drunken skirmishes late at night with the local village lads. Apart from Steve himself, and then only when we're working together, I steer clear of them. For the rest – including the girls – there's a mix of British, Australian, Brazilian and American, mostly students.

In Phil's eyes, having screwed up so early on, I start from the position of 'lazy bastard' and have to work doubly hard to climb in his estimation. But as I settle in, he gradually warms to me, initially because when he takes the micky out of my accent, I laugh. He considers himself something of a mimic, doing constant imitations of Terry-Thomas.

Phil's true raison d'être, however, is women. He loves them; all of them. At twenty-seven, he is a self-proclaimed expert and, night after night like Scheherazade, with pride and great detail he goes into each of the three hundred or so women he has allegedly 'shafted'.

'She was amazing!' He relates this one evening as we're cashing up. 'I tell you, James, there's *nothing* she wouldn't have done! Give you my word! Frontwards, backwards, sideways – she . . . was . . . gagging for it! And then,' and he leans forward, continuing in a half-whisper, 'you'll never believe it . . .'

'What?' I'm transfixed; as much by the fact that he's taking me into his confidence as by what he's saying.

'Her room-mate comes in, doesn't she . . .'

'Really?'

'Yeah, and you know what she does?'

'No.'

'Only gets her bloody clothes off and jumps in *with* us!'

'No!'

'Yup!' And with a deep sigh of satisfaction, hands behind his head, he leans back in his chair, thrilled with himself.

I can see it. The three of them, between silk sheets,

swimming almost. Phil, naked but for his gold medallion, grappling simultaneously with two nymphomaniac brunettes, bringing them smoothly, effortlessly to orgasm – to me, an unthinkable event; to Phil, just another couple of notches in the bedpost of the Elder Statesman of Sex, Abba King Shag, the Bedclothes Brute.

At twenty, with only two conquests to my name – and one of those didn't really count – I'm terribly impressed. I can learn from Phil, I realise. He's a man, and yet somehow I feel comfortable with him. He seems to accept me. I don't feel judged by him. I defer to him; I want him to be my older brother. He seems to know how to 'do life', as well as how to seduce women. Maybe he can teach me. I should stick with him.

And it's his idea to get the piano.

One Saturday afternoon, a few of us go to Toulon, about an hour's drive away. As we're wandering idly, Phil spies a piano shop and drags me in. Not that I need any dragging. After several weeks without a piano, I've taken to whistling or humming to myself almost all day to compensate. Having the chance to play again makes me realise just how much I've missed it.

The long and short of it is that Phil gets the okay to rent a piano for me to play in the restaurant in the evenings. As a result, I now only have to work the morning shift in the supermarket. My problem is that I've only ever played classical music, film music and maybe three or four pop songs. I've never played in public before and although I can pick up a tune by ear fairly quickly, I know hardly any of the requests which are thrown in my direction by the campers.

'*What!* You don't know "My Way"? You must know "My Way"! You *know* – Frank Sinatra!'

221

'Sorry, don't know it.'

'Bloomin' 'eck!' She turns and shouts across to her table. 'Trevor! He doesn't *know* it!'

Inside, I shrivel.

''Ow about "As Time Goes By"?' Trevor shouts.

''Ow about "As Time Goes By"?' she asks me, as though half of France hadn't already heard Trevor.

'Erm, sorry . . .'

'What, you don't know that *either*!?'

'No, sorry.'

Shouting to Trevor again: 'He doesn't know that either.'

I shrivel a little more.

'Well, ask him what he *does* know,' Trevor shouts back.

'What *do* you know, then?'

'Erm – *The Sound of Music, My Fair Lady, Oliver*, that sort of thing . . . or anything classical.'

'Classical! We don't want classical! We're on 'oliday! Tell you what, give us a nice round of "Consider Yourself"!'

And, faintly relieved, I launch into one of the few non-classical pieces I *do* know.

One evening a visiting journalist – writing an article about the campsite for a holiday magazine – approaches the piano and we start talking. I should think he's about fifty and with his aura of quiet confidence he wants to know how I ended up here. I tell him a little about the Royal College and my accident, spicing things up to make it sound more dramatic.

He's friendly, intelligent and winds up by asking, 'So, if you had to choose five composers to sum up your musical tastes, who would they be?'

I warm to this question; it's far more subtle than the usual 'Who's your favourite composer?'

So I tell him: 'Beethoven, Mozart, Stravinsky, Brahms and Ravel.'

'What about five songwriters?'

'Flanders and Swann.'

'Yes.'

'Noel Coward.'

'Sure, but what about something more contemporary?'

'I don't like modern pop music; it's complete rubbish.'

He stares at me.

'That's quite a statement. Why's it rubbish?'

I think for a moment.

'I dunno; it just is. It's too . . . simple . . . and they can't sing properly . . . and I hate the drums . . . and all pop stars are on drugs . . .'

'And yet,' he says, 'since you've been here, how many people have asked you to play a Beethoven sonata?'

'Well, none, but that's just because they don't understand classical music.'

'Oh, you think they're ignorant?'

Calmly, he takes off his glasses, breathes on them, wipes them clean and replaces them. I find this slightly intimidating, as if he's a teacher, used to this kind of attitude from his pupils, such that he barely needs to think about arguing the point any more.

'Yes . . . no! . . . I dunno.' I'm struggling.

'Well, which is it?' he says quietly.

'I dunno; it's just that I get more from classical music than anything else, I s'pose.'

'Yes, but can you understand that other people might get what *you* get from a short song, rather than a symphony? And as for being simple, Beethoven's best tunes are incredibly simple; that's part of what makes them great, isn't it? I mean, how much "pop" music – as you call it – do you actually know? The Beatles, for instance; do you know "Yesterday"?'

'Erm, no I don't.'

'How about Elton John?'

'I can do "Yellow Brick Road".'

'Any others?'

'No.'

'What else?'

I think for a few seconds.

'I know a couple of Simon and Garfunkel songs.'

'Is that it?'

'Pretty much, yes . . . oh no, I like Abba.'

'Still, not a lot to make a judgement on, is it?'

'No, I s'pose not.'

I feel smaller than the smallest worm. It's the most civilised bollocking I've ever had, made worse when later on, walking past his table during a break, I overhear him saying to one of his dinner companions, 'That boy's got a completely closed mind.'

I begin to see just how many gaps there are in my musical education. It isn't that I haven't been exposed to popular music; I have – mostly in nightclubs and at school – but because I've always felt threatened by it, I've never taken the trouble to listen. Something inside me – probably my musical training – tells me I shouldn't (I'm not sure why this doesn't apply to Abba). Maybe it's because I can't stop myself listening analytically, critically, when what I should be doing is just *listening* – emotionally. Maybe I have become a musical snob.

The Sound of Music, *Mary Poppins* and *Chitty Chitty Bang Bang* are part of my childhood and don't count somehow, especially since *Chitty Chitty Bang Bang* is something the Beast uses to deal with embarrassment. But in any case, I don't think of them as pop music.

There's a jukebox in the bar which, as well as being well-stocked with French songs by Michel Sardou and Johnny Hallyday, plays the Beatles, Elton John, the Rolling Stones and countless others, plus Lou Reed and Leonard Cohen (who I can't *bear*, however narrow-minded that makes me). Taking on board what the journalist has said, together with the realisation that I *have* to expand my repertoire, I begin spending time each morning just sitting with a cup of coffee listening to and learning these songs.

Gradually, I introduce them into my set, and every couple of weeks, when the jukebox is refreshed with new songs, I learn them as well. Occasionally I am actually able to oblige someone with a request. Frank Sinatra's 'My Way' is still a problem, however, because I have to piece it together from the only available jukebox version – by the Sex Pistols – which is very different apparently.

But life is good and with Phil as my sexual mentor, I learn a few tricks and adapt them to suit me. I take to wearing a T-shirt when I'm playing the piano, to expose the ugly scar on my right arm from my accident. And if a pretty girl approaches the piano . . .

It takes a while, but sometimes it works.

'How did you get that?' she asks, wide-eyed.

'Oh,' I say, modestly, as though slightly embarrassed and wanting to play down the whole ghastly episode, 'I was deep-sea diving and got attacked by a shark.'

'A shark!' And her eyes register shock. 'God!'

'Well, it wasn't a very *big* shark,' I continue, still modest, 'quite painful at the time, though, I s'pose.'

'But . . .' she says, flustered. 'I mean . . . how did you get away?'

'Luck, really. He was only a baby, but even they can be fairly nasty, so when he wouldn't let go of my arm, I took my mouthpiece out and the air bubbles frightened him off. Still, there was a lot of blood, so it was quite a hairy swim back to the boat.' And I chuckle, then raise my elbow to give her a better look.

She breathes in sharply. 'But it looks really serious. Didn't it hurt you?'

'Well, yeah,' I say, regretfully, 'it bit through the nerves, so my arm was paralysed for about six months. Still, it could have been a lot worse.' And I smile philosophically.

'So how come you still play the piano?'

'I couldn't. Not to begin with, which is a bugger if you want to be a concert pianist; but what can you do?' And I shrug.

'Oh God! Poor you!'

'Yes, well, I've got most of the movement back, but not all of it,' I say, adding with feigned sadness, 'so I doubt I'll be playing at the Albert Hall now.'

'That's so sad. Well, I think you're brilliant; I don't how you *do* it,' she says, and gently she puts her hand on my shoulder.

'I had a lot of physiotherapy, but it's not so bad really, and there *are* other things I could do. I'm just doing this,' and I indicate the piano, 'for a bit of fun during my year off, but when I get home I'm probably going to carry on with my composing. I'm writing a piano concerto at the moment.'

'A piano concerto? Really?'

And if I'm lucky, she gazes at me with a third respect, a third protectiveness and (hopefully) a third lust, and as long as I keep my twitching to a minimum, in Phil's words, 'I'm *in* there.'

Fortunately, the Beast doesn't much care for the South of France heat and confines itself mostly to counting, tapping and stacking tins. There are still one or two little rituals involving flip-flops on the beach – whereby I have to scoop up as much sand as I can with the front of the flip-flop as I walk, which means that they frequently break – but apart from this I'm largely twitch-free. Of course it may be because there's a lot of cheap wine around, and like everyone else in the permanent holiday atmosphere, I find myself drinking more than I normally would, which, after the magical one or two glasses, sends the Beast to sleep in any case.

There are always new faces and, with a plentiful supply of girls, Jenny fades from my mind surprisingly quickly.

When the four months are up I come home, fit, upbeat and having caught the travel bug. I'm determined to get away again as soon as possible.

'Why don't you try the Altiport in Meribel?' Libby suggests on one of her rare evenings in.

'What's that?'

'Meribel? It's a ski resort, you moron.'

'I *know* it's a ski resort. I meant what's the Altiport?'

'Oh. It's a hotel. *And* it's got a piano.'

'But haven't they already got a pianist?'

'I don't know! I'm not psychic, for God's sake! Give them a ring and find out!'

So I do. I ring them.

'You are a *pianiste*?'

'Yes, a friend of mine was working in Meribel last year and told me you might need someone to play the piano.'

Short pause, clicks on the telephone line.

'Ha!' he half chuckles. ''As it 'appens, we do. Are you *professionel*?'

'Yes I am.' I remove the receiver to a safe distance while I complete a series of facial twitches, then return it, continuing, 'I studied music in London.'

'*Oui*.'

'And I've been playing in the south of France for the last four months.'

'Whereabouts?'

'Toulon.' Not exactly the truth, but saying I've been working in the bar-restaurant on an English campsite sounds a bit downmarket.

'Oh.' He doesn't sound unimpressed. 'What kind of music do you play?'

'Everything really, jazz, classical, pop.'

'Okay . . . *pardon*, what eez your name?'

'James.'

'James, okay. Well, James, we *are* looking for a *pianiste* but I cannot offer you anysing until I 'ave 'eard you, so if you want to come 'ere, I will keep the job open, but I make no promises.'

'That's fine, I can come out next week.'

Three days later, I fly to France, arriving in Meribel shortly before dark. It's grimy and impersonal, there's no snow and the lines of deserted ski lifts stretching up the mountainside seem out of place and pointless against the tundra-like slopes and dark brown rock. Depressing.

Next morning I'm stunned at the transformation; it has snowed heavily during the night, and while cliché after cliché trips across my mind, from white sheets to iced cakes and blankets, what I notice most of all is the silence, a deep, padded hush. Life seems to have slowed; it's almost funereal. People and traffic now move with ordered respect; mopeds – the sound of which always grabs my attention – no longer crackle past at high speed as they did last night outside the hotel, merely chugging by instead. The snow has brought a kind of cotton-wool civilisation with it.

In the end, my audition is barely an audition at all. I smile a lot, chat away as best I can, force the Beast temporarily into a straitjacket and play a token song on the piano. I'm hired, not only as a pianist – playing in the bar from seven till eleven each evening – but also as a night guard, which means sleeping on a camp bed behind the reception desk to greet any late arrivals. These, fortunately, are rare.

If I enjoyed the South of France, I *love* Meribel . . . despite the fact that, once *out* of its straitjacket, the Beast flourishes in the cold climate; not so much in physical twitching terms as in the compulsions.

We learn to ski, the Beast and I.

I learn to ski, anyway. The Beast, being the monster it is, discovers a whole new world of disruptive possibilities.

I nearly die.

Not from embarrassment – although there *are* times – one in particular towards the end of my visit when, schussing at high speed towards a café-bar at the bottom of the slope, the Beast won't allow me to stop until it 'feels' right. Unfortunately, it still doesn't feel right by the time the snow has ended and the café-bar has begun. I tear a ligament in my knee, but kindly they don't charge me for the table or the other breakages.

No, the reason I nearly die is because each time I climb into a chair lift I have the nearly unquenchable urge to lift the safety bar and jump off when we reach the point at which I'm furthest from the ground. I should think many people at some time in their lives – at the top of a high building, for instance – have had thoughts akin to this, when the discomfort of vertigo makes you want to throw yourself off, but for me it's the thought of the incredible 'flump' sound my body would make when it hit the ground. It would be the ultimate compulsion; the only true compulsion to satisfy the Beast once and for all.

It would, of course, be the *last* compulsion; which is perhaps why I am able to resist it.

But short of artistic suicide, the Beast has plenty of other toys with which to amuse itself: boot fastenings, gloves, goggles, two skis, two poles, button lifts, cable cars and snow. I even twitch – or rather, have a compulsion – in French for the first time. It's something I hear one of the hotel chefs say about sausages – 'saucisses' in French. I don't catch the whole sentence but he ends up with something like '*les saucisses sont là*'.

The Beast grabs '*saucisses sont*' – which, when you repeat it endlessly, sounds like a train in a hurry – and for weeks it accompanies me on the ski slopes.

The piano itself causes trouble as well. To achieve that truly professional 'cocktail' effect in my dinner jacket, I have to play with the piano lid open, which gives me a constant view of its inner workings. Perhaps it's the temperature, but when I'm playing I notice that some of the dampers – the small felt-lined objects above the strings which rise and fall as you press the notes – go higher than others. It disrupts the overall pattern and after a while it begins to infuriate me. Various fruitless attempts using drawing pins and putty fail to allay the Beast, so I hit upon the idea of taping the neatly wrapped hotel sugar lumps to the offending dampers to weigh them down and make them move evenly. It looks ludicrous but it keeps the Beast happy, and by spouting supposed technical jargon at the management, I convince them it's absolutely necessary.

The Altiport is a five-star hotel and therefore attracts the well-heeled. In addition to my salary I make a decent amount in tips, something I'm not used to. The rule is: the Brits don't tip – ever; Europeans do – often. Europeans also practically always buy you drinks; several times in an evening if they can force it down you. By the time I finish my stint at eleven each evening I'm usually quite drunk, but I grow accustomed to it.

Later, when they too have finished their stints, groups of English chalet girls come to the Altiport for a drink or twelve, and since the bar is in plain view of the reception desk I'm able to party while still technically being on duty. Late nights become the norm and I average about five hours' sleep a night.

In April 1981, about two days before I'm due to come home, I begin feeling very sick and so tired I can barely summon up the energy to move, let alone twitch. By the time I get back to England, my face and the whites of my eyes have turned nicotine yellow and my throat feels as though it's lined with glass shards.

A trip to the doctor and a blood test confirms it's hepatitis and glandular fever. 'How much do you drink on an average day?' he asks, puzzled.

'Very little,' I lie. 'I mean, perhaps a tiny bit more than I normally would because I've been working in a hotel.'

'What were you drinking?'

'Wine mostly.' Another lie. I can't tell him that I drank everything on offer night after night.

'Hmm,' he says. 'Unusual. Your liver's a bit of a mess.'

He prescribes total rest, a fat-free diet and no alcohol at all. At which point I go home to my parents.

I stay in bed, sleeping most of the time, eating boiled fish, boiled chicken and boiled vegetables. I'm too tired to read and all I can manage in the brief periods I'm able to concentrate is television. I catch up with afternoon soap operas and *Blue Peter*, discover *Grange Hill* and feel a little as though I'm revisiting my childhood.

The Beast loves television.

BEANZ MEANZ HEINZ.

There is a tantalising symmetry to it. Everything is odd numbers.

Five letters in 'Beanz', five in 'Meanz' and five in 'Heinz'.

Add them together – fifteen; plus three – one for each word – eighteen; then one more for the entire phrase; nineteen.

To satisfy the Beast, first say the whole phrase five times, very fast, accentuating certain words, like shooting an air rifle.

Beanzmeanzheinz! **Beanz**meanzheinz! **Beanz**meanz heinz! **Beanz**meanzheinz! **Beanz**meanzheinz!

Then the adding, again very fast, this time using numbers.

Fivetenfifteen! **Five**tenfifteen! **Five**tenfifteen! **Five**ten fifteen! **Five**tenfifteen!

Add the three.

Fivetenfifteeneighteen! **Five**tenfifteeneighteen! **Five**ten fifteeneighteen! **Five**tenfifteeneighteen! **Five**tenfifteen eighteen!

Plus one for the whole thing.

Fivetenfifteeneighteen**nineteen**! Fivetenfifteeneighteen **nineteen**! Fivetenfifteeneighteen**nineteen**! Fivetenfifteen eighteen**nineteen**! Fivetenfifteeneighteen**nineteen**!

Finally, distil 'Beanz Meanz Heinz' into a single staccato sound. It often sounds nothing like the original, but it's the release mechanism.

'BeeYah! BeeYah! BeeYah! BeeYah! BeeYah!' – which I must shorten still further, until it becomes 'Byah! Byah! Byah! Byah! Byah!'

I've said each shortened word five times, making ten in total, which is too even. To make it an odd number, I intend to say the final 'Byah!' one last time, but the Beast is sometimes uncomfortable with ones, so I carry on repeating 'Byah!' until I reach an odd number it can live with. Or sometimes it just runs away with me and I shout 'Byah!' again and again for as long as it takes.

Obsessive counting has made me an expert at seeing a word and knowing exactly how many letters it contains. Words which contain 'sub-words' are irresistible. The word 'television' is rich in sub-words, and therefore contains almost endless counting possibilities.

'Television' has ten letters. At first sight, it's made up of 'tele' – which I can count as a word, although it's obviously a prefix – and 'vision'.

However, underneath the bonnet there's:

'Tel' which is a common shortening of the name 'Terry'.

'e', which is a Yorkshire expression of surprise.

'Vi', short for the girl's name 'Violet'.

'Si', short for 'Simon'.

And finally 'on', as opposed to 'off'.

Depending on my mood, in the middle section I

sometimes go for:

'Vis' as in 'vis à vis', which then leaves:

'I' and 'on'.

So what we end up with, using this second scenario, is:

Tel-e-vis-i-on! Tel-e-vis-i-on! Tel-e-vis-i-on! Tel-e-vis-i-on! Tel-e-vis-i-on!

Thus, numerically:

Three-four-seven-eight-ten! **Three**fourseveneightten! **Three**fourseveneightten! **Three**fourseveneightten! **Three** fourseveneightten!

Then you have to add the total number of sub-words, which is five:

Threefourseveneightten**fifteen**! **Three**fourseveneightten **fifteen**! **Three**fourseveneightten**fifteen**! **Three**fourseven eightten**fifteen**! **Three**fourseveneightten**fifteen**!

Plus one for the whole word 'television':

Threefourseveneightten fifteen**sixteen**! Threefourseven eightten fifteen**sixteen**! Threefourseveneightten fifteen**six teen**! Threefourseveneightten fifteen**sixteen**! Threefour seveneightten fifteen**sixteen**!

Which of course won't do, because sixteen is even, so we add one more:

Threefourseveneighttenfifteensixteen**seventeen**! Threefourseveneighttenfifteensixteen**seventeen**! Threefourseveneighttenfifteensixteen**seventeen**! Threefourseveneighttenfifteensixteen**seventeen**! Threefourseveneighttenfifteensixteenseventeen!

Then it's the staccato version:

Tvn! Tvn! **Tvn! Tvn! Tvn!**

Even more so:

Tn! Tn! **Tn! Tn! Tn!**

Then I continue as before.

The Beast has extended this process to phrases from films or real life. In simple everyday speech such as 'James, would you like a drink?' this presents no problem; each word is a single syllable and therefore free of sub-words and relatively easy to get 'right'. I dread words ending with '-ation' or '-ility' or '-able'; '-ation' has four sub-words in it, '-ility' has three, of which the 'y' (being the French for 'there') is one, and '-able' has two, the 'a' and 'ble' to which I add an acute accent, creating the French for corn, 'blé'.

Apart from counting, the Beast seems as exhausted as I am, confining itself to gentle taps on coffee cups and furniture, rearranging my shoes on the floor and violently poking the buttons on the television remote control with my forefinger. Occasionally it is enraged by the delicate balance of a plateful of food on the flimsy tray my mother brings my meals on and a heavy bash sends boiled plaice and broccoli leaping on to the sheets, but by and large it is subdued.

Gradually, however, the days of feeling well begin to outnumber the days of fatigue and after six weeks I am fit enough to go back to London. Unfortunately, I can't return to the flat. The other residents in the building, each of whom own a share in the freehold, have ganged together after my previously disruptive behaviour and insist that if I return they will force my parents to sell.

I move into a rented flat in the King's Road.

The End

I must achieve *something*.

    Sit at the piano in my dressing gown.

    Replace telephone receiver. Forgot last night.

    Legs crossed, first cigarette of the day . . .

    Which grates against the hangover.

    But we *have* to get through it . . .

    Past it . . . out the other side.

    Got this great tune.

    A golden syrup tune.

    About eight notes of it, anyway.

    Play it.

    One two three four five six seven eight!

    Don't know what to use it for, though.

    Sounds vaguely Russian.

    Probably because I was listening to Stravinsky, whenever it was.

    Can't remember.

So is that influence or plagiarism?
Fuck knows! But I panic about that.
More than anything else, if I'm honest.
Not to have one's own voice . . .
Would be hell. Making me pointless, redundant, a parasite.
I hate parasites, spongers, greed.
People who take too many chips off a communal plate.
Fuckers!

Chapter 12
Don't Shoot Me

I hate walking into this place. Always feel ashamed somehow.

Lawton's bar, restaurant and nightclub. I'm just the pianist, the hired help. Rock stars come here. Younger than me. They've made it.

Valerie the receptionist smiles at me, but there's no warmth there. It's a tolerant smile. The really nice smile's reserved for the punters.

'Hi, Valerie,' I say, far too enthusiastically, wanting to irritate her.

'Hello.' Polite but dismissive – cold. No 'Hi, James' just 'Hello.' She's attractive, in a rigid, statuesque, 'flawless make-up' sort of way, but she knows it.

'Hi, Felix,' I say, embarrassed.

He nods but doesn't smile. Felix is the bouncer, a frighteningly huge Jamaican.

I lied to him. Dreadful lies.

Christ! How *could* I have fed him such bullshit! We used to get on well. He's genuine, calmly self-confident and non-judgemental. He felt like an ally. When I asked him how he'd got into being a bouncer, he told me he had a black belt in tae kwon do.

I can't *think* what came over me, but I told him I had a first dan in karate.

Which would have been fine, except that he then asked if I'd like to come to his gym in south London and give a demonstration to 'the kids'.

Panicking and losing the plot completely, I said I'd accidentally killed someone who was trying to mug me. I went into all this rubbish about how: 'when the mugger attacked me with a knife, I just went into automatic mode – you know how it is, mate – and although he managed to "nick" me,' which I prove by showing him my scar, 'the training kicked in. I wasn't scared, it just happened. Next thing I knew, this guy was lying there, dead. Broken neck.'

I tried to look suitably regretful, as if this was just one of the unavoidable pitfalls in the life of a trained killer – as inevitable as 'friendly fire' in a war.

'But consequently,' I told him, 'causing the death of another human being shook me to the core, such that I took a vow to give up karate altogether.'

We were killers together, I thought, Felix and I. Companions. He'd understand.

I just wanted him to like me. I wanted to appear special in his eyes.

A strange look came over his face – as much disappointment as disbelief.

I avoid him now, though. He usually nods when I walk from the reception area where he stands into the bar itself.

Christ, it's noisy in here.

Mind you, it's always noisy; they don't really need a pianist, you can never hear it at the far end anyway, unless I'm thumping out 'Rhapsody in Blue' or something. The floor is dark shiny wooden; the tables are dark shiny wooden; the bar is dark shiny wooden; the lights are dimmed.

First thing, shuffle through the hordes, make straight for the bar to get the first of my two free drinks – Coke; I'm still off alcohol after the hepatitis.

'Hi, Fabio. How are you doing?' Fabio is one of the Italian barmen.

Or sometimes I say, 'All right, Fabio?' It's street-speak I learned on the campsite. When I first arrived in France, I always greeted people politely with a 'Hello, how are you?' But cockney Steve said I sounded like a wanker and that 'All right, mate?' or just 'All right?' or 'How are you doing?' was the current thinking. The habit stuck.

'Hey, James.'

Fabio thinks we have an understanding, a kinship, workers together. He knows what I drink and automatically reaches for the Coke bottle, which he half empties into an enormous cocktail glass.

'How you doin', man?' he asks.

'Not bad – you?' I say, resisting the urge to smash the delicately thin glass on the hard woodenness of the bar.

'Pretty good,' he says, and leans conspiratorially over the bar and whispers in my ear. 'Hey man, look at that!'

I follow his gaze to where a stunning blonde in a breathtakingly short, blue silk dress is standing, smiling flirtatiously at a man old enough to be her father. She looks perfect. Her perfect bronzed legs are long and slim, tapering seamlessly down to her delicate high-heeled shoes; her perfectly proportioned breasts could be filled with helium, judging from the way they seem to want to escape. Her perfect face is beautiful, her perfect skin is flawless and unlined, her perfect hair is shining, styled and brushed to – well – perfection.

And her eyes . . . those beautiful, blue eyes . . . are dead.

And still she smiles . . . but the old man doesn't see it.

Or perhaps he doesn't care.

'God,' whispers Fabio, 'beautiful . . . look at those legs! What I wouldn't give to fuck that . . .'

'Mmm,' I murmur, nodding as though in complete agreement, smiling at him in pretend lasciviousness, on one level flattered that Fabio, like Abba-clone Phil before him, sees me as a fellow hot-blooded male and therefore chooses to confide in me, on another level, uncomfortable because he's so unashamedly blatant about it. But he's right; she is beautiful, and given the chance, I probably *would* like to fuck her, but not, somehow, with quite the brutality it seems Fabio would.

I pick up my drink and start to move off.

'Hey, James,' Fabio touches my arm, 'you play "Return to Sorrento", yes?'

Fabio was born in Sorrento. He asks me to play the song at least once a week.

I find it hard reconciling Fabio the sex fiend with Fabio the romantic patriot.

I nod and he winks; then I fight my way towards the piano, say 'excuse me' to a man standing right next to the piano stool and sit down.

Put the glass down. Once, twice, three, four, five . . .

Don't smash it. **Pour** it over the piano keys. No, **don't!** **Leave it!**

This is my haven, my security zone. A sea of animated faces above and around me, glass sitting on the closed lid, I think about what to play first.

It's not easy to combat the boredom of playing to a room in which one is little more than a distant sound effect. Some nights it's so loud I know that if I was replaced by a chimpanzee playing a series of unconnected notes, nobody would notice. I used to pluck songs out of the air in no particular order, but there was never a sense of structure or purpose. Nowadays, in an attempt to give the evening a sense of direction, I plan a 'concert' in my mind.

I might start with a sort of overture, where I play all the songs from *South Pacific* or *West Side Story*. This usually takes about three-quarters of an hour and has the added bonus of my not having to think of what to play next. There is an order to it. I like the order. I know where I am. Then, to round off part one of the concert, before the 'interval' – my break – I might play the whole of 'Rhapsody in Blue', which lasts about half an hour.

From a nine-thirty start, all this takes me up to ten forty-five, when I could – if I wanted – take my official break and have another Coke, but I try to extend the first part for as long as I can as somehow it feels like a bonus. It's a kind of internal competition.

And when I play, I watch.

The Cocktail Pianist's People Guide
Type 1: The Genuinely Nice Person

I should think she's about forty. She's standing about five feet away, relaxed, arms crossed, resting her elbows on the closed piano lid, her cocktail glass in front of her – nothing too exotic, gin and tonic perhaps, something simple. She's by herself, but doesn't appear bothered by it. The jacket draped loosely around her shoulders gives her an air of quiet sophistication and relaxed confidence.

She's been there for about five minutes, listening; really listening, enough for me to go off autopilot and put some heart into my playing. Occasionally our eyes meet and we exchange smiles.

Finally, waiting until I've finished, she leaves her drink where it is and moves around the piano towards me.

'That was lovely.' She still has her arms crossed, but with her right hand she unconsciously plucks at the jacket, pulling it further over her shoulder, as if cold. It's an elegant gesture somehow.

'Oh, thanks,' I say.

With a frown and leaning forward slightly, she says, 'What was that you were playing? It sounds so familiar but I can't think what it's called,' and she places her hand against her forehead, thinking.

'"What I Did For Love"; it's from *Chorus Line*.'

'Tst! Yes, of course it is!' And she smiles again. 'I *loved* that show.'

The trouble with sitting at the piano is that you always have to look up at people when you speak to them. It gives me a distinct disadvantage, but somehow she senses this and, resting her hand on the piano lid for support, she crouches on her knees, joining me.

'That's better. Now I can see you. So you're a bit of a musicals fan, are you?' She seems genuinely interested.

'Yes I am . . . quite . . . I used to hate them.'

'Really? Why?'

'Well, I was trained classically, and there's a kind of dreadful musical snobbery among "serious" musicians which says that anything that isn't Beethoven or Prokofiev is rubbish. At the time I believed it.'

'What made you change your mind?'

'Well, to do *this*,' I say, gesturing at the piano, 'I had to learn something a bit more contemporary. I couldn't just sit here playing Mozart, so I went out and bought a whole load of records and listened to them. I bought everything – you name it – but it was the musicals I liked.'

'Such as?'

'Oh, all sorts. There's some really good stuff out there: *Cabaret, Chicago, West Side Story* . . . *Chorus Line*.'

'Oh, do play something from *West Side Story*.'

'Okay,' I say, putting my hands together and pushing them down between my knees. It's a half-nervous thing I do before I start playing something. 'What would you like?'

'How about . . . "Maria"?' As I start playing, she stands up and moves to retrieve her drink, returning a second or two later to watch. And when I finish, she says, 'Thanks so much,' and, indicating her glass, 'Can I get you a drink?'

'Thanks,' I say, and she smiles. I wish there were more like her.

There's a small supermarket close to the flat.

One Friday afternoon in winter, feeling dreadful and running a temperature, I grab a trolley and stock up with everything I could possibly need until Monday morning. By the time I get to the front of the checkout queue, an equally long line has formed behind me. Between sneezes and twitches, I unload my shopping on to the counter. I remove the last two items, a packet of Ready Brek and a bottle of milk from the trolley simultaneously, one in each hand.

As I'm about to place them on the counter, I have a twitch-sneeze. This is very unusual. I'm accustomed to the twitches and I'm used to sneezing – when I have cold – but I'm not prepared for both at once. I can't cope. Burdened with the Ready Brek and milk, I'm powerless to put hand or handkerchief in front of my nose and mouth. The resulting jet of snot ejaculates across the counter and hits the till. Splat!

It's not one of those modern McDonald's jobs either, covered with thick plastic that can be cleaned with a single wipe of a J-cloth. It's a close relation of my old organ teacher's Imperial typewriter, where you hammer a couple of levers and are rewarded by a distinctive metallic 'ding' as the drawer beneath it springs open to liberate the change. Great gloops of snot hang in impossibly inaccessible strands among the intricate workings of the machine. A jeweller with time on his hands and dozens of packets of cotton buds would be hard-pressed to remove it.

Oh . . . my *God*!

I've been twitching in supermarkets for years, tapping yoghurt pots in the dairy section so hard they split, pulverising packets of those infuriatingly delicate circular Dutch crispbread things, not to mention punishing carefully stacked pyramids of baked beans at the end of aisle three.

Another frozen, enduring image is added to my 'life' photo album, framed alongside the clapping incident on my first morning at the Royal College. Time again slows. Even the attendant Muzak ceases . . . all is quiet.

Everybody – me, the checkout girl, the people standing behind me in the queue, plus three or four accidental observers who happen to be standing close by – look at *it* . . . clinging, shining, motionless . . . then at *me* . . . clinging (to Ready Brek and milk), shining (with sweat), motionless . . .

And the appalling chemical reaction that is soul-deep embarrassment races through my body, starting in my legs, ending triumphantly on my face, crimson with shame.

Time resumes . . . and I run; out of the shop, back to the flat.

'Bugger bugger shit shit,
Chitty Bitty Gang Chang!
Oh Jesus!'

I never go there again, preferring to walk several hundred yards out of my way to a different supermarket.

The Cocktail Pianist's People Guide (cont.)
Type 2: The Star Maker

A middle-aged, slightly overweight, balding man approaches the piano. Dark glasses, open-necked shirt, gleam of gold medallion nestling among chest hair.

He looks confident. He looks successful. He smiles.

On his wrist he's wearing a pretty girl; short mini skirt, stiletto heels which clackety-clack hectically on the wooden floor.

Without waiting for me to finish what I'm playing, he puts his open hand right in front of my face. 'Dave Smiff,' he announces, interrupting my flow, in a voice which suggests that all my troubles are over.

I stop, take his proffered hand without thinking and look up at him.

'He's a bearded ponce!' says the Beast. 'Go on, call him a

fucking ponce! And she's his tart! Dolly bird, tarty farty marty larty garty! Tart! Tart! Tart! Tart! Tart!'

Shut up!

We shake. I smile. I don't *feel* like smiling. I don't much like the look of him. He's too confident. But I smile anyway. He looks important.

'Hey man! Really loike the piana playin'.'

'Thank you.'

He moves in closer as though about to impart a great secret.

'Look, mite, oim seerius. Oi bin lissnin' to ya. Yore dead good. Yer *sound* good. Yer *look* good.'

He beckons to his wrist accessory. 'Oi Trice, come'n 'ave a listen.'

She moves in closer and I catch a whiff of cheap scent.

'Trice,' Dave says, 'meet' – he pauses – 'wha's yer nime?'

'James,' I say.

'Jimes. Right. Meet Tricy.'

'Hello,' I say.

'Nah listen, Jimes,' he says before Tracy can reply, 'I dunno if you know vis, but ver's a bloke in Europe at the moment called Clayderman. 'E's a piana player, right? 'E's mikin' a bluddy fortune over there. They luv 'im! But 'e 'asn't got 'ere yet. No one over 'ere knows 'oo 'e is. An' it occurs to me there's a big market to be tapped. See where I'm goin'?'

I can feel flutterings of excitement. When I was in France, teenagers and grown women were always asking me to play 'Reeshar Clayderman', so I know who Dave's talking about.

'Yes I do,' I say, pound signs and groupies already dancing before my eyes.

'You interested?'

'Erm, yes. Very.'

'Good. Well, look, 'ere's me card. I know vis may seem loike a flash in the pan, but give us a bell tomorra. We'll 'ave a chat. Awroigh'? I've got some grite ideas. But . . . let's keep it between us, yeah?'

'Great,' I say, stunned. Thrilled. 'Thanks.'

'S'okay. Sorry, can't stop. Come on, Trice; gotta go. We'll be lite,' and waving, he exits.

Tracy gives me a sweet, patronising smile that says, 'Hey, I'm part of the Dave Smith empire too,' and turns to follow him.

For the rest of the evening I'm floating on a cloud.

I buy myself a couple of extra glasses of Coke to celebrate. I deserve it.

Everybody is lovely, everything is wonderful. I'm *going* to be James the piano star after all. I pretend I *am* James the piano star and work my way through Richard Clayderman's greatest hits.

When I get home at three in the morning I can barely sleep for excitement, and the next day the Beast goes on the rampage in 'fortune-telling' mode.

Don't spill a single drop of water when I'm pouring my cup of coffee or Dave Smith won't work out. I'll fail.

When I clean my teeth, I have to brush for longer than a minute, but I have to guess how long a minute is. If I look at my watch and it's been less than a minute, Dave Smith won't work out. I'll fail.

Open the fridge; shut the fridge; open it; shut it; hold the door open, then shut it very very very very very slowly. Watch the rubber seal. Try and find the *exact* point where the magnet on the door starts working. Do it again. Do it seventeen times. No mistakes, or Dave Smith won't work out. I'll fail.

Cut the toast in half with just *one* cut and one cut only. If it doesn't work, throw the toast away and make some more. *One* cut only or Dave Smith won't work out. I'll fail.

Finally, I sit in the kitchen clutching Dave's business card, watching as the clock creeps agonisingly slowly round to 10 a.m., when I can ring.

DAVE SMITH – PRODUCER, the card says, in thick black lettering, plus a telephone number.

At 10:02 – rather than at 10:01, which might seem a bit keen – I ring.

A woman's voice. 'HMV, can I help you?'

HMV! Christ, he must be important. Jackpot! Terrifying.

'Yes, erm, I'd like to speak to Dave Smith, please.'

'One moment, sir, I'll put you through.'

Couple of clicks then more ringing.

'Record department.' Another woman's voice, presumably his secretary.

'Hello,' I say, 'can I speak to Dave Smith, please?'

'Sorry, he's with a customer at the moment. Can I get him to ring you back?'

'Erm, is this his direct line?'

'Yes it is, but as I say, he's with a cu . . . oh no, wait a minute . . . Dave?'

'Yeah?' Distant.

'Phone . . . for you . . .'

More shuffles and clicks, then: ''Allo, Dave Smiff.'

'Hi, Dave – James McConnel.'

''Oo?'

'James McConnel . . . I was playing the piano in Lawton's last night . . . you gave me your card.'

Silence.

'Oh yeah . . . Jimes . . . erm . . .'

More silence.

'Look, mite . . . I . . . er . . . tell ve troof . . . (deep sigh) . . . I was 'avin a bit of a joke wiv me girlfriend . . . sorry 'bout that. No 'ard feelins, eh? Yor a grite piana player, by the way . . .'

Bastard.

I must have got something wrong.

Maybe the fridge.

God knows.

Shit!

One weekend, I go to stay with a friend in Suffolk. I knew Fiona in the hostel and we've stayed in touch.

Her father is an ex-army doctor. At dinner on Saturday evening, having refused wine, he asks me why. I tell him about the hepatitis and glandular fever.

'How long have you bin orff the booze?' he asks.

'About two years.'

'And how do you feel?'

'Fine, most of the time.'

'Well then, your liver's probably right as rain by now; couple of glasses won't hurt you,' and he pours . . .

The Cocktail Pianist's People Guide (cont.)
Type 3: Go on, Charlie, show 'im what you can do

'Dat's a rere gift y've got dere, sir.'

Irishman, tall, middle-aged, smiling; not drunk, but certainly cheerful. The woman with him could be his wife. But I'll bet she's his mistress. Demonstrative in a way that married people aren't. Unless they're newlyweds, of course. He's wearing a wedding ring but she's not.

They look as though they're borrowing time.

'Thank you.'

'Bin doin' it long, have yer?'

'Quite a while. About three years.'

He's so tall and standing so close I have to strain my neck to look up at his face.

A pause.

'No,' he sighs, ''tis a great gift.'

Another pause. He turns and winks at the woman, who giggles and says, 'Oh come on, Charlie, stop teasing; show 'im what you can do!' London accent.

'No no no no no no no,' he says, waving his hand at her, 'it's *his* gig.'

'Yeah, but he won't mind; ask him.'

I wait, knowing what's coming.

She looks at me. 'You don't mind if Charlie has a quick go, do you? He's really good.'

'No, not at all . . . please . . .' I say, getting up from the stool, heart sinking.

'Oh well, if you're sure,' Charlie says, and he sits while I stand beside him like a pupil watching his teacher.

He heaves a great sigh, interlocks his fingers, reverses his hands and stretches out his arms in preparation for take-off.

Then he turns to me, puts his forefinger in the air like a cricket umpire. 'Now . . . they don't write dem like dis any more, so.'

And, hands on the keys, head slightly raised, he starts to sing 'Danny Boy', his eyes half closed in glazed ecstasy.

I love 'Danny Boy'. If I'm ever asked, it'll be on my *Desert Island Discs* list. I can't imagine anyone not being moved by it. Charlie is obviously a kindred spirit. His raw emotional outpouring is almost palpable, and his performance is faultless, but for two tiny details – his playing and his singing.

He thumps the keys as though wearing boxing gloves. Wrong notes scatter and flee in all directions and his expressive – though tuneless – voice soars above the crowd of startled drinkers.

Charlie's girlfriend is gazing at him adoringly, her head swaying gently. She glances over at me, smiling dreamily, her expression saying, 'Isn't he wonderful?'

And as the song builds, so do the sporadic shouts from various quarters.

'Give it a rest, mate!'

'Shuuuuu-dup!'

'Fucking noise!'

And I stand, hideously embarrassed, a fixed smile on my face, trying both to look appreciative for Charlie's girlfriend's sake, and to convey sympathy to the increasing number of aggrieved faces turned in our direction. It feels rude just to walk away, so I'm stuck here, rooted to the spot until Charlie, having built to an excruciating crescendo, comes to an end, eyes now glistening.

He pauses, overcome with emotion, and then slowly gets up from the piano, leaving 'Danny Boy' lying dead on the floor.

His girlfriend flings her arms around his neck and gives him a huge kiss. 'Charlie,' she says, 'you're so talented, you should've been a musician not a builder.' She turns to me. 'He's so talented, isn't he?'

'Yes,' I say, 'he really . . . *feels* it, doesn't he?'

But it doesn't matter. Charlie buys me a drink; which makes it a good night.

My two free glasses – of wine now – plus Charlie's – three: plus (maybe) an extra from Fabio if I play the Sorrento song.

Four.

I relax.

Two free drinks doesn't always get me through the evening nowadays.

It used to.

Four just about does the trick.

'James?'

'Yes?'

'Hi, it's Jenny.'

'Jenny! Christ, it's been months! How *are* you?'

'I'm fine, really well. What about you? What've you been up to?'

'Oh, this and that. I'm still playing the piano.'

'Great. Now listen, someone's given me a couple of tickets for some show in the West End, and since you're about the only musical person I know, I wondered if you'd come with me.'

'Really? What is it?' I ask.

'Oh. Hang on a minute, I've got the thing here.' She puts the phone down and makes rummaging noises before coming back on. 'It's called . . . *Sweeney Todd, the Demon Barber of Fleet Street*,' she says slowly, clearly reading.

'Never heard of it,' I say. 'Who wrote it?'

'Erm . . . chap called . . . Stephen Sondheim, music and lyrics.'

I've never heard of *him* either, but later, as I'm sitting in the theatre reading my programme, I see he was responsible for the lyrics of *West Side Story*.

The theatre is an interesting gauge as to what people are prepared – or not prepared – to put up with. Normally, I drive my immediate neighbours, front, back and sides, to distraction. Something about being in a confined space – aeroplane seats do it too – causes me to kick the floor and try to push my foot through the back of the seat in front of me. I sniff, cough, make faces and grunt. I slap the arm rests and if I use the opera glasses I can't help bashing them against my nose, the Beast toying with me, delaying the gratification of actually seeing anything. Then there's the clapping, of course. Still thirty-seven times.

If the performance isn't sold out, people usually move during the interval and when I return for Act II with my tub of ice cream I often find myself alone in a little oasis of red velvet – which is rather nice.

But on this occasion – Jenny beside me – from the moment when, in the dimmed Victorian stage setting, the chorus first sings 'Attend the tale of Sweeney Todd', shivers run up my spine and I sit, electrified – the Beast becalmed – captivated by the sheer theatrical brilliance, the lyrical and musical originality of it. A musical thriller, truly frightening at times, side-splittingly funny at others, nodding at shows like *Oliver*, but much darker, much more uncomfortable.

The critics adore it; it's already won Tony awards on Broadway, but the public over here stays away in droves and it closes within five months – not though, before I've seen it a further five times, nearly bankrupting myself in the process.

I buy the record, playing it again and again, day in, day out, until I know every note, every word by heart.

I buy the score and sit for hours studying it. I play vast tracts of *Sweeney Todd* at my gigs. I've never had a live hero;

a few dead ones – Beethoven, Mozart, Ravel. I buy all Sondheim's other stuff, much of which is equally brilliant. I become obsessed with Stephen Sondheim. I write to Stephen Sondheim. I dream of meeting Stephen Sondheim. I worship at the altar of Stephen Sondheim. I want to *be* Stephen Sondheim. I want to write musicals – like Stephen Sondheim.

To hell with piano concertos; I never got very far anyway. This is what I *really* want to do.

So *what* if I know nothing about the theatre? I'll buy a book and learn the basics.

And so what if I've only ever written essays at school and at college, plus a few thank-you letters? I'll do the lyrics as well. I'm all set. All I need is a suitable story to adapt.

Trouble is, although my musical education is fairly rounded, I know bugger all about literature. My reading habits thus far have been confined to Alistair MacLean and Dick Francis. I've got O level English literature but *Richard II* doesn't sound like a great idea for a show.

I need to educate myself.

I start reading: Saki and Jane Austen and Oscar Wilde and the Brontës and Daphne du Maurier and P.G. Wodehouse and Evelyn Waugh and Anthony Trollope (yuck) and Henry James and Proust (double yuck) and Victor Hugo and Dickens and Maupassant and many more.

I spend my days reading in the flat. I take a book to my gigs and read during my breaks, which dilutes the boredom. I really enjoy it. I wish I'd read more at school.

On my evenings off I go to the theatre and see all the musicals I can; plays as well, the Beast ruining each performance for at least four other people. I buy records of musicals from a specialist shop in Covent Garden. I steep myself in them.

And after about four months I read an enchanting short story by Oscar Wilde. 'The Canterville Ghost', a comedy about an American family who buy a large English stately home, the resident ghost of which has terrified successive aristocratic residents to such a degree that they're forced to sell up. The joke is that the Americans turn the tables on the ghost, an ancestor of the previous owners, by not being in the slightest bit fazed by him, to his immense outrage. Various shenanigans ensue, and all ends happily.

I love it. I start to write.

Everything I produce, the music, the lyrics, sounds like second-rate Stephen Sondheim. I have no sense of my own style or sound in the way that he does, or Gershwin or Cole Porter do. I don't worry about it; I'm just happy I've found something I want to do. I may now not compose the greatest piano concerto ever written, but as a (slightly less) tragic genius, surely I can take the theatrical world by storm.

The Cocktail Pianist's People Guide (cont.)
Type 4: I Don't Know What the Hell I'm Gonna Do

I'm doing a two-week stint at Selfridge's Hotel, Oxford Street.

Very different from the Lawton's hellhole. True cocktail pianist stuff. Quiet, carpeted atmosphere. Clinical and polite. This is suits and briefcases and choreographed waiters. Tiny white dishes with only nine peanuts in them. Restraint.

No free drinks.

I have to play quietly here. The piano should complement, never dominate. Heaven forbid I should play with any feeling, in case it's too loud.

The Beast urges me to shout something staccato. Doesn't matter what. Anything – 'Sming!. Ba! Gobstoppers!' It wants me to shout so badly I can't help giggling. I try and compromise by punching the piano lid, but it doesn't satisfy. I look around to see if anyone's watching. There's a man sitting by himself at the other end of the room.

Then I whisper 'Ba!' But it's no good.

I say 'Gobstoppers!' very fast again and again under my breath . . . 'GobstoppersGobstoppersGobstoppersGobstoppers Gobstoppers!'

But I can't do it fast enough, it's a bugger of a tongue-twister and even reducing it to 'Dobdobdobdobdobdobdob dob!' doesn't work.

I'm saddled with it.

I slap the music stand in frustration and play 'The Windmills of My Mind'.

The lone man gets up, comes over to the piano and watches.

'Hi there,' he says when I've finished.

American; businessman. Greying hair, fifty maybe. His eyes are red-rimmed. He looks miserable rather than drunk and his dark blue shiny suit is badly creased.

'Hello,' I say.

He gestures to my empty wine glass. 'Can I buy you a drink?'

'Thanks. Vodka and tonic, please.'

Finally, some anaesthetic. Goodbye, Beast!

Hope he's not a poof . . .

Are you a poof! Shh! Think gobstoppers!

He waves to a waiter and orders my drink, plus 'Scutch un the rucks' for himself. Then he pulls up a chair and sits next to the piano at right-angles to me.

Never actually heard an American order scotch for real before. Only in films.

Does America really exist? I've always wondered.

I know it does on one level. You can't get away from it, whether it's watching *Starsky and Hutch* or Jimmy Carter on the news standing outside the White House. But can you actually prove it?

America could just be a film set at Pinewood.

Like history. Did the Battle of Hastings really happen?

It sounds ridiculous, but sometimes I don't believe it.

Or World War II?

Or Queen Victoria?

Or my parents' childhood?

Did they have a childhood? Or did everything start when I was born?

If I'm in a museum and I see, say, a mediaeval sword, or a World War I gas mask, I think, did people really use these things?

'Jim,' he says, holding out his hand.

'James,' I say, shaking it.

'Hah!' He chuckles with irony. 'There's a coincidence.'

Then he says nothing, but sits looking uncomfortable.

'Would you like me to play something?' I ask, feeling uncomfortable myself.

'Er, no. It's fine.'

More silence. This is getting a bit weird.

'So . . . are you American?' Can't think what else to say.

He sighs. 'Ya, from the States.'

'Whereabouts?'

'Milwaukee,' he says. I get the impression he wants to say something but hasn't plucked up the courage.

'Are you here on business, then?'

'Er, ya.'

'What sort of business are you in?'

'I'm a baker.'

A flashback.

I'm ten. There's a diarrhoea bug going round the school and I've got it. Practically everyone's got it. I'm sitting on the lavatory just vacated by a boy called Baker. As I sit there, I find myself inwardly repeating the word 'baker' again and again – ten, a hundred, a thousand times. Round and round it goes in my mind and gradually it loses its meaning completely. It changes and becomes something else, until finally I don't know what 'baker' is any more. I get to the heart of the sound until the sound is the only thing that has any meaning. But the word itself, the 'breadness' the 'cheerful man in the white-coatness', the 'oven-ness' the 'baker-ness' of 'baker' no longer exists. This has something to do with listening to its constituent parts. When I say 'baker', it's a soundbite, an all-in-one package. Repeating it, you begin to hear the subtle differences in the noises that 'baker' makes, the different words that burst out of it.

B (as in 'burr').

Ba (as in 'bay').

Bay.

Bake.

Ay.

Er.

The sound that comes before the 'b' is fully formed.

The sound that comes between 'b' and 'ay'.

The sound that comes between the 'ay' and the 'k'.

And the 'k' before, during and at the end as it exits to the 'er'.

K.

Ker.

Erb.

Kerb.

Kerbé.

Kerbay.

Kerbayee.

Baykerbay.

'A baker?'

'Ya, I have a chain of, ah . . . bakeries. I'm over here to, ah . . . ree-search and development, you know . . .'

He says this distractedly, as though he's just discovered he's wet himself and as well as trying to keep up a conversation with me, is wondering what best to do about it.

'Oh, that's interesting,' I say, wanting to jolly things along. 'Don't think I've met a travelling baker before.'

'No.' He seems to sink into a daydream.

Silence.

In desperation I doodle a few notes with my right hand. Then, when he says nothing else, I add my left hand and start playing quietly.

After a minute or so: 'Would you mind?' he says, coming to.

'Sure.' I stop.

And sit.

Just the two of us; the distant hum from the air conditioning the only sound.

And wait.

Then our drinks arrive. Jim signs for them and thanks the waiter, who retreats. Jim takes a gulp of his 'scutch', the 'rucks' rattling like dice. I do likewise. He sighs again, as if having come to a decision.

'Sorry, James,' he says, 'I just needed some company; hope you don't mind.'

'Not at all, that's fine,' I say, still feeling awkward.

Yet more silence.

A baker prepares . . .

To spill the dough.

Dough dough dough dough dough!

Doe.

Doe a deer, a female deer.

Dear dear.

Doe doe deer dear dear!

Doe doe doe doe da! Doe doe da! Doe da! Da! Da da da da!

Stop it!

Maybe I should hit him. Punch him on the nose, or slap his face.

What would Jim the baker do?

Jim . . . Jimjimjim . . . jim . . . jiiiiiiiiiiiiiiiiiiiiiiiiiiiiiiiiiiiiiiiiiiiim!

Oh *fuck*, he's crying! Christ, how embarrassing! What the hell do I do?

Jim, one hand on his forehead, wipes away tears with the other.

'Sorry, James,' he says again and fishes in his pocket for a handkerchief.

'It's okay. What's the problem?' Should I be asking?

He sighs again and looks down and to his left, not really focusing.

Pause.

'The problem, James . . . is women. Women, James . . . women . . .'

'Yes,' I say wisely, crossing my arms, unconsciously switching from pianist to therapist. I can feel the vodka going to my head.

'My wife, to be exact,' he continues.

'What's wrong with her?'

A beat.

Another sigh.

'Nothing. She's perfect.'

He has a sudden coughing fit.

'She's perfect,' he repeats, mid splutter. 'But it seems,' he says, recovering, 'that I'm not perfect . . . for her.'

'Oh,' I say.

'Dear,' I add.

'She wants to divorce me.'

'Why?'

He glances at me. 'Ha.' Then he looks away again. 'Good question . . .'

Pause.

Then, in a rush, 'I don't know what the hell I'm gonna do.' And it all comes tumbling out: 'The separation . . . can't understand it . . . out of the blue . . . two lovely kids . . . thought we were happy . . . beautiful house . . . her friends . . . that bitch Sonia, her sister . . . why I came to England . . .'

And I listen and I make sympathetic noises, but Jim is not a natural raconteur. He mumbles monotonously, so quietly sometimes that I miss whole paragraphs. I lose interest. I don't want to hear all this; I'm not an in-hotel-psychiatrist; it's embarrassing and tedious. And although I sit with him – offering little (non Beast) grunts of encouragement from time to time – after a while I find myself sympathising with his wife. But he keeps the drink flowing and flowing and before long I don't care either way.

* * * * *

'James McConnel!'

I look up from the piano.

Birtwistle! Across the room.

What's *he* doing in Lawton's?

Rimmington Hall. He was in my house but he left the year before I did; went travelling, I think. Not an ex-bully, but never much liked him. Never had much to do with him, come to that. One of the rugger buggers, first eleven cricket, athletics team . . . sporty type. Cheeky.

He's with a girl I know, Bella. She waves, eyebrows raised.

They approach the piano.

'Piers,' I say, standing, trying to sound as if I'm greeting a long-lost friend. Feels weird using his Christian name. I only ever called him 'Birtwistle' at school. And suddenly I see us as we were then: thirteen-year-old boys in our camouflage-green uniforms, queuing in the tuck shop, struggling with trunks and tuck boxes on the first and last days of term, rushing to lessons, shouting, spitting, flicking V-signs at the back of hated prefects or masters, throwing food at mealtimes, words and phrases like 'creep', 'spastic' and 'pinch, punch, first day of the month' integral parts of our vocabulary.

And I compare the image of the Birtwistle I knew then with the one in front of me: a taller, broader, hairier Birtwistle, a smoking, leather-jacketed Birtwistle in his 'grown-up' uniform.

'How you doing?' He smiles. 'Good to see you,' and he holds out his hand, which I shake. He really seems to *mean* it.

'You too,' I say, not sure I mean it, pushing on with a 'Hi, Bells' with rather too much enthusiasm to cover the uneasiness at encountering Birtwistle in *my* world.

'James,' she says, surprised, 'what are you doing *here*?'

'Playing,' I say, indicating the piano and leaning forward to kiss her cheek. 'What about you?'

'Oh God.' She closes her eyes. 'We've just been to an in*credibly* boring dinner party round the corner; so we left early and came here for a drink.' She giggles guiltily, glancing at Piers, and brushes her fingers through her long red hair. Then, wagging a finger between Piers and me, says, 'How do *you* two know each other?'

He and I exchange glances.

'Rimmington Hall,' I say.

'School,' he says, clarifying.

'Really! How funny,' she says. Then, losing interest and looking round the room, she adds with mild distaste, 'It's a bit *dark* in here, isn't it?'

'How did you get in?' I ask. 'It's supposed to be members only.'

'Got a friend who's a member,' Piers says, smiling, tapping the side of his nose in feigned arrogance. 'Gave his name at the door. That bouncer's a big fucker, isn't he!'

'Who, Felix?' I say.

'Yeah. Built like a brick shithouse.'

'Black belt in tae kwon do, but he's a nice bloke.'

'Hang on a minute, James,' says Bella, 'is this what you *do*?'

'Yes. Have done for ages. Well, it's not the *only* thing; I'm actually writing a musi—'

'God, I had no idea,' she interrupts. 'I knew you played the piano.'

'Yes, but I really want to write musi—'

'What d'you want, Bells?' Piers interrupts.

'Dunno, er . . . vodka? Tonic?'

'James?' And again, it feels odd hearing him use my Christian name.

'Oh thanks, white wine.'

'Okay.' He goes to the bar.

'What time d'you have to play till?' asks Bella, clearly not interested in my theatrical career.

'About two o'clock.'

'That's *ages*!' she says, looking at her watch, faintly outraged.

'I know. It's one of the late ones; I don't get home till about three.'

'Well, you can have a drink with us, can't you?'

'No, not really, I've just had a break and the manager's a complete bastard, he keeps checking up on me. Actually, I'd better get back, sorry.'

'Well, look, I'll tell you what, what are you doing tomorrow night?'

'Nothing much. Got the night off. Why?'

'I've got people for supper; why don't you come? Piers'll be there and you can reminisce about school.'

'I *hated* school.'

'Did you? Oh well, you can reminisce about how ghastly it was then. Come *on*, it'll be *fun*. About eight and it's not smart.'

'All right, thanks.'

The Cocktail Pianist's People Guide (cont.)
Type 5: The Lone Ranger

Because I'm fixed in one place, I become public property. Waiters can move around, but the piano is stuck to the floor and I'm stuck with it. I'm neutral ground. I'm a good excuse for the lonely. Anyone can come and talk to me or stand near me; there's no need for an introduction.

The Lone Ranger usually introduces herself by asking me to play something. Often in her late twenties or early thirties, she appears rude, hardened, bitter – wounded; desperate to hide her desperation. Rarely does she say 'Hello,' or 'Hi' or smile. Not at first.

She stands by the piano, her face a mask, chain-smoking, a little drunk, watching me, but not *really* watching me, using the piano as a security prop. She's made a huge effort with her appearance, but something's not right.

She doesn't know it's not right, and flaunting her mistake makes her look ridiculous.

It could be an inappropriate dress that she thinks will 'make a statement', or it could be a violent shade of lipstick, or even that the lipstick is smudged. Unlike the Dave Smiffs and the beautiful blondes in blue dresses who lie to others but ultimately *know* who and what they are, she's lied to herself for so long she no longer has an identity. All is make-believe.

'Who shall I be today?'

'What shall I be this evening?'

I know how she feels.

There is an unconscious space around her. She is avoided. But still she scans the room, smoking, looking at her watch occasionally for effect, as though waiting for someone.

And finally, when nothing happens and no one talks to her and she won't allow herself simply to walk out because it would feel like failure, eventually the prop becomes the main event, and she settles for second best.

Without any preamble, still unsmiling, ashamed at having to resort to talking to the piano player, she says something, almost aggressively, like: 'You play any Beatles?' Trying to be off the cuff.

I match her aggression by being 'cool' myself, as though I'm used to it.

'Sure.'

'How about –' she makes a small throwaway gesture with her hand – '"Yesterday"?'

And I play it, coolly, wanting to look as though I don't really care how it sounds, smarting inwardly at being treated like a coffee machine, but she's already scanning the room again, one final time – just in case. The Beast wants to undermine my coolness by trying to get me to force my right foot through the piano leg. I press, push, hard as I can, keeping my face impassive.

But I understand her.

I really do.

Deep down.

Underneath *everything*, though I would never admit it to anyone . . .

Even myself.

We're alike.

Not completely.

Close enough.

And I hate that fact.

But she's my soul-mate for the evening.

There's something missing in her. She's seeking a fixer; and *her* particular fix is an emotional doctor who'll take her home and fuck her brains out; to take away the pain for one night.

And eventually, finally, finally having given up hope of

finding any alternative, she allows herself to connect with me. She drinks . . .

And I drink . . .

We drink a lot. And she pays, then I pay, and Fabio looks on and he winks at me when he brings the drinks.

I budge up and she joins me on the piano stool and we laugh and we giggle and we forget to ask each other's names, and I sing Flanders and Swann songs and they're not her thing because she's not really interested in comedy, but my prop status is forgotten and we flirt and we touch and we leer and we convince ourselves that this is fun – which it is. And we recognise that something in each other.

At two in the morning, both of us very drunk, I give her a lift home, driving incredibly carefully, but not too slowly, to her tiny basement flat in Kensal Green and I go in for a 'cup of coffee', which turns out to be more booze, and for an hour – before we both fall asleep in a spinning, drunken haze in her chaotic, uncarpeted bedroom – we fuck each other's brains out – and we say things like 'I love you' and 'darling' and 'you're wonderful', longing for it to be true, stamping out, pushing away, ignoring the rising tide of mutual self-disgust. And the next morning I drive back to the flat.

And I never see her again.

So, alcohol.

Chartreuse . . . white wine . . . vodka.

One-time rescue remedy, confidence booster and purveyor of guts. I could take it then leave it, couldn't I?

But it's changed . . .

In my *mind* . . .

And my body.

It still calms the Beast. But it's promoted itself while my back was turned. It's becoming the need, in its own right.

Like the need to twitch.

The need . . . to drink.

When did it happen? When was the actual moment? When was the flick of the switch? When did companion become compulsion?

When did it change from:

'I like a nice glass of wine when I'm playing the piano . . .'

To:

'A glass of wine on the piano helps me get through the evening . . .'

To:

'I need a glass of wine on the piano to help . . .'

To:

'I need a glass of wine . . .'?

You see . . . with booze inside me . . . it's great! The piano just works . . . by itself. The notes press themselves. And my head goes away somewhere. I don't need to put anything in at all. I can float in a lovely comforting cotton-wool haze of goodwill.

I work . . .

Who *me*, sir?

What *me*?

There *is* no *me*.

Me is gone . . .

For the moment.

Yippee!

It's so exciting.

The Beast is gone.

Me is gone.
It's easy.
And I belong.

The End

Ninth note, tenth note, eleventh note, twelfth note!
    Just like that! Yes! Done it!
    11.30 a.m. Fantastic!
    How about squeezing out a couple more?
    Play it all.
    Again.
    Again.
    That's so good!
    Genius!
    But no more.
    I've done enough . . .
    But it's brilliant!
    Hit my forehead . . .
    One, two, three, four, five, six, seven times!
    'Na! Na! Na na na na na! **Na! Na!'**
Yes!
    'They can't take that away,

They can't take that away . . .'
God, I love Gershwin . . .
Bastard!
And now I can relax . . .

Chapter 13
Vita and the Woolf

My jacket's too tight. The Beast hates wearing black tie. It's constricting; I want to burst out of it. I make wide, circular 'boxing' movements with my right arm, fist clenched. But I'm careful these days. When I was about nineteen I accidentally elbowed someone standing behind me in the face on a backswing.

I'm at one of those parties where money's no object. Where, inside the Harrods-sized marquee there are two cascading fountains of champagne and a twenty-piece jazz band flown over from New York. Where there are legions of waiters dressed in traditional Arab costume, force-feeding the thousand guests intricate canapés, the type of delicate little filo-pastry thingummybobs the Beast would love me to flatten with a slap of my hand. Where everything is exceptionally beautifully done and careful thought has clearly gone into every possible detail.

Dinner's finished. There's a piano over there; the pre-dinner pianist has gone.

I wander over to it and sit, self-consciously at first, hoping everyone realises I'm a guest and not an employee. Just in case, I try looking as guest-like as I can, slouching a little, cigarette in my left hand while I play – one of my party tricks.

But always the show-off, and ever hopeful of the potential pulling power of my fingers, I launch into Fats Waller's version of 'Ain't Misbehavin''. It isn't that hard, but it sounds impressive. In the years since my accident, my 'devised' piano technique has become second nature; I know when approaching notes or runs are going to be too much for my right hand and I adapt accordingly.

Towards the end of the piece, a girl peels herself away from the edge of a small group of people and approaches the piano in a casual 'I'm quite interested, but don't want to overdo it' kind of way.

'Hiya,' she says. Cool. Fabulous dress – silver – unusual cut. Brown hair, good figure, nice face. Smiley. I like that. She leans in, unconsciously seductive, crossed arms resting on the piano.

'Hi,' I reply.

'I love Fats Waller . . . nice playing.'

Hey, she knows Fats Waller!

'Thanks. Just mucking about really,' I say, faking nonchalance. 'I *am* a guest, you know,' I want to say, but don't.

She hums along, moving her head rhythmically from side to side, singing the words occasionally, but too quietly for me to hear whether her voice is any good.

'How about some Gershwin?' she says when I've finished.

'Sure.'

Go on, hit her!

No! Piss off!

The Beast does.

I play 'Someone To Watch Over Me', and again she sings, but louder this time. She knows all the words and by the end of the song I realise she has a good voice. Extremely good.

'Here's a challenge,' she says. 'Do you know any Sondheim?'

There is a God . . .

'Yup! He's one of my heroes.'

'Really?' she says, excited. 'Mine too! Come on, let's do something.'

'Are you a singer?'

'Actress, but I've done cabaret as well.'

'Well, what about, I dunno, "Broadway Baby"?'

'Ha!' she exclaims. 'One of my audition songs.'

Which is all that needs to be said, and as I begin the sassy intro, her posture shifts almost imperceptibly and she slides into performer mode. She knows what she's doing. There's an instant rapport. Without having to look, I know instinctively where she wants to slow down or speed up, where she wants to build, or relax a little. Like riding a tandem, our pedal pushes synchronise. It's exciting and sensual.

Gradually, a small crowd gathers around to listen, and during the enthusiastic applause when we finish, the tiniest of glances passes between us; a glance which says, 'We're both in our element here, performing and being applauded . . . and . . . we'll end up in bed together tonight.'

Which we do.

Her name is Miranda, and I become instantly addicted.

*   *   *   *   *

During the first couple of months, revelling in the novelty of a new relationship, we do everything that new couples do; mostly at weekends because she's still at drama school and on weekdays she rehearses late into the evenings. Given my working hours, this should fit nicely, but in reality she's almost always too tired to do anything except go straight to bed.

But at weekends we learn each other. We spend hours around my piano, singing Gershwin, Kern, Porter, Sondheim – all our heroes. I play her some of the songs from my still unfinished *Canterville Ghost* musical.

I'm happy. The Beast doesn't appear to bother her; like Jenny was at first, she seems intrigued by it, despite the fact that, as my drinking has increased so too has the Beast's activities when I'm sober. I'm checking the door latches now, tapping them in odd numbers to make sure they're shut properly. I'm checking light switches, buttons on my radio and cassette machine, not convinced they're off even though I can plainly see they are. I don't trust electricity.

I'm compelled to memorise the number plates of parked cars as I walk along the street, the challenge being that having memorised five sets of numbers, one after the other, I have to try and remember the first one again. If I can't I have to walk back to the first car to check its plate again. I must look odd walking up and down the street, retracing my steps for no apparent reason, bending over each snugly parked car in order to see its number plate. But I have no choice. I think of some future undecided event in my life, and if I can remember the first number plate, then the outcome will be favourable. If not, then it will go badly for me. If I get it wrong, I have to do it again and again until I get it right. That way, in some strange manner I feel able to control my destiny.

I am still able to work. I'm still writing *The Canterville Ghost* but the music comes far more easily than the lyrics. I don't think I'm cut out to be a lyricist; but I am making progress. It's hard work. Much harder than Stephen Sondheim or Richard Rodgers or George Gershwin or Cole Porter or Jerome Kern or Kander and Ebb or Cy Coleman or Noel Coward or Lionel Bart or Julian Slade or Sandy Wilson or Frank Loesser or Leonard Bernstein make it seem.

But Miranda is the first person ever to comment on my drinking.

One Sunday afternoon after lunch, we decide to go for a walk. As usual, on the way out of the kitchen I touch the fridge several times to make sure we have a safe trip. On top of the fridge is a half-empty bottle of whisky. Without really thinking, but somewhere in the back of my mind feeling it might look quite sophisticated, I pick it up, open it and take a short swig, put the top back on and replace the bottle.

Turning, ready to leave, I see Miranda standing quite still, staring at me.

'What are you doing?!' she asks, incredulity in her voice.

Feeling suddenly guilty, like a naughty schoolboy who's been caught stealing sweets, I look over at the bottle, then back at her.

'Just having a quick swig,' I say, grinning, surprised at her surprise.

'A quick swig!' she echoes. 'That wasn't a quick swig; that was a gulp!'

'It wasn't a gulp!'

'Yes it was.'

She studies me for a moment and comes to some kind of sudden conclusion, as if seeing something in me she's never seen before.

'Do you realise,' she says, pointing at the whisky, 'you've just drunk straight from the bottle!'

'So what!' I shrug. 'What's wrong with that?' I'm defensive now, embarrassed.

'What's wrong with it? It's not normal; that's what's wrong with it! James,' she says, suddenly patient, as though explaining something fundamental to an impetuous child, 'normal people don't drink straight from the bottle . . . they just don't; specially in the middle of the afternoon.'

''Course they do! It was only a quick after-lunch swig, for God's sake.'

'It's not normal, James,' she says, shaking her head gently from side to side, 'it's not.' A beat. 'That's what alcoholics do . . .'

'Alcoholics!' I say aghast, anger rising. 'Alcoholics! I'm not an alcoholic! Alcoholics sit on park benches swigging meths! I am *not* an alcoholic!'

Silence. She looks shocked at my outburst.

She backs down, sighing resignedly. 'Okay . . . sorry . . . come on then, let's go.'

But I can't leave it like that. Guilt – or the fear of losing her – makes me need to finish it, to make it right with her. I put my arm round her shoulders as we walk up the street, anger giving way to a need for reassurance.

'Darling,' I say, chuckling as though the idea were ridiculous, 'I'm not an alcoholic; honestly I'm not.'

She doesn't reply and we continue in silence. As we walk, the Beast makes sure that my footsteps are in time with hers – seven steps exactly together or I won't marry her. Okay, how about nine? Good, now eleven. Great! I'll marry her. I'm going to marry her . . .

Seven-sixteen-twenty-seven, seven-sixteen-twentyseven, seven-sixteen-twentyseven, seven-sixteen-twentyseven, seven-sixteen-twentyseven. Sess sess sess sess sess sess sess!

'Fine!' I say, hating the silence, still wanting to make it right. 'Okay, maybe it is a bit unusual not using a glass . . . but you can't seriously think I'm an alcoholic!?'

Another pause.

She sighs again.

'So, where are we going?' she says, changing the subject.

Miranda has the same tantalising reticence I found so magnetic in Jenny. Somehow, however close we get, she holds part of herself back. I'm not even sure she knows she's doing it, but slowly she draws me further into her web until I'm emotionally bound and gagged.

She never seems to need me the way I need her. I think about her all the time. I want to be near her, to be able to touch her. I want to wear her – like clothes. She is the obsession I can never get right. Every night I ring her – from a phone box in Lawton's if I'm working – hoping beyond hope that this will be the one night during the week that she won't be too tired and she'll let me go round to her flat.

But gradually, as with Jenny, the first fragile excuses begin to appear; the tiny symptoms of distancing emerge. The kiss that's not as passionate as it used to be. The cuddle that's not quite so enthusiastic. The lovemaking that feels almost dutiful. As with Jenny, I agonise over her, dream up ways to get her back, imagine scenarios in which I do, rescuing her from rape and death at the hands of muggers, saving her from fire, from drowning, from a nuclear attack. But finally, one Saturday morning, when I turn up at her flat unexpectedly to take her out for a 'surprise' breakfast, she comes to the door . . .

'James!' She seems genuinely surprised, shocked almost, and quickly half-shuts the door behind her so I can't see into the flat. 'What are you *doing* here?' She's speaking unusually quietly.

'I came to see you. I just thought I'd take you out for breakfast. Sort of surprise.' I grin, though I'm desperately nervous.

'Oh, darling, I'd love to, but we didn't finish until midnight last night and I'm not feeling too good this morning. Can I ring you later? Sorry.'

'Well, can't I have a cup of coffee?'

'Not now, darling,' she says, too quickly. 'I think I've got some kind of bug, I really want to go back to bed. Do you mind?'

I see movement through the crack in the door behind her; just a flicker, but it's enough.

'Who's that?'

She glances hurriedly behind her, then back at me. 'No one,' she says dismissively, now anxious herself. 'Look . . . please, James, can I give you a ring later? I can't talk now.'

'Why not? Who is it in there?' I'm starting to feel sick because I already know the answer.

There's a long, long pause, during which her body noticeably slumps and then she sighs, defeated.

'A . . . friend,' she says again, this time closing her eyes, adding, 'from college.'

We stare at each other.

'I'm sorry, James,' she says finally.

There's nothing else to say. I can't think of anything to say *anyway* except 'bitch' or 'slut', but they only come to me as, heart pounding, I'm walking numbly down the street a few minutes later.

Fucking bitch!

Slut! Slag!

Slut slag! Slut slag slut slag slut slag! But I can't do it properly.

And then I smile.

As wide as I can; and the Beast Brigadier interrupts:

'It's all rather fun, really!'

'Rather good fun!'

'I *must* say! It's all really rather fun! Don't you think? Mmm?'

'Rather fun!'

'Fun! Fun! Rather good fun!'

I sink into a quicksand of depression, self-pity and anger.

I begin lone drinking in the daytime. Not every day. Not to begin with.

Every time I think of Miranda, of my humiliation on her doorstep and the bastard who's now sleeping with her, I get attacks of rage, and when I'm drunk I scream and I punch the wall with my fists as if the wallpaper itself is to blame.

I feel directionless. I feel as I always have: as though I've missed something; as though I've got life terribly wrong somewhere. I watch through the downstairs window as smart, suited city-boys my age walk by or drive in their new Golf GTIs, having learned the 'how to do life' thing, happy, secure, confident.

'Fuck 'em all!' I think. 'Fuck . . . them . . . all! And fuck *her!* Bitch!'

I'm still able to function, I'm not a complete physical wreck, and my spirits lift a few months later when a friend introduces me to budding lyricist Kit Hesketh-Harvey. He's one half of an up-and-coming cabaret duo, Kit and the Widow, and when we discover we both want to write musicals, he gives me tickets to a Kit and the Widow gig at the King's Head theatre in Islington.

I'm bowled over by his cabaret lyrics, which fairly hum with technical brilliance and wit. They demonstrate the extent to which I am limited in my own lyric-writing abilities. I'm desperate to collaborate with him, but when I meet him after the show, I adopt a rather patronising professorial tone.

'What did you think?' he asks.

'Mmm,' I say, 'there's some nice writing there. I liked the song about Spain . . . and the one about Norwegians on the Underground, but . . . I dunno . . . it's a bit "wordy" sometimes; you might want to think about making it a little simpler.'

'Oh,' he says, as if I'm some sort of theatrical oracle, 'maybe you're right.'

But I'm not right. I'm lying. I don't want him to know just how brilliant I think he is, in case he thinks I'm too easily impressed. I feel so stupid afterwards.

However, I send him a tape of some of my songs. He says he likes them, which amazes me, so we meet up again to think of ideas for a musical. At first I suggest that he might like to rewrite my lyrics for the (now abandoned) *Canterville Ghost* but he doesn't seem that interested.

From the beginning, he takes my obsessions and twitches in his stride, but I remain convinced that once he 'finds me out', once he discovers that I'm not up to his intellectual level, he'll ditch me and find another composer. By now, I think of myself as quite well-read, but in these first days and weeks, trawling through literature, searching for a suitable story to adapt, I realise I'm hopelessly out of my depth. Kit's conversation is littered with one-liners and literary jokes. Half the time I don't know what the fuck he's on about but I try to make sure I laugh in all the right places so I don't look like an idiot. He never means to confuse or belittle and he isn't trying to impress. I think he naturally assumes I'm as knowledgeable as he is – which, I suppose, is a compliment.

He treats me as an absolute equal and does far more than he probably realises to boost my self-confidence as a composer.

We're very different – me, the obsessive, unable to do anything by halves; him, the calm, self-assured, erudite charmer.

Kit turns out to be a bit of a sucker for lavish frocks and anything where questionable gender issues crop up. Aiming too high, in my view, but bowing to his 'why ever not' approach to life, I finally go along with his suggestion that we tackle the Virginia Woolf novel *Orlando*, as well as examining Woolf's relationship with Vita Sackville-West in parallel.

I read it.

The story: boy lives for four hundred years, becoming girl halfway through.

It's a huge, sprawling thing that demands sumptuous sets and costumes and a vast cast. There are gypsy scenes, dockside scenes, English country-house scenes, a court in

Constantinople, a frost fair on the Thames, eighteenth-century tea parties, nineteenth-century ballrooms and many others. I become obsessed with it.

As with piano playing, composing leaves me twitch-free. Though not in the same way. Playing a piano piece is a 'whole' thing. I start, I play for however long the piece lasts and then I stop. It is an uninterrupted process; there are no gaps – mistakes notwithstanding. Thus, for the duration of the piece the Beast is quiet.

Composing is not an uninterrupted process. There are numerous little stops and starts and in some ways it mirrors the process of twitching. I start with a three- or four-note phrase. I don't know where it comes from; perhaps it emerges; I can never remember, but somehow it presents itself. So there I have it. Three or four notes. I play those three or four notes over again and again, like a compulsion, adding harmony in my left hand, then trying different variations in the harmony.

Eventually, the next note or notes just appear, for no apparent reason, and tack themselves on to the end of the three- or four-note phrase. Sometimes they're right, sometimes they're not, in which case I dismiss them and go on until another, better possibility appears. So I now have notes five and six. I repeat the process from the beginning and go on repeating it until it feels 'right' and I get notes seven and eight. This, for me, is composing. It's a series of ever-increasing repetitions, just like the twitches and compulsions.

While I'm actually composing, that is, playing the repeated phrases to myself, I'm as twitch-free as I am when I play a piano piece. The twitches occur *between* the phrases: I come to the end of a phrase, then I need to tap the piano or kick one of its legs or hit my head or make a face.

The Beast also appears within the music. It can be an isolated event, a note or a chord which musically juts out – not ridiculously so; it must fit. Or it can be something in the tone of the song's accompaniment: a jolt, a hit or a 'pressing' feeling. It's a twitch, a compulsion, and without it the music feels incomplete.

Finally I write the music down in pencil on cream-coloured manuscript paper. I write it obsessively neatly, which takes for ever because the Beast is never happy until it's absolutely perfect. I get through rubbers far more quickly than pencils because one note can sometimes take up to ten rubbings-out to get right. The result, visually, is always perfect.

Kit, however, isn't perfect. At times he drives me mad.

I've become so obsessed with *Orlando* that I'm interested in little else. I either sit at the piano bashing away or I pound the streets of Battersea where I now live, walking 'in rhythm' for miles sometimes, trying to resolve a troublesome phrase going round and round in my head.

Kit, on the other hand, is in increasing demand from other quarters. He and the Widow are on the up and up, which means that K and the W's paid gigs take precedence over what he and I are doing 'on spec'. Consequently, there are long stretches when he's unable to give any time to *Orlando* and I get way ahead musically. I ring him constantly.

'Please, *please* can you finish the Gypsies lyric, I need a couple of extra lines in the last verse and I can't finish it without them!'

'Sure,' he says, 'give me a couple of days.'

Which in Kit-speak, could be two weeks.

He's so bloody reasonable and laid-back about everything! Doesn't he *realise* that at twenty-eight we're about to make theatrical history?

Occasionally I use my frustration as an excuse to revert to 'misunderstood genius', sign off for the day and sit morosely with my friend Mr Carlsberg for the afternoon watching old black and white films on television.

Something my mother says – on one of the increasingly rare weekends I go home – makes me realise that my alcohol intake is becoming even more noticeable to others. They are having a dinner party, and before the guests arrive my mother takes me aside.

'Now, Jamie, please behave nicely tonight, will you, darling?'

'Yes, Mum,' I reply in a laboured tone.

'And, darling, *please* don't drink too much.'

I know she's right. I know I drink too much, but stopping is unthinkable.

I *can* control it. That's the point. I *can* stop if I put my mind to it, I really can; for three or four days in a row sometimes.

But then I can't. Not once I start. One drink seems to set me off on a kind of rollercoaster which I can't stop until I'm completely drunk.

I know it's not about soothing the Beast any more. I know that.

But I can't help it and I *hate* that I can't help it.

And I know it's affecting me.

In small ways, at first.

Like my concentration, which seems to have deteriorated. My mind wanders off somewhere and suddenly I come to and realise that quarter of an hour has passed . . .

But I'm still playing at Lawton's, so it can't be that bad.

And my perfect pitch – the ability I have to identify any note just by hearing it – has also deteriorated, becoming fuzzy. Listening to a piece of music on the radio, I can no longer be absolutely sure what key it's in. I get it wrong sometimes. I never used to . . .

But Kit is feeding me lyrics at last, and I *am* working and *Orlando* is coming along, so it's not *that* serious.

Then there's my short-term memory. I don't have a diary or a telephone book. I've never had one. I can remember whole rafts of numbers and dates, so I've never needed them. Until now. I even forgot my *parents'* telephone number briefly the other day . . .

But *Orlando* is nearly finished and when we hear about a newly established competition, the Vivian Ellis Prize, to find up-and-coming musical theatre writers, we submit it.

And sometimes, when I've driven somewhere, I arrive and suddenly realise I can't remember the journey . . .

But *Orlando* survives the first round and from the original five hundred entries it makes it into the last one hundred, which is fantastic.

And I'm okay first thing in the morning – even with a hangover. I can still write music. My mind's clear and the ideas flow. Until lunchtime, that is, when it stops . . .

But *Orlando* survives the second round and gets through to the final fifty, which is amazing.

And I get tired easily and when I go to the shops I wonder if I'm being watched, which is ridiculous because I know I'm not but I can't shake the feeling and I get angry with roadworks and aeroplanes and passing cars and neighbours and the oven and the fridge and coffee lids and teaspoons . . .

But *Orlando* gets through to the final five musicals, extracts from which will be performed in front of a live audience at the Guildhall School of Music and Drama in London.

Which is incredible.

The End

There's a Greer Garson film on.
    They're doing a season of her films at the moment.
    Vodka and Garson.
    She loves Ronald Colman so *completely* . . .
    I could love like that.
    If I found the right person.
    I can feel tears . . .
    Because it seems such a waste.
    Not to have someone to love.
    Oh fuck it!
    One day . . .
    For now . . .
    Just pour . . .

Chapter 14
The Downhill Schuss

Christ, I'm nervous.

My body's pumping with it.

Pulsating like a speeded-up electric fence.

Phwoom, phwoom, phwoom, phwoom, phwoom.

I've got a terrible hangover and I'm sweating slightly.

Violent head twitches, side to side.

I'm trying to push my foot through the seat in front.

Its annoyed occupant turns to stare.

'Sorry,' I say.

Sit rigidly still.

Shit! Ashamed.

Shit,shit,shit,shit,shit.

He turns away again.

Why can't they hurry *up*?

It's been half an hour, for God's sake.

What's *keeping* them?

The audience is restless . . . expectant.

Except Kit, of course . . . next to me; un-fucking-fazed as usual . . . cool as face cream.

Probably planning dinner or something.

Nothing seems to *worry* him . . . ever!

'Wonder why they chose purple,' he says idly, examining the seats.

'Kit, how can you think about the fucking *seats*?'

No answer; then he says, 'I think blue would've been better.'

Urghh!

How come *I'm* always the one who panics?

Never *him*.

Is it nature?

Nurture?

Valium in his cot?

Cot.

Kit.

Cot Kit.

CotKit**Cot**.

I've got my **Cot**kit.

My **cot**kit is **cooked**.

I'm cooking my **kit**cot.

Kit! My cot is cooked!

Cot! My cook is Kitted!

Cotkitcotkitcotkitcotkitki-ki-ki-**ki-ki-ki-ki!**

Oh **fuck** off.

I could do with a drink.

Vodka . . . bitter lemon.

I *love* . . . bitter . . . lemon.

Oh come *on!*

How long does it *take* to judge a competition, for fuck's sake!

You've *heard* the music, *heard* the lyrics, *heard* the story, given your comments.

Just . . . fucking . . . ***choose***!

One of the judges is Tim Rice.

It was all I could do not to shout when he was talking.

Anything would've done . . . just to wreck it.

'*EVITA*'S UTTER CRAP!!!'

Evita's not crap, but that's not the point.

I didn't *want* to wreck it; of course I didn't.

I just wanted to know what would have *happened*.

Would he have ignored me?

Maybe he'd have come back with a crushing reply.

Maybe I'd have been thrown out of the building.

It was just the sight of the nine of them.

Sitting there . . . grave.

Nine judges in a semi circle at the front of the stage.

Suited and smart.

Formal.

Balanced.

Deciding my future.

'MY MILKMAN'S A LESBIAN!'

Stupid! Really *stupid*! Not even clever!

Maybe if they all took their trousers off. And stood with their ties and shirt tails hanging down over their pants, it would undercut it and I wouldn't need to.

Ah! At *last*!

I tap Kit on the shoulder. 'Here they come.'

He looks up.

In they walk again . . . the nine.

The chosen ones . . . to choose.

Clipboards under arms, overflowing with gravitas, to deliver the verdict.

My nerves ratchet up a notch; my heart's pounding in the way it does before you kiss a girl for the first time. Mum – a few rows in front – turns to me and mouths 'good luck'. She looks as nervous as I feel.

And the judges sit; except Don Black, the chairman, who walks to the microphone and such is the state of my nerves I find it impossible to hear anything clearly.

But I get snippets . . . while I fidget. And the Beast feels like a caged animal.

'Very difficult decision . . . high standard of work . . . should all be very proud . . . achievements . . . wonderful performances . . . Guildhall students . . . talent . . . Rasputin (huh!?) . . . lunch afterwards . . . now we come . . . wish you all . . . we decided . . . originality . . . but the winner is . . . *Orlando* . . .'

Applause.

Huge.

Whistles.

Shouts.

Kit stands, but I hesitate.

It *can't* be me.

What if I've got it wrong?

What if it's some other *Orlando* – nothing to do with me?

What if it's a ghastly mistake?

I'll walk through the audience, on to the stage and there'll be a sudden dreadful hush.

'Erm – terribly sorry,' Don will say, 'I didn't mean *your Orlando*, I meant the *other* one.'

Or: 'Oh heavens! Did I say *Orlando*? I'm sorry; what I meant to say was ——.'

And I'd have to walk back to my seat, past all those faces, having failed.

But I follow Kit, hastily tapping the arm rest of my seat seven times in panic and for luck, down through the audience, pausing to tap my right foot three times on the edge of the stage before stepping on to it, still not believing it.

And we walk over to collect our certificates and our prize money and I shake hands with all the panel members and we're photographed and the audience is still clapping and when at last I can see that it's not some huge mistake after all, I start to relax and suddenly I realise ... I've actually *achieved* something. These people are clapping *me*! I have a certificate which proves it in gold lettering:

The Performing Right Society Limited
is delighted to award The Vivian Ellis Prize
to James McConnel and Kit Hesketh-Harvey for Orlando.

We're standing there, alone now, centre stage, the theatre lights so bright on my face I can't see the audience at all and I wonder what I look like. And for this moment ... this one, glorious, celestial moment, I'm completely ... completely ... happy.

Kit seems quite pleased, too.

I ... feel ... like ... celebrating!

There's lunch. Lots of lunch.

And lots of booze.

I sit with my parents and Polly.

Complete strangers are coming up to me and saying 'Well done' and 'Congratulations' and 'Here's my card' and my mother looks on proudly as if I've finally arrived and ...

For some reason, I feel left out.

When my parents leave to catch the early train home and

Polly has to get back to work, I find myself watching Kit cruise the room in that effortless way he always does.

I go and sit with the actors – feeling more comfortable with them than having to talk myself up to producers and directors – and I drink and I drink and I drink.

And I think: I've done enough for one day, it'll all be fine tomorrow; but for now I can relax . . . and celebrate.

A month later, I receive a letter from the Guildhall School of Music and Drama saying that in the light of the Vivian Ellis Prize, and because the Barbican are this year focusing on music by British composers, they are considering mounting a full-scale production of *Orlando* for their end-of-year student production and would Kit and I be interested?

'Oh that'd be nice,' says Kit.

'Fuck off. It's bloody brilliant!' I say, and promptly go out and buy a bottle of vodka to drown my happiness.

And *Orlando* goes into rehearsals.

It may be a drama student cast, but it's run as if it's a professional production.

I keep wondering when they're going to find me out, realise that in fact I'm not a real composer after all and that somehow I've pinched the music from somewhere else and passed it off as my own.

And how am I going to sit for hours in the rehearsal room without twitching and causing a distraction?

The first week is given up to music rehearsals for the actors to learn the songs. Aside from the Vivian Ellis workshop performances and one or two sessions in a recording studio to make the demo tape, this is the first time

I've ever heard a whole chorus singing something I've written. They're actually singing my music. They're singing the very notes I spent all those hours writing down in pencil at my green piano in my little Battersea house, and somehow it's coming out of their mouths exactly as I'd intended. It works! It really works!

And . . . what's more, they're taking it seriously – as if it's *real* music.

God, it's weird.

But exciting . . . and the Beast is likewise far too intrigued to interrupt much.

But when we get to the drama itself, when two or three intense, uninterrupted hours creep by while a couple of actors go over a non-singing scene with Peter the director, requiring great concentration, repeating it, honing and changing it . . . I can't sit still.

In the hushed rehearsal atmosphere, knowing I absolutely *have* to makes it impossible.

Neck jerk, head jerk, face-making. I can't relax.

Even Kit, who has the concentration of a bomb-disposal expert, shoots one or two impatient glances in my direction.

I have a new compulsion.

I have to close my mouth, puff out my cheeks and try to compress the enclosed air as hard as I can so that my cheeks bulge to bursting point. Once the pain reaches a certain point and it feels 'right', I can relax again.

Occasionally, as now, my lips simply can't take the pressure, they part slightly and the resulting explosive 'fart' makes everyone jump.

Pairs of eyes and heads swivel in my direction.

Shit.

'Sorry.'

I work out a coping strategy. I always make sure I sit at the end of the table nearest the wall, as often as possible with Kit sitting next to me on the other side. Using the musical score as a shield – I've printed it out extra-large in A3 format – I stand it on its end, open, in front of my face, and when I need to twitch, I lower my head, pretend to examine some musical detail and am therefore free to make faces without being seen. It doesn't stop the 'farting' explosions but it probably mutes them a little.

It doesn't always work – it can't – and before long, everybody begins to notice, but after the initial peculiar looks, people seem to get used to it.

Gradually the show takes shape. The actors learn their lines, the atmosphere becomes heightened and urgent and we have 'run-throughs' without costumes, then run-throughs *with* costumes, then run-throughs with costumes and sets, then run-throughs with costumes and sets and the orchestra, then run-throughs with costumes and sets and the orchestra and the lighting, and then the first night with an audience and second night and third and fourth and so on, and I'm nervous and excitable and manic and happy and impatient and I hear clapping and laughter and shuffling and coughing and the Beast is going haywire and I wreck the performances for my neighbours but I'm on a high so I don't give a shit and because I know every word off by heart I mouth along silently waiting for the really good bits and at the end of each night's performance I go up on stage with Kit and the audience applauds us and cheers us and says 'More' and people come up to me afterwards and say 'Well done' and 'Congratulations' and 'You've got a bright future' and we do interviews and the critics come and they write about us and our names appear in the papers and mostly they like it and there are parties and parties and parties and once it's all over and all the excitement has died down . . .

There's a sickening lull.

Which feels as though someone has died.

And I go back to Battersea.

And I sit, missing the fact that for a while I belonged, I truly belonged to something which no longer exists and I wonder what the fuck will come next.

And again . . .

And again . . .

And again . . .

I seek solace with my friends.

The Carlsbergs and the Smirnovs.

I have a routine.

First thing in the morning, if I've been out the previous night, I ring my host . . . just in case. Because I can't remember.

Did I do anything?

Did I?

'Hi.'

I feel terrible.

'Just wanted to say . . . sorry . . . if I did anything . . . ghastly last night.'

And I grit my teeth and close my eyes . . . shit.

Sometimes it's, 'Darling, what on *earth* are you apologising for? We were *all* absolutely *out* of it; I don't think you were worse than anybody *else*, were you?'

I don't *know*. Was I? Wasn't I?

But increasingly there's a stony silence, followed by a quiet but firm, 'All right . . . but *please* don't do it again.'

Guilt; sudden. 'Oh God, I'm sorry; what did I do?' Panic now.

Pause.

'Look, it doesn't matter . . . James . . . you're a lovely guy, you really are . . . but when you drink too much . . . you're just . . . horrible.'

I sit in fogged, hung-over shame, trying to remember.

And some of it returns.

'*Christ*, you're ugly!'

It sounded so *funny* at the time.

How could you have said that!?

Jesus! Poor girl.

And I cringe . . . and I curl.

'Bitty Chang Chang, Bitty Chitty Bang Chang, we love you,' I mutter.

Ah! God! Fuck!

Breakfast: two or three paracetamol for my head, washed down with several cups of strong coffee.

Can't do food in the mornings; makes me feel sick.

Think of cheese soufflé – thick . . . cheesy . . . sick-making . . . soufflé . . .

Make yourself feel sick.

Concentrate on cheese soufflé.

Visualise the yellow nellow kellow rellow zellow-ness of it.

Come on, climb *inside* the cheese soufflé.

Bathe in cheese soufflé.

Become cheesy weesy meesy feesy keesy soufflé.

Be the very essence of soufflé-ness.

Stop it!

Then a bath.

I always have a bath. I can think in a bath. The bathroom's a different world and sometimes I have three baths a day.

It's peaceful; unconnected; safe.

Until the Beast wakes – to play with the soap. It's slidey and slippery and indecisive.

And when I slam it down it doesn't stop moving immediately.

It moves. It always moves. Just the tiniest amount.

So I slam it down again . . .

And again . . .

And again . . .

And I keep on slamming down until it doesn't move. Until it's fucking dead! Until it's right! Until it does as *I* command!

Bastard soap!

And bastard lavatory.

Lift the top lid: up down up down up down and check and check and look look look look look for spiders and rats and crocodiles and psychopathic gannets . . .

The Birds. Ever since I saw the Hitchcock film, I imagine birds coming up through the U-bend to peck, to zoom up my bottom, to kill me.

Same with the bottom lid. Examine the porcelain, really *examine* it, close up. Any dot of dirt or hair or . . . anything . . . *has* to go. Wipe it away, scrub scrub scrub scrub scrub.

A rush, a rustle of water and something could grab me; a piranha.

Check it check check check check . . .

Then in my dressing gown, towel draped round my neck, hair wet, I sit at the piano for an hour, or maybe two.

Until about twelve o'clock.

Or until I've achieved something. Even one new note.

As long as I've moved on from where I was the previous day.

Progress, however small.

Then I deserve it.

And I can **think** . . .

Of the first **drink** . . .

Oh what'll it **be**?

Tee hee **hee**!

But there's always a brief internal skirmish, and never any shortage of good reasons.

I've been working hard, I deserve a reward . . .

For heaven's sake, you're only young once, live a little . . .

What would Toulouse-Lautrec do . . . ?

I haven't got to go to work tonight, I can celebrate . . .

I'm feeling low, I need a pick-me-up . . .

The Beast is driving me insane . . .

I'm a genius . . .

And once dressed, I trot.

Or maybe I jaunt.

Yes, I jaunt, excited, overflowing with 'tee hee hee', to the small supermarket at the corner and buy a newspaper and three cans of Special Brew.

It has to be three.

I can't buy anything in even numbers, be it bananas, light bulbs, or blank cassettes.

Anything.

Shoes and socks come in twos, but as a pair they count as one. Most things are bought in ones, particularly expensive things. I don't know how I'd cope if I had to buy in even numbers – the house would be full of useless duplicates; two typewriters, two fridges, two stereo systems.

It wouldn't, of course, but it would feel uncomfortable.

Mrs Patel at the checkout smiles; she never comments. She just smiles; and says, 'Good morning!'

Like Julie Andrews.

Mary Poppins-Patel.

I smile back. It's a neighbourly smile. A cheerful, jovial smile.

I'm a happy neighbour . . . I'm Dick Van Dyke.

'Oh, it's a jolly 'oliday with Missis Patel . . .'

I'm just a local resident who comes into her shop every morning and buys three cans of Special Brew.

That's all.

Perfectly normal. Happy happy happy . . .

I *like* Mrs Patel. She's attractive; elegant.

Mrs Patel, I think, likes me.

She smiles as though she likes me.

I expect she likes everyone.

She probably smiles at everyone too.

Guilt.

Mrs Patel is non-judgemental.

She's letting me buy these things and she doesn't say a word.

Not: 'Having a party, James?'

Not: 'Gosh, you really like your beer, don't you, James!'

Not: 'Haven't you got a fucking job to go to, James?!'

Except she wouldn't say that, because I doubt Mrs Patel swears.

Ever.

She smiles. That's what she does.

I've bought tampons from Mrs Patel (for Miranda). She smiled then too.

And nail varnish.

'A pound of dog shit and two kilos of heroin please, Mrs Patel.'

I know she'd smile.

Opening the first can is a ritual.

The Beast delays that first glorious swig. I poke at the top of the can countless times with my little finger.

This can take up to three minutes to get 'right'.

It's painful and frustrating and sometimes I cut my finger on the sharp edge and I get irritated with the can and the Beast and myself and I swear because I'm angry.

Hit! **'Stop it!'** Hit! **'Just fucking stop it!'** Hit hit! 'Fuck . . . **off!'**

I won't drink more than one. I know I won't. Just one.

I'm not going to get drunk, after all.

Well, okay, but I certainly won't have more than two.

The Beast is gone by now.

Somewhere in the middle of can three I give up.

And come to a decision.

Having run out of booze and having never planned it this way, I go to a different off-licence. I can't face Mrs Patel; I can't bear to see her smiling, non-judgemental face again until tomorrow. I buy a bottle of spirits, either vodka or gin, or . . . anything.

I mix it with whatever's in the fridge, be it tonic or Coke or orange juice. Tomato soup or consommé sometimes, if there's nothing else. There's always a can of consommé in the kitchen. I don't know where it comes from or who buys it, but there it sits at the back of the cupboard, often for months or years gathering dust. But whatever I do there's always *one* left.

Then I organise myself.

I like to be very organised before jumping aboard the Oblivion Express.

I close the curtains. I take off my shoes. I check the door. I check it again. Locked.

The postman's been.

Brown envelopes and letters from the bank go in the wicker waste-paper basket.

Kick the basket. Crush it with my foot. Then stroke it with my big toe.

Nothing must be too far away from my chair. The newspaper, the TV remote control, my cigarettes and lighter . . . the drink.

I'm calm. I sit.

And I settle in for the two- or three-hour journey to Oblivion.

The train makes various stops on the way:

Confidence

Fuck the bank! Only two thousand quid overdrawn. Deal with it later. It's fine! One day when the bastards realise *just* how much of a genius I am they'll come crawling to me *begging* to lend me money! But I won't need it. Ha!

Enthusiasm

God, this feels fan*tastic*! Vodka after beer. Nothing like it.

'Oh, it's a jolly 'oliday with Missis Patel . . .

Missis Patel makes the world go round . . .'

I quite fancy Mrs Patel.

Mrs Patel is elegant.

Me and Mrs Patel . . . wonder what her first name is.

'And here is a picture of Mr and Mrs James McConnel-Patel on their wedding day. Mrs McConnel-Patel wowed the crowd in her Safeway uniform as the number 45 bus whisked the happy couple away . . .'

Maybe she's called Rani Patel, or something like that.

Can't think of any other Asian names.

Not even sure if Rani's a name *anyway*.
Probably muddled it up with Maharaja and Maharani.
Yes. Course it is. Ha!
Patel.
Patella.
Kneecap.
Kneecap Patel.
Leg Patel.
Wholebody Patel.
What about . . .
Melanie Patel.
No way!
Karen.
Karen Patel.
Karen . . . Patel.
That works, but it can't be her name.

Hope

Fuck it. It'll all be okay tomorrow.
Just enjoy it. Seize the moment!

Anger

'Oh turn that *fucking* noise off!' (Loud bass beat next door from the neighbours.) And I jump up out of the chair and I scream and I shout and I kick the wall again and again and again until I kick a hole in it. I hate.

Curiosity

What would happen if I never woke up again?
Would I mind?
Would I?

Lying

The phone rings.

'Hello.'

'Hello, darling.'

'Oh hi, Mum, how are you?' Concentrate, just concentrate . . . sound normal.

'I'm fine. Haven't spoken to you for while, that's all. Are you all right?'

'Yes, I'm just . . . sort of . . . quite busy really . . .'

'Oh good, what are you up to?'

'I dunno. Reading; Kit and I are looking for new ideas.'

'Well, that's rather exciting, isn't it?'

'Yes. We just can't find anything.'

'Oh well, I expect something'll turn up. Are you *all right*, darling? You sound a bit funny; are you eating properly?'

'I'm *fine*; just a bit tired.' Get off the phone!

'It's probably all those late nights you have; I'm sure it's not good for you. You *will* try and get some sleep, won't you?'

'Mum, I'll be okay.'

'I know you will, but I *do* worry sometimes, you work much too hard.'

'I'm fine, Mum, really I am.' And I hang up.

Despair

No, I wouldn't much care if I never woke up.

And there's grime on the window.

And the sky's overcast.

And I'm safe in my little house with its hideous brown carpet, so what does it matter?

So fuck it! Just die . . .

*   *   *   *   *

And we pull into Oblivion City at about two thirty . . .

    And suddenly, all's well.

    Until much, much later.

    When I wake.

    And it's a *Coronation Street* night again.

    Like so many times before.

    And the chair's wet *again*.

    And my trousers are wet *again*.

    And this time something has shifted.

    Changed gear.

    Downwards.

    And I know that if want to live . . .

    Because that's one choice . . .

    If I really *do* . . . want . . . to live . . .

    And not die . . .

    Because that's the other choice . . .

    Then I can't do this any more.

    I CAN'T DO THIS . . . ANY MORE.

Chapter 15
Summer Pudding and Friends

'Welcome to this meeting of Alcoholics Anonymous. My name's John and I'm an alcoholic.'

How can he just *say* that?

He doesn't even *look* like an alcoholic. Suit and tie; he looks too healthy.

Late middle age, respectable.

There's a grey-haired woman next to him, about fifty.

'Hi, John!' everyone says enthusiastically.

I look round, slightly startled. Christ, hope this isn't a happy-clappy cult. The woman on the phone sounded normal enough.

'I've asked Rachel to read the preamble.'

What's the preamble?

No one's said a word to me yet, apart from a 'hello' at the door.

'Hi. My name's Rachel and I'm an alcoholic.'

I turn in the direction of the voice.

Now, she *does* look like an alcoholic. Fuck, she looks *terrible*! Her face.

'Hi, Rachel!' everyone says, equally enthusiastically.

Go on, urges the Beast, shout **'BET YOU'D ALL LIKE A LARGE WHISKY!'**

Stop it!

Rachel reads: *'Alcoholics Anonymous is a fellowship of men and women . . .'*

FACE LIKE A SUMMER PUDDING!

Summer pudding! Summer pudding! Summerpudding! Smuddng! Smng!

' . . . who share their experience, strength and hope with each other . . .'

A parody of the lyrics from the musical *Grease* pops into my head.

Summer pudding, had me a blast . . .

Summer pudding, happened so fast . . . SPLAT!!!

Shut up! Concentrate . . .

' . . . that they may solve their common problem and help others to recover from alcoholism . . .'

Recover? What d'you mean 'recover'? I'm not ill! I just drink too much.

Hate this Styrofoam coffee cup . . . too delicate . . . yuck . . . want to crush it . . .

Smash it . . .

Stop it!

Calm . . . **down.**

'The only requirement for membership is a desire to stop drinking.'

Christ yes, I want to stop drinking.

Feel terrible. I've been drunk for three days. A final fling.

'There are no dues or fees for AA membership . . .'

My God! That woman over there! I know her!

Can't remember her name. Shit! What's she doing here?

' . . . *we are self-supporting through our own contributions . . .*'

She's seen me.

She's smiling at me! Mouths 'Hello.' Why doesn't she look surprised?

I smile back – sort of . . . then look away.

'*AA is not allied with any sect, denomination, politics, organisation or institution . . .*'

Oh my God! *That's* where I've seen her.

She's a friend of my parents!

Alcoholic! Her! *She* can't be an alcoholic! She's been to *stay* with us!

They'll have a *fit* when I tell them.

Except I can't tell them.

' . . . *does not wish to engage in any controversy . . .*'

Thirty-seven (I counted) losers in a room.

Drunks! Alkies!

They don't look much like losers; they seem quite happy.

' . . . *neither endorses nor opposes any causes . . .*'

Well dressed, most of them.

Classy drunks.

The Beast Brigadier interrupts:

'I must say, you get an **awfully** good class of drunk in Kensington, these days!'

'**Awfully** good class . . .'

'Awfully awfully **awfully awfully awfully awfully awfully awfully awfully** good class of drunk. **WAITER! BRING ME A LARGE BRANDY!**'

Shush!

Why is it *them*? Them and me?

313

It should be us. Thirty-*eight* losers in a room.

'*Our primary purpose is to stay sober and help other alcoholics to achieve sobriety.*'

Come on, concentrate!

'Thank you, Rachel,' John says.

John indicates the grey-haired woman.

'Today, Susan has kindly agreed to come along and share her experience, strength and hope.'

'Thanks, John. My name's Susan and I'm an alcoholic.'

Gentle Scots accent – reminds me of Samantha at the Royal College.

'Hi, Susan!' Everyone.

Susan clears her throat. 'By the time I came into AA I was putting away two bottles of cooking sherry a day. I was a mess.'

God, that's brave too.

I poke a hole in my empty cup.

A **chock** sound.

Quick glance from man next to me.

'I'd lost my friends; I'd lost my self-respect; I was on the point of losing my job and I was in debt to the bank. I couldn't see a way out. I knew I had problem with alcohol but I couldn't imagine life without it. However hard I tried to control it, I just couldn't stop.'

She doesn't look like a drunk *either*. I dunno what she is; retired games mistress?

'For years I made excuses; I blamed pressure of work, my relationships, my failed marriage, stress. My motto was "If you had *my* life, you'd drink too!" I blamed everything and everybody except myself.'

May be true for you, Susan, but you haven't got a fucking Beast breathing down your neck twenty-four hours a day.

But she's riveting. I can't take it all in, but key phrases resonate . . .

'. . . felt different . . . childhood . . . alone . . . obsession . . . the next drink . . . criticism . . . paranoia . . . escape . . . fear . . . anger . . . tired . . . compulsion . . . selfish . . . alcohol . . . the solution . . . admit . . . self-pity . . . hangovers . . . hiding bottles . . . off-licence . . . powerless . . . rock bottom . . . special and different . . .'

And when she finishes, other people speak about themselves.

Happy, sensible people with similar stories.

And, yes, I recognise myself.

Some of myself.

The alcohol part of myself.

The anger and obsession and frustration and hangovers and fear and escape and loneliness.

And they say they're not bad or weak-willed, they've just got a disease (which sounds like a cop-out to me).

And they talk about powerlessness and defeat and getting well again . . .

And to stop drinking, you have to change . . .

And believe in something greater than yourself (Oh fuck! Not God!) . . .

And they tell stories, and there's laughter . . . and biscuits . . .

And everyone's smoking . . . me included . . .

And when it's finished, my parents' friend, who's called Marion, takes me for a café coffee and she doesn't judge and she's wise and kind and accepting . . .

And I go to another meeting that afternoon . . .

And I go to meetings every day . . .

And I begin to understand about alcoholism . . .

And it's slow but I quite enjoy it . . .

And I **don't . . . drink.**

Which is nothing short of miraculous when I think about it. It's exciting not to have to drink, and I can't work out why I don't. I can't work out what's different, what's changed.

And people say: 'Don't question it, just accept it and be grateful . . .'

And I get a 'sponsor', someone who guides me through these *Twelve Steps to Recovery*, which I don't understand either . . .

And Anthony my sponsor is patient and sympathetic, because I worry that without the drink I won't be able to compose . . .

And day after day, at least three times a day I ring him to say things like I think Toulouse-Lautrec would have been a crap painter if he hadn't been drunk and so maybe I'll be a crap composer without the drink and the ideas will dry up and that all geniuses are screwed up anyway and that if I get too 'sober' I will just be normal and boring.

And Anthony listens and never complains about the amount of times I ring and he offers help and advice. I listen but I don't really believe what he says about trusting the process. I can't let it go. And I sit at my piano in a panic, terrified I'll never be able to write anything ever again.

But apart from this I follow his suggestions and I feel so much better.

And amazingly, I learn one or two of the **rules!**

One or two of those **life** lessons I thought I'd missed out on long ago.

One of which is that I thought I was 'less than'.

In every way.

And I'm not.

Even though I don't quite believe it yet.

And I explain about my twitching and compulsions . . .

And Anthony chuckles when I twitch but he never ridicules . . .

And we become good friends . . .

And I find myself laughing again . . .

And I **don't . . . drink.**

Which is fantastic because it's been six weeks and my body feels terrific.

But the Beast, freed from the bondage of booze, goes on the rampage. On and on and on it goes, unfettered, unhindered and unheeding, seemingly taking revenge for all those countless occasions when it was cowed by the gin and the vodka and the lager and the wine and I count and I make faces and I grunt and I growl and I grin and I grimace and jerk and kick and punch and obsess . . .

But amazingly . . .

In spite of it . . .

I don't *mind* so much . . .

And I'm still going to meetings every day . . .

And for some reason, I don't *hate* the Beast the way I used to . . .

Which is very strange, because it's always been the enemy . . .

And I make new friends . . .

And see old acquaintances who I didn't know were alcoholics . . .

And then suddenly it's six months . . .

That I **haven't . . . drunk.**

And then **I'm** the one in the chair one day, being Susan . . .

And people identify with **me** . . .

And they say: 'Thank you, James, I was just like you . . .'

And: 'I sat alone in a darkened room getting pissed too . . .'

And: 'I thought I was special and different too . . .'

And: 'I was a terrible people-pleaser as well . . .'

And: 'I never had any self-esteem either . . .'

And: 'I felt alone as a child . . .'

And: 'I thought I was weak-willed because I couldn't stop drinking . . .'

But however much better I feel . . . and I do . . . *so* much better . . .

NO ONE mentions light switches or numbers or grunts or face-making or leg jerks or hitting or tapping or sniffing or coughing or shouting or copying or checking for men in blue coats and Italian taxi drivers or Beasts or Controllers.

No one.

Not even the tiniest sminiest piniest finiest kiniest riniest hiniest little reference.

And yet I belong . . .

I do.

In ways I never did before.

But I *don't* belong either . . . not quite.

I still feel partly alienated from these people, with whom I have self-destruction in common.

But it doesn't matter quite as much as it used to . . .

Because the Beast feels different somehow . . .

Softer . . .

Less threatening . . .

Less . . . angry.

Even though the twitches are as bad as ever.

And I've been sober a year.

*   *   *   *   *

I'm giving a dinner party, a 'James-warming' party, the new James, alcohol-free.

I've invited nine people, many of whom I haven't seen for some time. At the last minute one of them rings to say she's ill. In a mild panic, I ring up one of the other guests and ask if she can bring along an extra girl to make up the numbers.

'I know,' she says. 'I'll see if Annie's free; I'll ring you back.'

Five minutes later she calls me to say that Annie can come.

I sit Annie next to me at dinner. She's an artist. We talk about her work. I talk about my composing. Each of us gives the other a potted history of ourselves. Then I proudly tell her about my alcoholism, something I often do with strangers at dinner tables to make myself appear special and interesting. And the Beast is under control.

When she says, 'I had a boyfriend who was an alcoholic,' we warm to our mutual subject.

I'm careful to try and appear calm and balanced, as if 'all that' is far behind me, and that I'm talking from the perspective of someone who has come through it, having emerged into the sunlight of reality, now living a life as contented as a Tibetan monk.

After dinner, keen to impress my guests, determined to leave them in no doubt that I'm finally back on the straight and narrow, I do my piano bit, pulling out all the stops, singing my best cabaret numbers and doing my special party trick, asking my audience to name a well-known tune and a composer, then playing *EastEnders*, for example, in the style of Schubert.

319

A couple of days later, Annie rings and asks if I'd like to go to a weekend party she's having at her parents' house in Yorkshire. 'And,' she says, 'we've got a really nice piano.'

Which turns out to be a bit of a disaster really.

Annie's devout Catholic parents live in a large country house, not far from Leeds. My allotted, Wembley-sized bedroom is a compulsive checker's nightmare. The bed alone is huge, the cavernous space underneath it taking about five minutes to inspect fully. There's a giant wardrobe with countless drawers and odd little spaces. There are various cupboards, occasional tables with more drawers, antique cigarette boxes, letter-writing boxes, blanket boxes and sash-window locks, any and all of which could harbour malicious blue-coated men or Italian taxi drivers. It's nearly an hour before I can finally allow myself to twitch-switch the light out and attempt sleep (door ajar, passage light on).

After dinner the next evening, dressed in our best, we all move into the drawing room, where once again I reprise my party piano tricks. All is going smoothly: I'm singing silly songs, I'm the centre of attention and – caffeined-up with several cans of Coke – in my over-excited element. So much so that, without thinking I burst enthusiastically into the Tom Lehrer classic 'The Vatican Rag', a song which gently takes the piss out of Catholicism and the Pope. '*Ave Maria! Gee, it's good to see ya, doin' the Vatican Rag*' may be a little close to the bone, but it's not *that* bad.

One or two little titters from those who are too polite not to laugh, but stony-faced disapproval from the rest (except Annie).

And there the evening ends.

Next morning, from her sickbed – via Annie – her mother asks me to write out the lyrics for her to inspect. Certain that in the cold light of day they will surely seem less offensive, I dash them off and send them up to her.

Half an hour goes by and Annie reappears, having been told that she is Beelzebub, hand-maiden to the Devil himself (me), corrupter of souls, bringer of evil, and that we shall be damned throughout all eternity!

She will, however, pray for us.

So that's nice.

Back in London, and as an apology by proxy, I take Annie out for lunch a few days later.

Walking through Brompton cemetery afterwards, idly twitching on an overhanging branch – seven taps and a stroke – I notice her watching me. She turns her head away and looks back at the path, then after a few seconds she says quietly, 'James, can I ask you something?'

'Sure.'

Pause.

'Will you tell me about your twitching?'

A jolt. I wasn't expecting that.

'Was it that noticeable?' I say.

'Well, yes.'

'Oh.' I thought I'd been quite good at hiding it in Yorkshire. I'd given the Beast a kind of pre-weekend pep talk; but clearly it hadn't listened.

'You don't mind, do you?' she asks.

'No, not really,' I say. 'Why? What was I doing in Yorkshire?'

'It wasn't that bad in Yorkshire,' she says, 'but you were doing it a lot during lunch just now.'

'Yes I was, wasn't I.'

Pause. I'm still not a hundred per cent comfortable talking openly about the Beast.

'Well,' I begin, 'it started when I was about six . . .' And I go on to explain about the twitches and the counting and the obsessions.

She listens without interrupting and then says, 'You know, the reason I ask is because I know someone called Richard who has a friend called Philip who does exactly the same sort of things as you do; *he* twitches and makes funny noises.'

'Really? Poor bloke.'

'Yes,' she says, 'but Richard thinks Philip's got something called Tourette's Syndrome.'

'Tourette's?' I'm puzzled. 'Never heard of it. Sounds like French cough sweets. Anyway, how does he know?'

'Because he has *another* friend who's a neurosurgeon, a Tourette's specialist and he thinks that that's what Philip's got, even though he's never seen him. The problem is that Philip won't do anything about it. He won't even *talk* about it.'

'But how can twitching and face-making be a medical thing?'

'I don't know . . . but I've met Philip and . . . well . . . you're very similar.'

She pauses.

'You could meet him if you like. I don't think you'd be able to talk about it but it might ring a few bells. What d'you think?'

'Christ, I don't know.'

What if I start laughing?

I'm sure I'd laugh if I saw someone *else* twitching . . . although Jason at the Royal College wasn't funny exactly.

After all this time, the idea that the twitching and obsessions could be medical feels really peculiar. Fine, if you go to the doctor and say, 'Doctor, I've got bronchitis,' he'll probably put you on antibiotics. If you say, 'Doctor, my leg's broken,' he'll put it in plaster. But to say, 'Doctor, I have this terrible urge to crush boxes of vibrating eggs, touch fridges, check under the bed for men in blue coats, check in lavatories for arse-pecking birds, smash glasses, count baked bean slogans, tap light switches, copy things people say, hold my breath until it hurts, jump off ski lifts, smash teapots, jerk my leg, arm and neck, sniff almost everything, cough, make faces and grunt like a pig. Oh, and by the way, I've always felt different from everyone else *and* I'm a recovering alcoholic, what can you suggest?'

That sounds ridiculous!

But somewhere, the idea that there might be a genuine reason for the Beast; that there could be a legitimate, logical explanation for it, that it might even have a scientific *name*, grabs at my guts and my heart quickens.

'Are you sure about this?' I ask.

'No, of course I'm not, but wouldn't you like to find out?'

Philip looks normal. Richard's brought him round to Annie's flat.

I'm nervous, desperately hoping he doesn't twitch, in case I do start laughing. Introductions all round, and we sit.

I'm watching him surreptitiously, trying hard not to appear to be doing so, but at any moment half expecting him to explode or produce an axe.

He's talkative but intense, and seems preoccupied somehow, as though in reality he's a mongoose who, having suddenly been transformed into a human, can't quite understand what's happened or what he's supposed to do.

I find him intimidating.

But when minutes go by and nothing happens, I start to relax.

I don't dare twitch myself; or rather, I rein in the Beast.

CLACK!

In mid sentence, his knees, having been apart, suddenly slam violently together like the jaws of a mantrap, followed immediately by a loud sniff and a head jerk. I feel an instant wave of adrenaline, partly from the shock of it, partly because this guy is clearly a weirdo, probably dangerous with it, and partly because it feels so . . . well . . . familiar.

He barely seems to notice what he's just done, carrying on completely unaffected.

'Is that *really* what I look like?' I ask Annie when they've left.

'Yes, frankly; plus, you've got all that obsessive stuff. Actually, he *may* check things as well; I don't know.'

A pause.

'Annie, do you think you could find out about this neurosurgeon? I think I'd like to see him.'

''Course I will,' and she smiles.

Chapter 16
Life's a Twitch

I feel extremely uneasy.

I've been feeling uneasy ever since I boarded the train to come here.

Don't know why.

Nothing I can put my finger on.

Just general . . . unease.

And I'm desperate for a pee.

But I'm not allowed to get up.

They've given me a lumbar puncture. Having had what felt like a macaroni-sized needle inserted into my lower back to remove some spinal fluid, I have to lie flat on my back for about four hours to recover.

One hour to go. Let's try again.

I've got a bottle to pee into, but in this position I can't convince my brain it's okay to let go. It's very uncomfortable. I push, I strain; I try to relax . . . nothing. It reminds me of Angélique and Anna in France. A knock at the door and in walks Michael the neurosurgeon, clipboard under his arm.

'How are you getting on?'

'Fine,' I say, 'but I can't make myself pee.'

He chuckles. 'Never mind; won't be long now; then you can get up. In the meantime I've got some good news: it's not syphilis.'

'Syphilis!? What made you think it was syphilis?' I must sound appalled because he chuckles again.

'I didn't. Not really. But syphilis can mimic almost anything you can think of, so we always check just in case. That's one of the reasons you had the lumbar puncture.'

'What was the other reason?' I ask. 'Gonorrhea?'

'No,' he laughs, 'I wanted to see if there was anything abnormal in your spinal fluid, but you'll be glad to hear there isn't. I wasn't expecting there to be, really.'

When I arrived at the hospital, Michael led me to a small consulting room for a chat. At first it was unnerving, almost surreal. We sat, me sipping coffee, him taking notes, his face strangely impassive while I went through a catalogue of the Beast's crimes to date.

'. . . and I stare at things so hard I try to *become* them, like a radiator or concrete.'

This sounded so bizarre and ridiculous I was half expecting him to bolt. But all he said was, 'Mm hm.' Which was the first time I'd ever had such a reaction, or rather, non-reaction from anyone; not that I've ever mentioned *that* particular compulsion before. I found it disconcerting. And then I wanted to impress him.

'. . . and sometimes I feel like I'm an unwilling puppet.'

'Mm hm.'

'. . . and I sniff petrol and teaspoons and envelopes.'

'Mm hm.'

'. . . and I copy things people say, words or phrases, and I can't stop until it feels right.'

'Go on.'

'. . . and I jerk my head, my neck, my arms and legs.'

And gradually feeling safe in his presence and slowly allowing myself to relax, I began letting the Beast illustrate as I talked. Michael hardly seemed to notice.

'. . . and I make faces and grunt, sniff, snort and cough.'

'Right.'

'. . . and I always have to check the lavatory seat in case there's a snake or a rat under it, or a piranha in the water or a bird that's going to fly up my bum . . .'

'Yes.'

Still no reaction, even to this, and, inexplicably, I felt a bit miffed. Shouldn't he have been a *tiny* bit impressed?

I wanted him to say, 'My God!' Or, 'Really!' Or . . . *something*.

'. . . and I count things. Almost anything, but mostly it's words, these days.'

'Mm hm.'

'. . . and if I don't constantly check light switches or door locks, I'm convinced the house will catch fire and I'll die.'

'Okay.'

'. . . and I have to check every nook and cranny of my bedroom before I go to sleep in case a man in a blue coat or an Italian taxi driver in a chef's unform is hiding, waiting to jump out and kill me.'

'Yes.'

'. . . and I've always felt as though I don't belong. It's as if everyone else is playing chess and I'm playing backgammon. It's not as bad as it was. Being sober has helped a lot.'

'Being sober?'

'Yes . . . sorry, I'm a recovering alcoholic. Booze was one of the things that stopped the twitches; but then my drinking got out of control. I go to AA now.'

'I see. And how long have you been sober?'

'Just over a year.'

'Good,' he said.

Now, hours later, he says simply, 'It's definitely Tourette's, James; there's no question in my mind. Everything you've described is more or less classic Tourette's behaviour.'

'Right,' I say, still uneasy. 'What about the lumbar puncture, though? Wouldn't it have shown up?'

'No. Unfortunately, there's still no absolute clinical test for Tourette's. But, to be honest, you don't need one. I'm convinced.'

'Oh,' I say.

Pause.

'Well,' he continues, prompting me, 'what do you think?'

'I don't know,' I say. 'It feels very strange. Since Annie first mentioned Tourette's I've sort of come to accept I've probably got it, but now that you've told me . . . I dunno.'

'Well, it *would* feel strange! I'm not surprised. It's *you*, James. It's all the things you've been talking about. Must be a relief, isn't it, though? To finally know?'

'Yes, I suppose so.'

Or it should be.

I feel ungrateful.

'I'm just amazed you weren't diagnosed earlier. Didn't anyone say *anything*?'

'Yes, of course, all the time,' I say, 'but I don't think my parents ever saw it as anything more than an annoying habit.'

'What about other people?'

'Yes, they *noticed* it, obviously; at school, particularly; but until I met Annie it never occurred to me it could be medical.'

'That's fairly unusual, you know. I don't see many people your age coming in to be *diagnosed*. Most of my patients are children or teenagers.'

A beat.

'Anyway,' he says, 'you've definitely got it, so now we've got to work out what we're going to *do* about it.'

'What *can* you do about it?' I ask.

And again, the unease . . .

'Well . . . there's quite a lot of research being done in the States at the moment but there's no absolute cure, I'm afraid. There are drugs coming on the market now which seem to be quite effective, so I think we should start you on a low dose of one or two of those and see how you go. You're not allergic to anything, are you?'

'No, I don't think so. Except alcohol.'

'Good. Well, fortunately, you're not a desperate case, so they should help.'

'Aren't I? You mean there are people who have it worse than I do?'

'Oh, *much* worse. Some of my patients literally have *no* control over themselves at all. They swear compulsively in public, they smash objects, they spit, self-harm, any number of things. I'd say you're somewhere in the middle.'

'But *I* swear,' I say.

'Yes, but I don't think that's the Tourette's. There's a difference. When *you* swear, correct me if I'm wrong, you're talking to this Beast character, aren't you?'

'Yes.' I nod.

'When it's annoying you, you swear at it, you're telling it to shut up. People with genuine copralalia swear, not out of anger or frustration, but because they simply can't help it.'

And I don't know what to think. It's exactly the same as after my accident. I don't feel the way I think I *should* feel.

I should be happy, shouldn't I?

I should be ecstatic.

I've found the answer.

I've found a reason.

I'm not a freak, after all!

This should be a seminal moment in my life.

The relief should be overwhelming.

In the corny Hollywood version there would be a series of tableaux; images without dialogue in which the *music* would portray my reactions after the diagnosis, a huge, glorious, soaring orchestral theme breaking through the emotional clouds, bathing me in sunlight, smashing to smithereens the nail-biting tension in the rest of the film. Eyes glistening with relief and gratitude, I would pump the doctor's hand furiously and jump for joy, having at *last* discovered that there are *others* on the planet just like me, who do the same things as me, feel the same way I do, my Tourette's brothers and sisters, a universal clan of compulsives, and though I would know there wasn't a complete cure, I would twitch ecstatically off into the sunset, pills in hand, head held high because at least I would know that finally, miraculously, I wasn't alone any more.

Which is crap.

I sing one of the songs from *A Chorus Line* quietly to

myself on the train back to London, armed with an alarming array of Beast-repressing drugs.

'*And I felt nothing*
I felt nothing.
Except the feeling that this bullshit was absurd . . .'
I do.

I feel nothing . . . at all.

Except the same nagging unease . . . threat . . . fear, even.

But certainly not relief.

I was expecting relief.

I really was.

The lead-up was quite dramatic. I was excited at the thought that there might be a *name* for the Beast; that I could finally be categorised as something.

But I'm not.

Why not?

And, sipping my Coca-Cola and chewing on an impotent British Rail sandwich, the Beast conjures a lyric from somewhere.

Oh, I'm a Touretter,
And I'll never get better . . .
Oh
What
A
Fetter metter ketter netter hetter metter petter retter
poo!

I thought maybe I'd feel the way I did when I first went to AA.

That *was* relief.

Huge relief; not to have to drink any more.

Not to *want* to drink any more.

Even though I still don't feel *completely* at home there.

Maybe I should go to Tourette's Anonymous.

Or better yet, Alcoholic Tourette's Anonymous.

I try saying it out loud.

'I have Tourette's Syndrome.'

'I . . . have Tourette's Syndrome.'

'I, James McConnel, am a Touretter.'

'I am James Tourette's McConnel.'

'I have a condition called Tourette's.'

'I have a medical condition.'

'A condition.'

'A condition called Tourette's.'

Nothing.

And when I get home, I'm tired.

And still uneasy.

And the Beast is tired . . .

And nervous . . . and shows it.

I'll start the pills . . . tomorrow.

Then the phone rings.

'How did it go?' It's Annie.

'It *is* Tourette's. No question.'

'That's amazing!' she says. 'You must be thrilled, aren't you?'

Pause.

'Yes, it was extraordinary.'

No.

It wasn't.

'So, what are they doing about it?' she asks.

'He's given me a bunch of pills to take.'

'Has he? What kind of pills?'

'I dunno. Pills to stop me twitching, I suppose.'

Another pause.

'You don't sound very happy about it.'

'I know. I'm not.'

'Why not?'

'I don't know. That's what I've been trying to work out.'

I've spent years wondering what's wrong me, thinking about all the things that have happened, the way I feel because of this bloody twitch, and now that I know, now that I can pop a pill to stop it, the way that the booze or music stop it, I feel threatened.

It doesn't make sense.

The Beast is a pain in the arse.

It's *been* a pain in the arse for as long as I can remember.

Well, not quite. I can sort of remember a time when it wasn't there.

Only faintly, though, because although I can remember events, like the dentist and the piano, I can't really remember what it was like *not* to twitch because, at the time, I hadn't yet *begun* to twitch, so I wasn't on the lookout for it *not* being there.

But what if I'd had the pills at thirteen, for instance?

What would Thompson, Hargreaves and Carson-Scott have done for kicks if the Controller hadn't existed?

Would they still have picked on me?

Or someone else?

Maybe they'd have found another excuse.

Was it *just* the Tourette's that made me unpopular?

I don't know. Maybe.

Maybe not.

And the accident?

Would *that* have happened if I hadn't twitch-revved the throttle?

Almost *certainly* not.

Would I have become a concert pianist, then?

Would I have stuck it out at the Royal College?

Enjoyed it, even?

If it weren't for the Beast, perhaps Jenny would have stayed with me.

And alcohol . . .

Would I have become an alcoholic?

Would I have stayed a 'normal' drinker?

What would a Beast-free life have been like?

Better probably.

Much better.

Apart from anything else, I can't even *begin* to calculate the amount of time the Beast has wasted – twitching and checking, counting, touching, sniffing . . .

Hours and hours and hours, I should think.

And yes, at thirteen, I'd have taken the pills without a second thought . . .

If I'd had the opportunity.

If it had meant *not* feeling the way I did.

Of course I would.

So *now* . . .

I should be jumping at the chance to kill it off, once and for all.

But that was then. Childhood. Adolescence.

And the problem is, when I think about it, when I really stop to think, the Beast . . . is *part* of me. Yes, it may have started life as a parasitic weed, clinging like ivy, a permanent disruption, interfering with everything I did.

But I've grown up with it, and as I've grown, so it's grown. It's developed with me and, in a way, it has *become* me . . .

Not entirely, of course. It's not who I *am*. I'm not *Beast* and nothing else. But part of James *is* Beast . . .

I'm used to it. And although I hated it when I was younger – loathed it, wanted to beat it senseless, sometimes, still do, on occasion – now that I'm older, I can deal with it. In fact, it's more than that, it's almost . . . comforting sometimes. Well, perhaps 'comforting' is the wrong word. Familiar . . . part of the furniture – even *though* I still swear at it and it drives me mad.

But to lose it . . . would be like losing a rib . . . or a leg . . . or my piano . . .

An old favourite.

An ability, a talent.

What would I be then?

What would it be like if I *didn't* have to do these things any more?

What would going to bed be like?

I'd get into my bedroom:

And I *wouldn't* have to put my shoes *exactly* right by the bed.

And I *wouldn't* have to check behind the door seventeen times.

And I *wouldn't* have to check in all my drawers.

And I *wouldn't* have to look under the bed and then kick it seven times.

And I *wouldn't* have to put my clothes absolutely *flat* on the floor, in case pixie-sized versions of the blue-coated man or the Italian taxi-driver were somehow hiding under the sticking-up folds.

Because *they* . . . would no longer exist.

And I *wouldn't* have to scrape my left foot aggressively on the carpet until the friction burned the skin.

And I *wouldn't* have to mutter 'ba ba ba' at the toothpaste.

And I *wouldn't* have to lift the pillow high in the air, smash it down on to the mattress as hard as I can, then punch it again and again and again to kill any monsters lurking inside.

And I *wouldn't* have to stand on the bed on tiptoe to check on top of the picture rail for ant-sized monsters.

And I *wouldn't* have to throw the duvet off to check for snakes.

And I *wouldn't* have to bang the bedside telephone to make it *right*.

And I *wouldn't* have to risk electrocution by switching the bedside light off and on, off and on, off and on, again and again and again and again and again as fast as I can, as hard as possible.

And that would be fantastic . . .

Wouldn't it?

Or it might be.

I don't know.

But, yes . . .

I could stop it.

Right now.

Today.

I look at the two little boxes sitting on the kitchen table, instructions neatly written on sticky labels on the outside.

Box 1: *Take one tablet in the mornings after food.*

Box 2: *Take one tablet in the mornings after food.*

I open Box 1. I pull out one of the flat packets of individually foil-sealed, little round wonders.

Beast killer. Like weedkiller.

Twitch Paraquat.

Of course, standing here, it's not like Socrates before he swallowed the hemlock. Whatever I do, it's not life or death. It's not that dramatic. But just by swallowing a couple of these each day, I could banish the Beast, lock it out, send it to sleep. Kill it. The way the music does, or the alcohol did. But they were only ever temporary. This would be permanent. As long as I kept taking the pills.

Maybe I could be a part-time Touretter.

Maybe I could twitch from Monday to Thursday and have the rest of the week off.

I look at the pills.

'Go arrn! Stop shilly-shallying and get the buggers down you!' says the Beast Brigadier suddenly, clearly not understanding their significance.

And I smile.

'Go arrn, you bugger! Do it!'

And then I giggle. Because the Beast doesn't realise what it's saying. It's compulsing its own death sentence.

Which is funny.

And . . . touching.

Because it means, doesn't it, that it *isn't* out to get me. That it's *never* been out to get me. It's got nothing to *do* with getting or outing or mouting or houting . . .

It just **is.**

It just exists. A child, which knows *nothing*, with no agendas, no aims, no ambitions to disrupt. A part of me and yet *not* a part of me. As it always has been, right from the moment the Controller was born.

An identity in its own right . . . which, in reality, may just be a bunch of neurons or beurons or teurons, or whatever they're called, on an acid trip . . .

But that's not how it feels . . .

It's a child.

A disruptive child.

And since I've got sober, I don't *mind* so much any more, I really don't. I don't cringe the way I used to when people see it, because I don't care quite as much as I did about what other people think. It's not so important any more.

And I'm not as angry as I was.

The truth is . . .

These days . . .

I *like* the way I am . . .

And I don't want to change it.

Afterwards

It's been a year since I was officially diagnosed.

So much has changed.

My attitude to my Tourette's.

My attitude generally.

The pills went in the bin. All of them.

I enjoyed doing that.

It was ceremonial.

The Beast, like the Controller before it, has been reborn.

It's become the Brat, the wilful, naughty child that sometimes drives me mad with its constant demands, but there are times now when I'm almost fond of it. It *can* be comforting.

I can't think of a decent reason why I should have to hide it. I don't care who notices, nor do I worry about the reactions I get at the fish counter in Tesco's, where, for some reason, it's particularly mischievous. If it offends, well, too bad, although I've yet to meet anyone who is actually *upset* by it. Surprised? Certainly. Intrigued? Yes. But not offended.

I *am* James Tourette's McConnel. If people laugh, then so much the better, because when you think about it, it's bloody funny. It's so **ridiculous!** I just wish sometimes they wouldn't feel embarrassed for me and could get the joke a little sooner.

Anger still kills it. At least it kills the compulsions, if not the twitches.

Intense sadness still kills it.

And so, of course, would alcohol.

Mostly, if I do need a break, I just sit at the piano.

Occasionally I try to reason with the Brat, as if it's a separate, rational being. I can't; it doesn't work like that; it never has. It's ruthless and it's relentless. I *can* keep it at bay sometimes, for several hours if needs be, and during those hours I will not twitch or compulse. However, to resist for ever is impossible, much as it would be impossible to resist the impulse to rescue a toddler drowning in a paddling pool. But the point is, I don't see it as an affliction any more; rather, it's a quirky idiosyncrasy.

And there are definite advantages . . .

For one thing, the Brat keeps me on my toes – literally, sometimes – which means I'm quite fit. When it's on top form, constantly flexing the muscles in almost every area of my body feels akin to an aerobic workout.

I'm my *own* gym.

A James gym.

A Jim gym . . .

More importantly, I've found a practical use for the Brat. It still, for instance, comes up with nonsensical, unconnected words and phrases a lot of the time; but it's the very unconnectedness of them that I've learned to listen to,

340

especially when it comes to searching for ideas. Now that I listen, rather than immediately reject, I find I'm able to make spontaneous leaps in my mind that perhaps I might not otherwise make. This can be a huge advantage in problem solving. The Brat tends to think laterally, or at least it throws out random thoughts that I can either discard or, sometimes, use.

It works musically as well. I've always thought of music as being something that temporarily sends it to sleep but, increasingly, I feel it actually focuses the Brat, allowing it free rein to express itself in a non-destructive way. This is particularly true when I sit at the piano and improvise. As with words, it musically 'free-associates', sometimes wildly, dragging me along for the ride.

These are positive things. This is the *good* side of the Brat, and sometimes I wonder just how much of me is Brat and how much isn't. At what point does the Tourette's start? If I *had* taken the pills, would they have removed some of the traits I've never even associated with the Brat? I don't know. And I don't want to find out, either.

My recovery from alcoholism has made me realise that I'm *not* a tragic genius. Or any genius, come to that. What I've been missing most of all is a healthy dose of self-esteem. Knowing this and embracing the Brat has gone a long way to making me feel as though I belong, that I'm not a 'nearly' person. And a few more of those 'how to do life' rules seem to have sunk in.

Tourette's is like an iceberg. The tiny tip, the bit that protrudes above the surface – the twitches – barely hints at the monstrous monolith below that nobody sees – the obsessions and compulsions. It is these that are the most troublesome, particularly at bedtime.

If I decide to go to bed at eleven o'clock, for instance, I still have to build several extra minutes into my schedule in order to be in bed on time.

The Tourette's Bedtime Recipe
(Serves 1)
Total compulsion time: 9 minutes.

1. First, take an overview of all the kitchen light switches. Then, when you've stared at them as hard as you can until you've *become* them, lightly tap the microwave five times, three times with the right hand, twice with the left. Turn the switch off firmly at the wall socket, not forgetting to tap six times (to make eleven in all). Check that it is actually off – this is very important. If you're not absolutely certain, check it again.

2. Next, move over to the electric oven. Tap lightly as above then turn off the wide red mains switch. (TIP: I often like to bash the kettle several times against the hob *before* I turn off the mains switch, but that's just me.)

3. Once you are convinced the oven is really secure – actually you'd better check once more, just to be safe – walk to the television, banging your heels against the floor on the way. Now this is the tricky bit. What we have here is a double wall socket, one of which has an adapter with two additional plugs attached. Each of the three plugs must be tapped three times, then the adapter four times, making thirteen. Clearly, this will not do, as thirteen is unlucky, so I recommend a further four taps on the wall socket itself, making a total of seventeen, which 'safens' the whole thing up. If it still doesn't feel

right, tap until you lose count. This can take a while, but it's well worth the effort.

4. Next, move to the stereo system – if you get the chance to bang the table on the way, so much the better. There are four plugs connected to a plug strip here, which to the amateur Touretter may appear a little daunting. Fortunately, there is just one plug coming from this that goes into the wall. You will notice that, again, we have a double wall socket, and although nothing is plugged into the second socket, it must be thoroughly checked for offness, before continuing on to the Aga.

5. Making sure that nothing is too close to the surface of the Aga, in case of fire, touch-sniff-twitch each tea towel individually by pushing firmly against the nose before throwing it on the floor, ready to pick up again at breakfast. Repeat as necessary.

6. Finally, having let the dog out for a pee, lock and triple check the back door. Give the expectant dog his goodnight biscuits (seven only, please) and twitch-stroke him nineteen times, paying particular attention to his head and ears.

7. Finally, finally, check all light switches – especially the dimmer switch by the door to the back hall – shut the kitchen door firmly five times and make your way to the bedroom, where the bed and pillow and duvet and telephone and boxes and toothpaste and corners and carpet and picture rail and bedside light are ready, waiting for you.

Acknowledgements

Huge thanks go first to my agent, Mark Lucas, who's rather cuddly and who took me on purely on the strength of an idea.

Second, to everyone at Headline, particularly my editor, Jo Roberts-Miller – also cuddly. She nursed and nurtured, cajoled and encouraged and offered virtual Valium as required, throughout the writing process.

Third, to Val Hudson, über-publisher and helmsperson at Headline who hardly batted an eyelid when the Brat expressed an interest in her filing cabinets.

Fourth, to Stephanie who has helped to keep my golden syrup levels topped up.

Fifth, to a series of good friends and family who have offered help, love and support over the years: my parents, Polly and Chris, Caroline, Piers, Julian, Jason, Alexa, Tim and Mieneka, Adrian, Kit and Kate, Garlinda and Peter, Annabel, Johnny and Wendy, Katya, Paul, and many others.

Sixth, to my wife, Annie, a breathtakingly talented artist who, though we are shortly to go our separate ways, has never been anything other than encouraging.

Seventh, to Freddy and Daisy, our children. It was Daisy who, having clambered on to my knee while I was working at the computer, decided that fd4oh#kj'yp\3rh;6 would be a useful contribution to the book. Some may agree with her.

Last, but utterly not least, in fact as unleastishly leastish as it's possible to be, Marion Milne. Among a myriad other things, it was her suggestion that I write this book. She's been a wonderful friend and I owe her, big time.

P.S. I supose I ought to thank the Controller, the Beast and the Brat.

The Controller was a Pain.
The Beast was a bastard.
But the Brat can be quite sweet sometimes . . .

Except when it's not.

Without the three of them, life may have been different. With them, it's never been dull.